UML
Weekend Crash Course™

UML
Weekend Crash Course™

Thomas A. Pender

Wiley Publishing, Inc.

Best-Selling Books • Digital Downloads • e-Books • Answer Networks • e-Newsletters • Branded Web Sites • e-Learning

UML Weekend Crash Course ™

Published by
Wiley Publishing, Inc.
909 Third Avenue
New York, NY 10022
www.wiley.com

Copyright © 2002 by Wiley Publishing, Inc., Indianapolis, Indiana

LOC: 2002103278

ISBN: 0-7645-4910-3

Manufactured in the United States of America

10 9 8 7 6 5 4 3

1B/SQ//QW/QS/IN

Published by Wiley Publishing, Inc., Indianapolis, Indiana
Published simultaneously in Canada

Ⓦ**Wiley Publishing, Inc.** is a trademark of Wiley Publishing, Inc.

About the Author

Tom Pender is the author of six courses on the UML. He has taught throughout the United States and 12 other countries. He has over 20 years' experience in systems development in industries as diverse as coal mining, power plants, wholesale distribution, warehousing, insurance, investing, materials management, weather satellites, and retail. He has spent the past four years teaching and consulting with companies who are transitioning to object-oriented technologies. In addition to writing, Tom enjoys collecting silver-age comic books, and studying science and history.

Credits

*With thanks to Lynne Angeloro
for her support and friendship*

Preface

Welcome to the *UML Weekend Crash Course*. So why another UML book? The Weekend Crash Course series is designed to give you quick access to the topics you want to learn. You won't find a ton of reference material in this book. You won't find a book that assumes you have a specific programming background. Instead, you will find the material you need to get the job done, no matter what your background.

You are about to experience the joy of discovering and modeling a complete software system design from start to finish. You will be equipped with tools to work with client and technical professionals alike and to overcome so much of the confusion and frustration common to software projects. You will master one of the most practical and useful tools in current technology, the Unified Modeling Language.

Who Should Read This Book

This crash course is designed to provide you with a set of short lessons that you can grasp quickly — in one weekend. The book is intended for three audience categories:

- Programmers who want or need to learn more about design and specifically how the tools of the UML help in design. Perhaps you have seen the modeling tools used on projects and want to know how to use them yourself. This course provides 30 focused sessions on the most practical aspects of the UML modeling tools. You will learn the role of each diagram, the notations to draw them, and how to apply them using a realistic case study.

- Team leaders and analysts who need a tool to help communicate what the project is all about. You haven't written code in a while, but you know what you want the system to do for your clients. You need a way to express the requirements in a way that all the participants can understand and support throughout the project life cycle. The course sessions break down the diagrams to clearly explain why and how you would use them. I also provide tips on how to make sure that what you're doing is correct.

- Business analysts and clients who need to communicate with systems developers. One of the challenges in projects is finding a common language, a way to communicate effectively and consistently. The UML provides a common ground for business and technical professionals. The examples in the course are nontechnical yet very practical for establishing a common language to describe critical business systems.

To get the most out of this book, you should be familiar with software projects and the various participants. I don't cover project management or much of the technology used in projects. In fact, I assume you know the project-related concepts like code, databases, programs, requirements, business processes, clients, developers, and analysts.

What You Need To Have

The requirements for the course are very basic. You can create all the diagrams with pencil and paper. If you like, you can download any one of the modeling tools mentioned in the book. Nearly all vendors provide an evaluation copy for 15 to 30 days, more than enough time to complete the course and try out the tool. For a list of vendor sites see Session 30. I'll offer two cautions regarding the use of tools: First, there are a few free tools out there, but most of them are not complete and might get in the way of your work. Second, if you are struggling with the tool, go back to paper until you finish the course. Focus on learning the concepts, then work on using a tool. The concepts are more important than the mechanics of a particular tool.

What Results Can You Expect?

How realistic is it to try to learn the UML in one weekend? The UML is like many things you learn. Grasping the basics is easy, but it can take years to master the application. The UML defines ten diagrams. Five of those get used a lot; the other five are more specialized and are used less frequently. All of the concepts represented in the diagrams should already be familiar, concepts such as clients, business processes, and messages. The toughest part is learning the terminology. That is why the course focuses on giving you definitions and lots of examples.

There is more to the UML than I could possibly cover in 15 hours. But I can give you a solid understanding of the core concepts that will support 80 percent of your work. You will know the purpose of each diagram, how the diagrams work together, the entire notation to construct each diagram, and even ways to test your work. After you work through the examples and the case study, you should be able to immediately start applying your new understanding at work with confidence.

Weekend Crash Course Layout and Features

This book follows the Weekend Crash Course layout and includes the standard features of the series so that you can be assured of mastering the UML within a solid weekend. You should take breaks throughout. I've arranged things so that the 30 sessions last approximately 30 minutes each. The sessions are grouped within parts that take two or three hours to complete. At the end of each session, you'll find "Quiz Yourself" questions, and at the end of each part, you'll find part review questions. These questions let you test your knowledge and practice your newfound skills. (The answers to the part review questions are in Appendix A.) Between sessions, take a break, grab a snack, and refill that beverage glass, before plunging into the next session!

This Weekend Crash Course contains 30 half-hour sessions organized within six parts. The parts correspond to a time during the weekend, as outlined in the following sections.

Part I: Friday Evening

In this part, I provide the background of the UML and how you can approach it to get the most out of it. I cover a brief history of the UML and what exactly the UML defines. Next, I briefly cover some sample methodologies to explain the context in which you will use the UML. I also cover an overview of the diagrams supported by the UML and the fundamental object-oriented concepts used throughout the development of those diagrams.

When the background is complete, you will dive into the Case Study to gather requirements.

Part II: Saturday Morning

This part covers the application of the Use Case Model, from the diagram through narratives and scenarios to fully document user requirements. You will learn to identify and define Use Cases in terms that can be verified by your clients. You will explain the requirements of each Use Case so that they form the foundation for testing throughout the project. Then, based on the requirements, you will begin the construction of the Class diagram, including classes and associations.

Part III: Saturday Afternoon

In the afternoon session, you will learn the rest of the Class diagram notation and apply it to the case study. You will refine the Class diagram by applying aggregation, composition, and inheritance. You will then test the Class diagram using the Object diagram, applying test cases to validate your Class diagram notation. You will also learn to use the Activity diagram to model logic, such as business processes and complex system behaviors. Then you start modeling the interactions between objects using the Sequence diagram by bringing together the test cases and the resources defined in your Class diagram.

Part IV: Saturday Evening

You will continue your application of the Sequence diagram. Then you will learn another, complementary tool, the Collaboration diagram, to model object interactions. You will learn the unique properties of these diagrams and how they can work together to reveal holes in your design. For those objects that are constantly changing, you will learn the Statechart diagram so that you can fully understand and document their behavior over time.

Part V: Sunday Morning

The application of the Statechart will continue into Sunday Morning with lots of practical examples. By this time you will have seen a lot of diagrams. You will learn how to organize your work using Package diagrams. Then, when the design is reaching the point where you need to build the system, you will learn how to model the physical implementation using the Component and Deployment diagrams.

Part VI: Sunday Afternoon

Sunday Afternoon you will learn how the UML diagrams are applied to the development of a Web application. Finally, I will provide some information about modeling tools, including evaluation criteria and sources to obtain evaluation copies.

Features

First, as you go through each session, look for the following time status icons that let you know how much progress you've made throughout the session:

30 Min.   20 Min.   10 Min.   Done!
To Go   To Go   To Go

The book also contains other icons that highlight special points of interest:

This flag is to clue you in to an important piece of information that you should file away in your head for later.

This gives you helpful advice on the best ways to do things, or a tricky technique that can make your UML modeling go smoother.

Never fail to check these items out because they provide warnings that you should consider.

This states where in the other sessions related material can be found.

Accompanying CD-ROM

This Weekend Crash Course includes a CD-ROM. It contains trial software, a skills assessment test, a copy of the UML standard, and some supplemental materials I think you will find it useful. For a more complete description of each item on the CD-ROM, see Appendix B.

Reach Out

The publisher and I want your feedback. Please let us know of any mistakes in the book of if a topic is covered particularly well. You can send your comments to the publisher at Wiley Publishing, Inc., 909 Third Avenue, New York, NY, 10022 or e-mail them to www.wiley.com. You also can e-mail me directly at tom@pender.com.

You are ready to begin your Weekend Crash Course. Stake out a weekend, stockpile some snacks, cool the beverage of your choice, set your seat in the upright position, fasten your seat belt, and get ready to learn the UML the easy way. Turn the page and start learning.

Contents at a Glance

Contents

UML
Weekend Crash Course™

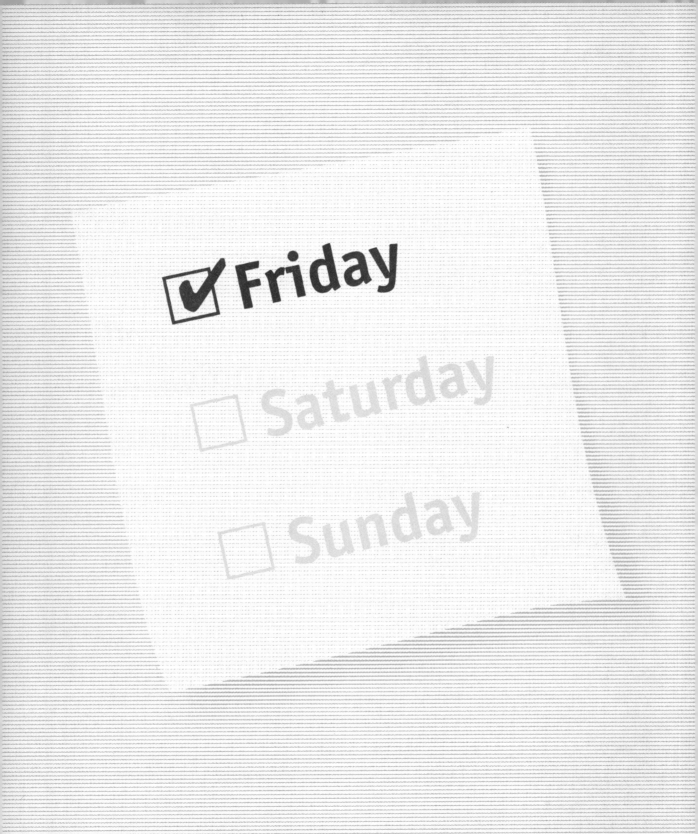

Part I — Friday Evening

Session 1
What Is the UML?

Session 2
UML and Development Methodologies

Session 3
How to Approach the UML

Session 4
Defining Requirements for the Case Study

PART

I

Friday
Evening

What Is the UML?

Session Checklist

✔ Explaining why the UML was created

✔ Defining what is and is not included in the UML specification

✔ Explaining the four-layer metamodel architecture

✔ Explaining the built-in extension mechanisms

✔ Describing how the UML is being refined and extended

**30 Min.
To Go**

The Unified Modeling Language (UML) is a hot topic in an even hotter industry. The whole software development industry has been explosive, partly due to the revolutionary nature of software itself, which is driven by worldwide business growth and competition.

Establishing Standards

For those who are responsible for delivering these revolutionary business solutions, the challenge is daunting. Every week new developments threaten to make our current skills and experience obsolete. Furthermore, the software industry is relatively young and hasn't yet established itself as a formal discipline. Consequently, most study is focused on programming rather than on engineering, with practitioners gravitating toward the tangible implementation products and away from the abstract analysis and design artifacts. But it is this very tendency that has led to many failed systems and disastrous problems.

This need for a more mature industry is behind the drive for the UML and other related standards. Our industry needs a framework for measurable and proven engineering techniques. The UML is one of the necessary steps in the right direction. This course helps you understand what this step is and how the UML can help you deliver solutions in a way that will help you and your clients reach a new level of systems development maturity.

The UML is a standard for the creation of models that represent object-oriented software and business systems. It combines the best diagramming practices applied by software developers over the past 40 years. The UML standardizes the notations but it does not dictate how to apply the notations. This approach to the standard provides the greatest freedom for developers' own styles and techniques, while ensuring consistency in their work products.

Some History behind the UML

The UML is the current stop on the continuum of change in software development techniques. The UML was created out of a storm of controversy over the best methodology to use to specify and to develop software systems. Dozens of methods were (and still are) in use, each with a loyal following.

In 1994, Grady Booch and James Rumbaugh, the two market share leaders in object-oriented (OO) software methods, formally joined forces to develop a notation standard. A year later, they published the Unified Method version 0.8. Ivar Jacobson, yet another leader in object-oriented development, joined the team. The team of Rumbaugh, Booch, and Jacobson were soon after dubbed the "three amigos" within OO circles. At the same time that the three amigos were working on their common notation, the Object Management Group (OMG) was establishing the Object-Oriented Analysis and Design (OOA&D) Task Force. The OMG is the same standards body that defined and still manages the CORBA standard. In June 1996, the task force issued a request for proposal (RFP) for a standardized *metamodel* to support the exchange of models among modeling tools. By October 1996, a number of the leading application and modeling tool manufacturers, like IBM and i-Logix, had partnered with the three amigos to sponsor the UML proposal to the task force.

What is and is not included in the UML Specification

The UML has a more limited scope than people may assume. The OMG's RFP was primarily concerned with the development of a *metamodel* for object-oriented modeling. A metamodel is a cohesive set of definitions for concepts and their relationships. The metamodel was expected to define an underlying language that could be transmitted between tools that support visual modeling, without constraining the vendors to support a particular methodology for developing the models.

The UML metamodel

This metamodel, or set of definitions, describes in fairly precise syntax the underlying meaning of each *element* used in visual modeling and the relationships among the elements. For example, in the UML metamodel, you find a detailed definition of what a class is; its component parts, attributes, and operations; and the relationships among them. You do not, however, find a process for finding classes or for evaluating a "good" class versus a "bad" class.

The UML standard actually defines four layers to the metamodel architecture: the user object layer, the model layer, the metamodel (2M) layer, and the metametamodel (3M) layer, shown in Table 1-1.

20 Min. To Go

Table 1-1 *The UML Four-layer Metamodel Architecture*

Layer	Description	Example
metametamodel	Defines the language for specifying metamodels.	Defines the concepts MetaClass, MetaAttribute, MetaOperation, and so on.
metamodel	Defines the language for specifying a model.	Defines the concepts Class, Attribute, Operation, Component, and so on.
model	Defines the language to use to describe a subject domain.	Defines the concepts Order, Shipment, Product, Product ID, Buy(), and so on.
user objects	Defines specific subject domain information.	Defines Order #74653, Shipment #87649, the product "CD-ROM 435", the price $50.00, and so on.

Starting from the bottom and working up, the *user object layer* is where you find a diagram, like a Sequence diagram or Object diagram, populated with the facts from the problem domain like Order #74653 that contains a line item for "CD-ROM 435" with a price of $50.00. The diagram is built following the rules defined by the next layer above it, the *model layer*.

The *model layer* fully explains the classes that describe the subject domain objects, for example, classes like Order, Shipment, and Product. It tells you what an Order looks like, the fields it contains, the operations it can perform, and so on, without ever telling you about any particular Order. These class definitions conform to the rules specified in the next layer above, the *metamodel (2M) layer*.

The *metamodel (2M) layer* defines what a class is so that the model layer knows how to describe the Order class. It defines a class as a concept having attributes, operations, and associations. It defines an attribute as having a name, a data type, a default value, and constraints. These definitions in turn conform to the specifications of the *metametamodel (3M)*.

The *metametamodel (3M) layer* is the realm of the philosophers and practitioners of the black arts who determine what makes up a language. Nearly all the definitions at this layer are abstract, that is, they are more like templates that can be used to build a wide variety of concrete concepts.

In case I managed to scare you just now, relax, all you really need to know is the metamodel. That is what this entire course is about, defining the diagrams and the elements used to construct them. Once you understand the diagrams defined by the metamodel layer, you will get enough practice building the model and user object layers to become quite comfortable.

The organization of the metamodel

The metamodel is a bit complex, so it helps to organize the elements into *packages*. A package is basically the UML version of a directory, a place to put things. At the first level you will find three *packages* called the Foundation, Model Management, and Behavioral Elements packages, as shown in Figure 1-1.

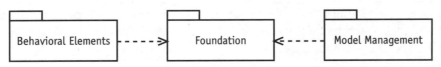

Figure 1-1 *Packages of the UML metamodel*

Figure 1-1 shows that Behavioral Elements and Model Management depend on the Foundation package. In other words, they won't work properly if they don't get help from the contents of the Foundation package (more on the Foundation package in a moment).

The Behavioral Elements package contains everything you need to model behavior like Use Cases, Collaborations, Statecharts, and more.

Model Management explains how to model packages, subsystems, and similar organizational structures.

Figure 1-2 represents the contents of the Foundation package. The Foundation package contains four more packages, the CORE, Auxiliary Elements, Data Types, and Extension Mechanisms packages.

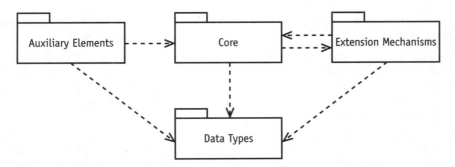

Figure 1-2 *The contents of the Foundation package*

The Core package defines all the fundamental concepts used in the UML diagrams like Class, Interface, Association, and Data Type. But it also defines some abstract concepts like GeneralizableElement, a high level definition for anything that can implement inheritance, like a class, a Use Case, an actor, and more.

The other three packages support the Core package with items like dependencies; primitive data types like integer, string, and time; and some built-in extension mechanisms that I'll talk about next.

**10 Min.
To Go**

UML Extension Mechanisms

The UML also provides some built-in extensions to the diagram notations. One such tool is called a *stereotype*. A stereotype appears inside of << >> (guillemets) and characterizes a type of element like a class or relationship without specifying its implementation. For example, you might stereotype a number of classes as <<user interface>> to convey that they are all used in the construction of a user interface. But, as Figure 1-3 shows, the individual classes could be as diverse as Frame, Button, and DropDownList.

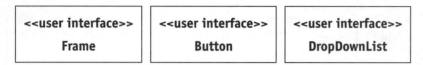

Figure 1-3 *A stereotype on a class*

There are a number of stereotypes already defined in the UML, but you are free to define and use your own. The existing stereotypes are specified in Appendix A of the UML specification.

Because no notation can cover every possible type of information, the UML also supports the use of *comments*. Figure 1-4 illustrates a sample comment icon. You may place as much text as needed within the symbol. The symbol can be placed anywhere on any diagram.

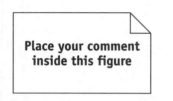

Figure 1-4 *Comment notation*

Another extension, called a *constraint,* is used throughout the UML diagrams to limit the use of a model element. You can always spot constraints by the use of { } braces around the text that describes the limitation you want to impose. For example, you might want to limit the values that can be used for the attribute "age" to between 21 and 120. The constraint might look like this: {age > 20 and < 121}. I'll cover the use of constraints with each diagram in the subsequent sessions.

There are two more mechanisms that reach beyond the scope of an introductory book, *tagged values* and *profiles*. A complete description is available in the UML specification.

Ten Diagrams

Ten diagrams are defined in the UML metamodel. Each is fully described using Class diagrams and textual narrative. A key to the successful application of the UML is in understanding that you can use the notation standard with any number of different development methods, process controls, and quality controls.

In Session 2, I explain the difference between a process and the UML, how they complement one another, and four very different yet popular processes to apply the UML. Session 3 provides an overview of the diagrams. The rest of this course is devoted to explaining the purpose and definition of each UML diagram and their relationships to one another. This understanding should prepare you to apply the models successfully in your own unique environment.

The Continuing Refinement and Expansion of the UML

From the outset, the UML was designed to be a public resource. It grew out of a long list of competing notations and methods and continues to be extended and refined. The standard is intended to be a reflection of best practices. Consequently, there is an ongoing need to improve the standard as practices improve and the application of the standard is tested in increasingly diverse and demanding applications.

For these very practical reasons, the UML standard is open for review and change by anyone who wants to contribute to it. The OMG evaluates feedback and incorporates changes into each new release. The OMG has established the UML Revision Task Force (RTF) as a clearinghouse for suggested changes. The suggestions are reviewed for merit, and often scheduled for incorporation into upcoming versions of the product.

The UML is currently in version 1.4. UML version 2.0 is not expected until about the spring of 2003.You can investigate the work being done by the RTF at the UML Revision Task Force Web site (`www.celigent.com/omg/umlrtf`). You may also access the UML specifications themselves and even download them for free from the OMG Web site: `www.omg.org`. You will want to refer mostly to the Notation Guide and the Glossary. The Notation Guide covers all the diagram notations and terminology covered in this course and more. It makes a good reference, and it's free. Regarding the Glossary, you may want to rely as well on the glossary in this text. I found a number of the definitions in the UML Glossary to be circular or simply too thin to be useful.

You can also try some online tutorials at `www.celigent.com/omg/umlrtf/tutorials.htm`. They aren't comprehensive, but for free it's hard to justify a complaint.

Done!

REVIEW

- The UML is a major step toward the standardization of software development. The UML standard has received widespread support from tool vendors and developers alike.

- The UML specification describes a metamodel that defines the elements of each diagram, how the diagrams may be assembled, and how they can be extended.

- The UML standard doesn't prescribe a process for applying the diagramming notation. Nor does the standard define the proper use of the notation to create "good" products, or guidelines to avoid bad products. The standard does not dictate how a vendor implements the standard.

- The UML metamodel architecture defines four layers: the user object, model, metamodel (2M), and metametamodel (3M) layers.

- UML extensions include stereotypes, comments, constraints, tagged values, and profiles.

- The UML Revision Task Force (RTF) of the Object Management Group (OMG) is responsible for coordinating and applying suggested changes to the standard.

QUIZ YOURSELF

1. Who sponsored the UML? (See "Some History behind the UML.")

2. What part of systems development does the UML define? (See "What is and is not included in the UML Specification.")

3. What part of systems development is not defined by the UML? (See "What is and is not included in the UML Specification.")

4. What is a UML stereotype? (See "UML Extension Mechanisms.")

5. What is a UML constraint? (See "UML Extension Mechanisms.")

6. How are changes made to the UML standard? (See "The Continuing Refinement and Expansion of the UML.")

UML and Development Methodologies

Session Checklist

✔ Explaining methodology

✔ Examining some popular methodologies

**30 Min.
To Go**

A methodology consists of a process, a vocabulary, and a set of rules and guidelines. The *process* defines a set of activities that together accomplish all the goals of the methodology. The *vocabulary* of the methodology is used to describe the process and the work products created during the application of the process. The *rules and guidelines* define the quality of the process and the work products.

The part of all methodologies that can be standardized is the *vocabulary,* often expressed in a *notation*. The UML standard is a common notation that may be applied to many different types of software projects using very different methodologies. The variations appear in the use of the UML extensions, like stereotypes, and the emphasis placed on different diagrams for different types of projects.

One of the challenges inherent in defining a methodology is that it is difficult, if not impossible, to define a single process that works for all projects. For a software development methodology, this would mean a process that works equally well on projects as diverse as arcade games, device drivers, banking, rocket navigation, and life support.

Consequently, even though the UML standardizes the notations gathered from a number of methodologies, the processes used to apply the UML notation are still as diverse as the environments in which they are used.

Some Current Methodologies

The rest of this session is devoted to a brief summary of four of the current methodologies: RUP, Shlaer-Mellor, CRC, and Extreme Programming. They represent the diversity of the current set of methodologies. I provide a brief summary and then try to point out what I see to be some strengths and weaknesses in each approach. This should give a fair idea of the opportunities available to you and the factors that may influence your choices.

The list of all methodologies is far too long to cover here, so at the end of the session I'll point you to a resource where you can check out many of the others and dig a little deeper into the methodologies presented here.

I have selected these four methodologies because they represent the diversity inherent in system development. The Rational Unified Process works well in large projects where quality artifacts and communication are critical. The Shlaer-Mellor Method was developed primarily to address the unique needs of real-time systems long before the UML existed, but has since adopted the UML notation. CRC is almost more of a technique than a methodology. It was designed as a tool to help people gain an understanding of objects and how they work. Extreme Programming tries to reduce many of the existing development practices to the bare essentials, attempting to optimize the relationship between developers and clients.

The Rational Unified Process

One method that has received a lot of interest recently is the Rational Unified Process (RUP). RUP is the latest version of a series of methodologies resulting from a blending of methodologies. You may have heard the names Objectory Process, the Rational Approach, the Rational Objectory Process, and the Unified Software Development Process. These were all predecessors and have been synthesized into the RUP. Actually, it gets a bit confusing because the Rational Unified Process was a proprietary process within Rational Software, Inc. The merged method was published in 1999 as The Unified Software Development Process. The method has since been made public and the name reverted to the Rational Unified Process (RUP).

The hallmarks of RUP are the two terms *incremental* and *iterative*. These concepts are part of most current methods, but RUP places particular emphasis on their value and their associated artifacts. The goal of the methodology is to deliver an executable release of a product, an increment of the product for every pass, or iteration, through the process. The motivation for this approach is to keep delivery times short and deliveries frequent. This prevents the historical problem of projects that run for months or even years before they actually produce anything. It also supports early review and early problem detection.

Note that in the very early increments, the concept of an executable release is a bit of a stretch. Typically, you might produce prototypes or layouts without anything executable until at least a few iterations into the project. The key is to produce some *verifiable output* for the clients.

The process is built around the two concepts of project lifecycle *phases* and process *workflow*. Figure 2-1 shows a two-dimensional matrix. The horizontal axis represents the progress of the project over time. The vertical axis represents the core process workflow. Using this visualization, you can see that in each *iteration,* or small step through the life of the project, the team is working through all the steps in the process workflow. In each subsequent iteration, the team digs deeper into each activity in the process workflow.

The workflow consists of a set of activities, business modeling through defining the environment. Each activity is associated with a set of *artifacts* or work products. In most cases, the artifacts are UML diagrams, but they may also be items like requirements documents, test plans, risk assessments, deployment plans, and much more.

Workflows	Phases			
	Inception	Elaboration	Construction	Transition
Workflows				
Business Modeling				
Requirements				
Analysis and Design				
Implementation				
Test				
Deployment				
Configuration and Change Mgmt				
Project Mgmt				
Environment				
	Initial	Iter #1 / Iter #2	Iter #3 / Iter #4	Iter #5 / Iter #6

Figure 2-1 *The Rational Unified Process, phases and workflows*

For example, the case study presented in this book refers to an inventory control system. The first iteration on this project might focus heavily on requirements and result in a risk assessment, a glossary of inventory control terms, and some screen and forms layouts for receiving and shipping to help the users visualize their requirements. The second iteration might create the Use Case diagram and a set of one or more prototypes from the original screen layouts. A few iterations later you might take one Use Case and actually build the application to support a screen to set the standards for the screen look and feel and to test the basic architecture of the application.

The iterative approach continues until all the requirements have been satisfied and the system is fully implemented.

You may have the impression that the Rational Unified Process is a standard like the Unified Modeling Language. The choice of the name might have been a smart marketing ploy, but that does not make it a standard. There are many other valuable methodologies to consider.

Strengths of the RUP

- The emphasis on iterative development and incremental deliveries is a time-tested and valuable approach that prevents many common project problems. However, it must be noted that this approach is common to most of the current methodologies.
- The process is well defined and supported by the Rational modeling tool.
- The artifacts and the roles of the project participants are also very well defined.
- The process combines many of the best practices from many successful methodologies.
- The process is comprehensive.

Weaknesses of the RUP

- In trying to be comprehensive, the RUP becomes very large and difficult, both to learn and to manage.

- It is easy to get so caught up in the rules for using the RUP that you forget why you are using it (to deliver software).

- A substantial amount of time is spent trying to customize the RUP for each project. Here, too, you run the risk of becoming a slave to the process and losing sight of the reason for the process.

- Tool support for the process is limited to Rational's own products, which are at the high end of the cost range. A few other vendors are now starting to provide limited support.

Shlaer-Mellor Method

**20 Min.
To Go**

The Shlaer-Mellor Method is based on an integrated set of models that can be *executed for verification,* and an innovative approach to design that produces a system design through a *translation of the analysis models.* The method is built on a set of well-defined rules for the construction of the diagrams and the translation of those diagrams from analysis to design and finally to implementation. In fact, the most recent generation of modeling tools, like BridgePoint (www.projtech.com/prods/bp/info.html), have created the ability to generate 100 percent of the code.

This achievement is ahead of most other methodologies that generate the operation declarations but cannot provide the method code, the implementation for the operation. The rigorous set of rules also supports verification through simulation. The diagrams can actually be executed to see if they work properly.

One of the primary concepts in Shlaer-Mellor is a domain. A *domain* is a subject area. Shlaer-Mellor defines three basic types of domains: the application domain, the service domains, and the architectural domain. Each domain has its own unique types of requirements and diagrams. Together they represent the entire specification for the system.

The Shlaer-Mellor process is broken down into the following steps:

1. Partition the system into domains.
2. Analyze the application domain using object information models, state models, and action specifications (action data flow diagrams — a non-UML diagram).
3. Confirm the analysis through static verification and dynamic verification (simulation).
4. Extract the requirements for the service domains.
5. Analyze the service domains.
6. Specify the components of the architectural domain.
7. Build the architectural components.
8. Translate the models of each domain using the architectural components.

The progression from step to step follows a fairly strict set of rules to guide the translation from each version of the diagram to the next. The process sets up a rhythm of build a little and test it, build a little more and test a little more, which helps prevent surprise problems from cropping up deep into the process.

The Shlaer-Mellor Method also places a great emphasis on iterative and incremental development. But this methodology reduces and controls iteration in analysis by confining it to a single domain at a time. Iteration in design is similarly controlled: Modifications to the design are made entirely in the architectural domain and propagated to the entire system through the standardized diagrams.

Reuse is yet another high priority. Because domains are kept completely separate from one another until the final construction steps, they can be transported intact to other systems. This applies particularly to the architectural domain: This domain is commonly reused for other systems that have basically the same loading and performance characteristics.

Strengths of Shlaer-Mellor

- By far the greatest strength of the Shlaer-Mellor Method is the ability to test your diagrams through simulation. You actually execute your diagrams.

- The process is extremely well defined in terms of rules that govern the construction and testing of the diagrams.

- The movement from one step in the process to the next (for example, from analysis-level diagrams to design-level diagrams) is also defined with enough precision to allow the generation of design diagrams directly from the analysis diagrams. This is a huge time saver and prevents mistakes in the translation. It also speeds up the process of applying changes because they can be propagated through the diagrams automatically.

- The method was developed for and maintains a strong emphasis on real-time systems design. As such, it provides support that is largely lacking in other methodologies that gloss over the unique demands of real time in favor of the more common business functionality.

Weaknesses of Shlaer-Mellor

- The strengths of the methodology can also be its weaknesses. Like the RUP, the tool support is limited to vendors directly associated with the methodologists. This is changing, but don't expect it to be quick.

- Learning the rules involves a definite learning curve and a serious investment of time and effort. Steve Mellor is currently leading an enhancement to the UML, called Action Semantics, to improve the definition of Statechart diagrams and build much of this knowledge into the UML 1.5 standard. Tool support for this enhancement should soon follow.

- The methodology was developed for real-time systems, so it places heavy emphasis on state modeling. Many business applications simply do not warrant a lot of work on state transitions.

CRC

CRC stands for *Class, Responsibilities, and Collaborators*. The CRC methodology was originally developed as a learning tool during the time when object-oriented programming was new; a lot of procedural programmers needed help making the transition to OO thinking. The goal was to provide the simplest possible conceptual introduction to OO modeling.

The heart of the method is the CRC card. A CRC card is a 3-x-5" or 4-x-6" lined index card. The physical nature of the cards emphasizes the division of responsibility across objects. The physical size of the cards also helps to establish limits for the size and complexity of the classes. The CRC card technique does not use the UML. Instead it is used to discover information about classes that is then placed into a UML Class diagram.

Figure 2-2 is a sample blank CRC card. The class name is written at the top of the card. The next two lines are reserved for the listing of superclasses and subclasses. The body of the card is divided in half. The left column or half lists the responsibilities of the class and the right column or half lists the other objects that it works with, the collaborators, to fulfill each responsibility.

class name	
subclasses:	
superclasses:	
Responsibilities	Collaborators

Figure 2-2   *A CRC card sample*

The CRC process requires a team that includes people in two distinct roles: domain expert and object-oriented technology facilitator. The domain experts provide knowledge of the subject area, and the OO facilitator coaches the team through the development of the cards and the eventual model.

The CRC process centers on working through scenarios. The process breaks down into four stages:

1. Before the Scenario Execution
   a. The Problem: Everyone agrees on the problem definition.
   b. Brainstorming for Classes: Based on the problem statement, the team identifies candidate classes using the vocabulary of the problem.
   c. Filtering Classes: The team works on definitions for each class, eliminating synonyms and conflicts.
   d. Assigning Cards: Each team member is assigned responsibility for one or more classes.
2. The Scenario Execution
   a. Each scenario expresses something that the system is supposed to do. The team walks through the scenario identifying the responsibilities of each class in the scenario.
   b. Each discovered responsibility is recorded on the card of the corresponding class.
3. During the Scenario Execution
   a. Grouping the Cards: The team identifies similar classes.
   b. Scenario List: The team reviews the scenario coverage for completeness.
   c. Collaboration Drawings: The cards are combined on a wall or white board to show how they cooperate in the execution of the scenarios.
4. After the Scenario Execution
   a. The team reviews the resulting model and plans the implementation.

Strengths of CRC

- The simplicity of the method has remained a major selling point and the method has been incorporated into many different methodologies. It is still a valuable tool for helping a programmer transition from procedural to OO concepts.
- It is extremely easy to use and very visual. It is difficult for any participant to claim he didn't know exactly what was going on.
- The technique is very responsibility-driven. It keeps the participants focused on the value of an object based on what that object contributes to the proper operation of the system. The result is a system with the minimum number of objects needed to make it work.
- The technique helps the participants think like objects and to understand why objects work well or work poorly. This understanding helps ensure a good design.

Weaknesses of CRC

- The most significant limitation, however, is also its simplicity. It only really addresses the problem of finding and modeling classes. There is a lot more to complete systems development. So the bulk of the work still rests on the programmers.
- The success of the process is very dependent upon the participants and especially on the facilitator. The simplicity can be very deceptive.

Extreme Programming

Extreme Programming (XP) shocked a lot of people, including myself, when it first showed up. The goal of XP is much like that of CRC (that is, keep it simple). This is not surprising when you learn that the originator, Kent Beck, was also instrumental in the CRC method. XP does not advocate the UML. I present it here because the goal of this session is to provide you with an understanding of the diversity of methodologies and the views or attitudes that various methodologies hold toward the application of the UML standard.

XP strives to strip away anything that is not essential. XP requires a complete and unwavering commitment from the clients to work side-by-side with the programmers. Working through stories or scenarios of how the system should work, the teams eventually develop the entire system. Every iteration of the project (typically one to four weeks each), the teams deliver something functional. The minimum deliverable is a set of tests.

XP basically says that the code is everything, so there is a very heavy emphasis on coding standards and design principles. The process includes numerous standup meetings to keep everyone on the same page. Furthermore, programmers work in pairs so that they can learn from one another, provide insights, share design alternatives, and generally help each other out.

Because XP is completely devoted to the code, there is very little use of up-front modeling. If modeling is used, it is usually thrown away when a decision is reached. XP does use the CRC method because of its simplicity and utility. Instead of design up front, the method encourages design through integration and refactoring. In other words, XP advocates believe that as you learn more about the code, you are in a better position to make the design decisions and update your code. In one sense, it could be seen as *bottom-up design*.

Strengths of XP

- XP is the first that I know of that truly cared about the programming environment and its affects on the participants. The bibliography for *Extreme Programming Explained, Embrace Change*, by Kent Beck, reads more like a sociology text than a programming text. No one since Tom DeMarco, writing the book *Peopleware*, has devoted as much time to finding ways to make the programming job livable.

- XP encourages an extremely close relationship between clients and developers.

- XP faces the fact that change is inevitable and often uncontrollable and builds that fact into the development approach.

- Kent Beck has been brave enough to describe what it really takes to create a high-caliber development environment instead of bowing to the status quo of impossible deadlines, inadequate user involvement, ill-defined requirements, and programmer isolation.

Weaknesses of XP

- XP relies heavily on setting up the ideal development environment. It starts from several questionable assumptions:

  - *Highly committed clients will spend huge amounts of time working side by side with programmers.* In my experience, projects are lucky to get access to true subject matter experts because they are considered too valuable to release from their current responsibilities.

- *Programmers work extremely well together.* In every shop I've worked in for over 20 years, programmers tend to be extremely individualistic and resist input from other programmers. I've mediated too many fights to be overly optimistic in this area.

- *Experienced programmers work with new team members to maintain the system ("Maintenance is the normal state of XP," says Kent Beck).* In every shop I know, the experienced people move on to new projects and the new folks get stuck with the maintenance. It's almost like a rite of passage. Plus, in XP there is no documentation other than in-line comments (that is, no overview documentation about how the design works or how the system fits together), which makes it extremely difficult to know how to modify a system.

- *Design is a skill that is common to every coder.* Not so. Many programmers have no concept of what good design is. Much of their coding is intuitive or simply "how they learned to do it."

Resources

The single best resource I've found to track down the various methodologies is `www.cetus links.org`. On the first page of this site, you will find a link to OOAD Methodologies. Click on it and you will be sent to a page with links to more than 50 different methodologies, lists of books, articles, conferences, and organizations worldwide.

Done!

REVIEW

A methodology is made up of a predefined *process,* a *vocabulary* used to describe the process and the work products, and a set of *rules and guidelines* that help define the quality of the process and the work products. The UML specifies only the vocabulary, the notation that describes the artifacts of the process. Each methodology decides if and how to apply the UML notation.

This session presented four leading methodologies that illustrate the diversity and commonality of the current techniques available for software development.

- The Rational Unified Process (RUP) provides a comprehensive plan for the activities and the artifacts required to complete the development process. The approach strongly emphasizes iterative and incremental development. The RUP is best suited for large projects.

- The Shlaer-Mellor Method emphasizes tight integration and simulation to verify the accuracy of the product throughout development. The Shlaer-Mellor Method is best suited for real-time systems.

- The CRC method emphasizes simplicity and role-playing to work out the class-level requirements for the design of the system. The CRC method is best suited for helping people learn about objects and object-oriented design.

- Extreme Programming (XP) attempts to address many of the personal issues involved in team dynamics and to create the most positive work environment for both programmers and clients alike. It emphasizes continuous testing, consistent standards, and a lot of communication throughout the process. XP tends to be best suited for small, fast-moving projects with high management and client support.

Each methodology has strengths and weaknesses. Choosing a method requires understanding your own environment and matching those strengths and weaknesses to your specific needs.

QUIZ YOURSELF

1. What are the three key elements of a methodology? (See Session introduction.)
2. What are the two hallmarks of the RUP? (See "The Rational Unified Process.")
3. Name the predominant strength of the Shlaer-Mellor methodology. (See "Shlaer-Mellor Method.")
4. What are the three key concepts that define the CRC methodology? (See "CRC.")
5. Name the three driving factors behind the success of the XP approach. (See "Extreme Programming.")

How to Approach the UML

Session Checklist

✔ Explaining the types of UML diagrams

✔ Explaining the concepts of views

✔ Organizing the diagrams into views by function

✔ Explaining the basic Object-Oriented concepts that support modeling

**30 Min.
To Go**

The UML includes specifications for nine different diagrams used to document various perspectives of a software solution from project inception to installation and maintenance. In addition, Packages provides a means to organize your work. The Component and Deployment diagrams describe an implementation. The remaining seven diagrams are used to model requirements and design. This session presents a way to organize these last seven diagrams to make them easier to remember and apply, and an overview of the principles that guide their development.

Views

One way to organize the UML diagrams is by using views. A *view* is a collection of diagrams that describe a similar aspect of the project. I very often use a set of three distinct yet complementary views that are called the Static View, Dynamic View, and Functional View. Figure 3-1 illustrates the complementary nature of the three views and the diagrams that make up each view.

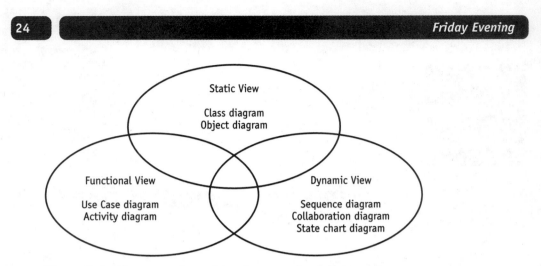

Figure 3-1 *Three complementary views or sets of diagrams*

To understand this approach, consider the process of applying for a job. When you interview for a job, you can find out what the job is about through a published description. A typical job description begins with a title and a brief definition of the job, usually in paragraph form. This would be the *static* part of the job description. It simply states what the job is.

The job description is usually followed by a list of duties detailing *what is expected* of you in the performance of this job. You could think of the listed items as demands placed on you throughout the course of your job. This corresponds to the *dynamic* part of the job.

After you get the job, there are often specific instructions on how to do your job (for example, policies and procedures to follow). These are the *functional* details of the job, for example, *how* to perform the job rather than *what* to perform.

Together, the three views provide a complete and overlapping picture of the subject you are modeling. I'll explain each view and the diagrams they contain. Then I'll explain the benefits of using the overlapping views.

Functional View

In the Functional View, I include both the Use Case diagram and the Activity diagram. I keep them together because they are used together so often and they both model how the system is supposed to work. Figure 3-2 shows that the *Use Case diagram* defines the functions that the system must provide. The functions are expressed first as goals. But then the goals are fleshed out in a narrative to describe what each Use Case is expected to do to achieve each goal.

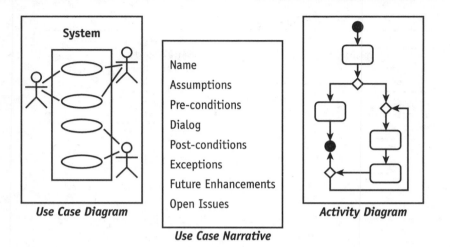

Figure 3-2 *Elements of the Functional View*

This Use Case description can be written, but I often draw the logic with an *Activity diagram,* a diagram that models logic very much like a flowchart. The Activity diagram is also useful for modeling a workflow or a business process. It can be very useful when working with clients to determine how things are or should be done. You can also use the Activity diagram to assess the complexity of the application, and to verify the internal consistency of your Use Case definitions. Later in the design, you need to specify the implementation details for methods. When the details become complicated, being able to draw them out using the Activity diagram makes the logic much easier to understand.

- The **Use Case diagram** describes the features that the users expect the system to provide.
- The **Activity diagram** describes processes including sequential tasks, conditional logic, and concurrency. This diagram is like a flowchart, but it has been enhanced for use with object modeling.

Static View

The Static View includes those diagrams that provide a snapshot of the elements of the system but don't tell you how the elements will behave. It is very much like a blueprint. Blueprints are comprehensive, but they only show what remains stationary, hence the term *Static View.* Figure 3-3 illustrates the two diagrams that make up the Static View, the Class diagram and the Object diagram. The *Class diagram* is the primary tool of the Static View. It provides a fixed look at every resource (class) and its features. It is the one diagram nearly always used for code generation and reverse engineering.

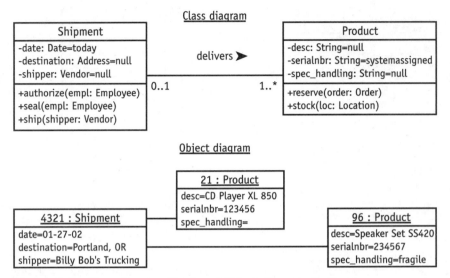

Figure 3-3   *Class diagram (top) and Object diagram (bottom)*

To support the Class diagram, you can employ the *Object diagram*. Consider: Have you ever had difficulty understanding a concept that a client was trying to explain? If so, what did you ask for to help you get a better handle on what she was saying? Typically, I ask for examples. Often, a few good concrete examples (objects) reveal relationships and information that were hidden in the more generalized description (classes).

The Object diagram is also used to test the Class diagram. Class diagrams are very easy to draw, and even easier to draw badly. Logical processes create objects and their relationships. Tracing the affects of a process on an Object diagram can reveal problems in the logic of the process. Drawing Object diagrams for test data can be just as effective as drawing them for examples. Hard facts will either confirm or deny the accuracy of your Class diagram. Session 7 provides a complete example of testing a Class diagram using an Object diagram.

- The **Class diagram** is the primary static diagram. It is the foundation for modeling the rules about types of objects (classes), the source for code generation, and the target for reverse engineering.
- The **Object diagram** illustrates facts in the form of objects to model examples and test data. The Object diagram can be used to test or simply to understand a Class diagram.

Dynamic View

I mentioned that the Static View was like a blueprint. In the blueprint of my house I can see the front door, a thermostat on the wall, a furnace downstairs, and I can even expand it to include my family members and pets that reside there. What I cannot see is how all these pieces work together. For example, stare as I may at the blueprints, I will never know what would happen if I left the front door open on a cold winter day.

If I could see a model of the *interactions* between all those things on the blueprint, I would know that if I left the front door open on a cold winter day, my wife would yell at me, the dog would run out the door, the thermostat would send a signal to the furnace, and the furnace would turn on. Now *that's* dynamic.

Figure 3-4 shows the three types of diagrams that make up the Dynamic View. The Dynamic View includes the diagrams that reveal how objects interact with one another in response to the environment. It includes the *Sequence and Collaboration diagrams,* which collectively are referred to as interaction diagrams. They are specifically designed to describe how objects talk to each other. It also includes the *Statechart diagram,* which shows how and why an object changes over time in response to the environment.

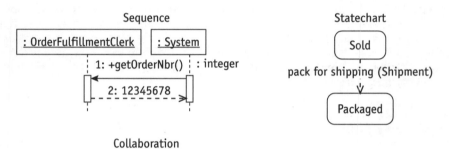

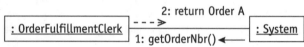

Figure 3-4　*Sequence, Collaboration, and Statechart diagrams*

- For modeling object interactions, the Dynamic View includes the **Sequence and Collaboration diagrams**.
- The **Statechart diagram** provides a look at how an object reacts to external stimuli and manages internal changes.

Three views

The big question that usually crops up about now is "Why do I have to do all of these diagrams? Joe next door has always just drawn Class diagrams." This question is valid. For small projects, you may not need to create all these diagrams. But I suspect that one of the reasons you're reading this book is because you don't work on small projects, and the projects you do work on get pretty complicated.

When the work gets complicated, you often move from one piece of the project to another in rapid succession. Coming back to something you worked on a few days ago often means hours of getting your head back into a pile of notes and/or mountains of code, much of it not your own. It also means that there is no realistic way to know how right you are until you get enough code to run tests. By then you have eaten up a large part of the project schedule, and justifying a lot of rewriting is difficult if you find problems. And let's not even talk about the challenge of dealing with user-requested changes.

So how do the three views help? Consider another example. Suppose you're in an accident at an intersection. A guy runs a red light and broadsides you. A police officer shows up, walks over to one of the witnesses, takes his story (which says you ran the red light, not the other guy), and leaves assuming he has the truth. How do you feel? Outraged, I imagine. The officer talked to his "client" and captured the facts just like we typically gather our requirements. So what's the problem?

The problem is that the officer did nothing to verify his facts. He should have asked the other witnesses for their perspectives. After he does that, he has a bunch of eyewitness accounts. If he compares the stories, he'll discover two things. First, some of the information from different testimonies will agree. He can reasonably assume that those portions of the account are true. Second, the portions that don't line up can't be trusted until he can find corroborating evidence.

Working with multiple, different views works in the same way. The diagrams each look at your problem in a different way, like different witnesses. The diagrams will overlap. If they agree where they overlap, you can relax knowing you've probably got it right. If they don't agree, then you have some homework to do to reconcile the differences. Now here is the other great benefit: When they disagree, you've pinpointed where you need to invest your effort. When everything agrees, you know you're done.

Object-Oriented Principles

20 Min. To Go

Next I want to visit the principles that drive most of the UML modeling. All the UML diagrams describe some form of object-oriented information. But what does the term *object-oriented* mean? The term itself sheds some light on the answer. It has something to do with viewing the things in the world as objects.

So what is an *object?* The simplest definition of an object is pretty much anything you can talk about. Look around you. Almost without thinking you may begin to recognize things you see and give them names: book, chair, lamp, room, and so on. An object can be a physical entity, like the things you see, but an object may also be intangible, for example, a concept like an illness, attendance, or a job. Even though a job is not something you can touch, it is something you can describe, discuss, assign, and complete.

(By the way, if you aren't already familiar with OO concepts, some of the language may sound a little odd. Be prepared.)

So what do you need to know about an object?

Abstraction

A software object is an *abstraction,* a representation of something in the real world like this book. An abstraction is a way to describe something where you only include the information about it that is important to you. When I need to contact my friend Victor, for example, I don't need to know everything about him. I just need his phone number or e-mail address. Thank heaven I don't also need to know his anatomy, his genealogy, and his music preferences! All those things are valid, but they don't help me contact him. Figure 3-5 shows Victor on the left, hard at work, and an object icon, my abstraction of Victor, on the right.

Victor : Person
name : Victor phone : 555-555-5555
call(integer): boolean

Figure 3-5 *Victor on the left (hard at work); abstraction of Victor on the right (an object icon)*

Here's the crux of the matter: An abstraction benefits you only in so far as it describes the information you need in order *to solve a problem*. So when you create an abstraction, you must first make certain that you know *why* you need it.

My own working definition for creating an abstraction is: *representing something in the real world in a useful manner to solve a specific problem.* Usefulness is measured by how well it helps you solve the problem you are trying to solve.

The representation is an *object*. The rules that define the representation make up a *class*. For comparison, think of the word *apple* in a dictionary and an *apple* in your hand. In software, the definition in the dictionary is a class, and the apple in your hand is an object. To make objects from classes, you must use the class definition like a template or a mold. Although each object may vary somewhat, all objects of the same class must conform to the class definition. That's why some people say that an object is an *instance* of a class. An object is created, manufactured, or instantiated (made real) from the class definition.

What an object knows

To function properly, every object has to know two kinds of information and two types of behavior.

Information

First, you can say that an object knows about itself. In other words, there is information that describes the object. For example, the pencils on my desk have a length, hardness, brand name, eraser, and so on. A book has pages, a cover, a title, an author, and so on. This is some of the information that would eventually be captured and manipulated in files or databases.

Second, you can say that an object knows its own current condition. This condition is formally called the *state* of the object. Simply put, the state of an object is a description of the properties of the object during a particular period of time. Consequently, when any of the properties of the object change, the state of the object is said to change.

- An object can describe itself.
- An object knows its current condition (or state).

Behavior

What an object can do is pretty easy to see when you're talking about animate objects. For example, you might expect an Employee object, like Tom Pender, to work, ask for time off, call in sick, complete a task, or accept an assignment. You would say that these are all things Tom can do as an employee type of object, and you would include these abilities in the object's description, for example, the Employee class.

But the pencil in the jar on my desk poses a different problem. What can a pencil do? It is tempting to say that a pencil can write, but is that really true? It isn't the pencil that writes, but a person who uses it to write.

You've discovered a second type of behavior. An object must know *what can be done to it*. There are a lot of people who can write with the pencil, including students, teachers, programmers, designers, and analysts. To do so, every class of objects in this list would have to include a description of the "write" behavior. There are a lot of problems with this approach, including redundant maintenance, possible conflict between the different class definitions for how to "write" resulting in possible misuse of the pencil, and the fact that all these objects would need to be notified of any changes to the pencil that would affect their ability to use their "write" behavior.

- An object knows what it can do
- An object knows what can be done to it

A better solution is to write one definition for the behavior in the pencil class. That way, anyone who wants to use the pencil to write goes to the pencil to find out how. Everyone gets the same implementation of the behavior, and there is only one place to make changes.

Encapsulation

The discussion so far leaves you with a lot of information and no way to organize it to use it effectively. Encapsulation provides the means to organize this information so that you can use it and maintain it efficiently. Here's what this organization looks like.

First, encapsulation says you need to separate everything you know about the object into two categories:

- What you need to know in order to use the object
- What you need to know in order to make the object work properly

10 Min. To Go

To use the object

Two years ago, I taught my daughter how to drive. My first challenge was to identify for her the minimum knowledge she had to have *in order to use the car*.

She needs to know about the ignition, the steering, the brake, the gas pedal, the gearshift, the mirrors, the gauges, and so on.

Should I include the universal joints, the spark plugs, and the fuses on the list? No, because she doesn't need to know about those things *in order to use the car*. In fact, she has been driving for two years and still doesn't know about them. The information that the car exposes so that someone can use the car is called the car's *interface*. The interface is how you communicate to the car that you want to use one or more of the car's behaviors. For example, when you press on the gas pedal, you're telling the car to go faster.

So in order to use an object, you need to expose the *interface* of the object, like the car interface in Figure 3-6.

Figure 3-6   *The interface for a car allows us to use the car.*

To make the object work properly

I remember as a kid our neighbors had the old shell of a car in a field behind the house. It had brake and gas pedals, a steering wheel, a gearshift, and so on. But wish as we might, the car never responded. An *interface* without an *implementation* doesn't do much. We could communicate with the object, but the object didn't have any way to respond.

In order to make the object work, you need to provide the mechanisms that respond to the interface. Here is where it all starts to come together. Remember back to the part about what an object knows? When you press the gas pedal, the behavior (the implementation behind that interface) needs to know how the car is put together and the state of the car. An object knows about itself, so the car would know how it is put together and its current state.

More than that, the knowledge must not be altered inappropriately or the behavior won't work properly. Consequently, encapsulation tells you that the information has to be inside the object with the behavior so that you can control access to it and protect its integrity. This is why encapsulation is often called *information hiding*. You hide the information inside the object, where the object has complete control. For example, Figure 3-7 illustrates the hidden, internal mechanisms that make an engine work properly.

In order to make the object work properly, you need to place inside the object:

- The *implementations* for each interface
- The data that describes the *structure* of the object
- The data that describes the current *state* of the object

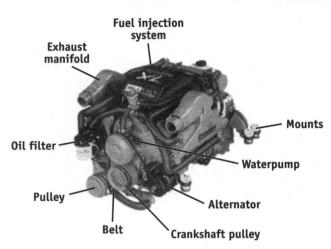

Figure 3-7 *Defining the internal design of an object so that it will work properly*

Giving an object purpose

If you leave encapsulation with this description, you have a bit of a problem. Many objects can have the same interface. Just think for a minute about all the objects you know of that share the interfaces accelerate, decelerate, turn, start, and stop, such as those shown in Figure 3-8.

Figure 3-8 *Purpose drives the design and use of an object.*

The go-cart and luxury car in Figure 3-8 share all these interfaces. But you would never use them both in the same way. If interface alone doesn't adequately distinguish objects, then what else do you need in order to define an object? Purpose. You need to know why that type of object exists, what it was designed for. The interface is designed to satisfy the purpose.

Encapsulation summary

Encapsulation of an object requires you to **expose**:

- Its *purpose,* so you can select the proper object for the application you have in mind
- Its *interface*, so you know how to use the object

Encapsulation of an object requires you to **hide**:

- The *implementation* that provides the behavior requested through the interface
- The data within the object that provides the *structure* that supports its behavior, and tracks the condition of the object, its *state,* at any given point in time

Done!

REVIEW

The UML includes specifications for nine different diagrams used to document different perspectives of a software solution from project inception to installation and maintenance. Packages provide a means to organize your work. The Component and Deployment diagrams are specific to implementation. The remaining seven diagrams are used to model requirements and the design. Views provide a means of organizing these seven UML diagrams by their features and applications, thus making it easier to identify the right tool for the right job.

- The *Functional View* employs the Use Case and Activity diagrams to describe the behavior of the system.
- The *Static View* includes the Class and Object diagrams to define all the resources of the system.
- The *Dynamic View* includes the Sequence and Collaboration diagrams, also known as interaction diagrams, to define how objects work together to respond to the environment, and the Statechart diagram, which describes how and why an object changes over time.
- An object is an *abstraction,* a representation of something in the real world.
- An object can describe its own structure and its current *state.*
- An object knows what it can do and what can be done to it.
- *Encapsulation* defines a way to organize an object definition (a class).

QUIZ YOURSELF

---

1. Why is the Static View called *static?* (See "Static View.")
2. Describe the purpose of the Class diagram. (See "Static View.")
3. What diagrams are used to represent the Dynamic View (See "Dynamic View.")
4. What is illustrated in the Sequence diagram? (See "Dynamic View.")
5. How can using multiple views help you? (See "Three views.")
6. What is an abstraction? (See "Abstraction.")
7. What does it mean to encapsulate an object? (See "Encapsulation.")

Defining Requirements for the Case Study

Session Checklist

✔ Explaining the concept of a problem statement

✔ Identifying types of requirements

✔ Explaining the process of gathering requirements

✔ Identifying common pitfalls in requirements gathering

**30 Min.
To Go**

I n this session, you begin work on the case study. The *case study* is a scaled down inventory control system. In a software project, as with many other problem-solving endeavors, the first step is to gather as much relevant information as possible. In most projects, you call this *gathering requirements*. But what kind of requirements do you need to build software?

The Case Study Problem Statement

To make all this talk of requirements and pitfalls a bit more realistic, I focus on a sample problem, the case study. Your goal is to gather enough information about the system to rewrite it by evaluating the *problem statement*. Typically, in order to start a project, there has to be a perceived problem to solve (or an opportunity to exploit). Users and/or management see something about the existing system as an obstacle to the goals of the company. In the case of a new business, the "problem" may be the lack of a system to do a critical function. The problem statement documents this perception.

The problem statement for your case study consists of the following four paragraphs titled receiving, stocking, order fulfillment, and shipping. Refer back to these paragraphs as you discover what kind of questions to ask to gather the requirements. For this chapter, you simply gather the requirements in the form of textual descriptions, that is, answers to questions. In the remaining sessions, you find out how to formalize these requirements using the UML diagrams.

Remember to pay close attention to the vocabulary.

Receiving

The receiving clerks receive incoming shipments by matching purchase orders against the products in the shipment. The incoming shipment documents are delivered to the supervisor for verification. The products may come from cancelled orders, returned orders, or received shipments. The products are offloaded from the trucks and placed into a staging area.

Stocking

The stock clerk looks up the correct location for each product, places the product in that location, and updates the inventory with the location and quantity. When the product is in the right location, the stocking personnel inform the supervisor, who delivers the receiving documents to the Accounts Payable Department.

Order fulfillment

Other staff members fill orders by locating the products required for the order. After they have filled the order, they drop the order at the clerk's desk. The clerk updates inventory to reflect the fact that the product has been removed for an order. There can be a delay of up to two days, causing significant problems with the reordering process and stock levels. They also notify the Order Processing Department that the order has been filled.

Shipping

When the orders are filled, they are then packed and prepared for shipping. The shipping folks contact the shippers to arrange delivery and give the paperwork to the clerk. The clerk also notifies the Order Processing Department when the order has shipped and updates inventory to reflect the fact that the products actually shipped.

Types of Requirements

In a software project, you're most often supporting business processes. But you may also be supporting automation of mechanical processes in a factory setting, or real-time processing inside equipment like a heart monitor. Given that this is a crash course with a limited amount of time, I focus in this section on business application requirements.

What types of requirements could you encounter in a business system? Much of what you'll discover falls into four categories of requirements: business process, constraints, rules, and performance.

Business process

Most systems are built in order to do something: place orders, issue payments, launch rockets, run a heart/lung machine, and so on. To use a system, you need to know how to interact with it and why. Business processes describe your relationship with the system in terms of interactions. You enter a shipment. The system validates the data about the shipment and gives you a set of error messages. You fix the data about the shipment and try again. The system validates the data again. Seeing that the data is valid, the system uses it to save the shipment to the database and update the associated orders.

A common challenge with gathering business processes is that it is difficult to distinguish personal preference or legacy practice from actual current need. So how do you avoid this trap? One technique is to look past the process to the *reason for the process*. Each process had a justification at some point, even if that justification no longer exists. You need to know the reason behind the process. For example,

- What result does logging the shipment produce?
- What would happen to the rest of the system if you didn't have a record of the shipment?
- Would another process fail (for example, would you be able to accurately maintain the inventory and Accounts Receivable if you didn't know what was shipped)?

Next, evaluate each process, both on its own and in its role in the system. Identify those processes that no longer produce valuable outcomes. Keep only those that are essential to the successful operation of the system. For example, evaluate the following interactions of the Inventory Control processes for Receiving, Stocking, and Accounts Payable:

- The stock is offloaded from the trucks and placed into a staging area. Why? Historically the same people offloaded the trucks and placed the products into inventory. They couldn't do both at the same time.
- When the product is in the right location, the stocking personnel inform the supervisor, who delivers the documents to the Accounts Payable department. Why do they wait to notify AP? Historically this was a manual process so the stock clerks waited until they had all of their other work done.

Then come back and evaluate those processes that, even though they aren't essential, may add value. Prioritize these contributions and allocate resources proportional to their value to the system and add them to the project plan. For example,

- The incoming shipment documents are delivered to the supervisor for verification. Why? After a few interviews, you find out that this practice was instituted because in years past the warehouse had serious theft problems. Is there still a problem that would justify the added cost and delays?

The goal in this evaluation process is to make conscious choices about how to spend the finite time and money available to the project to deliver the best possible system. The lesson: Focus on results rather than processes; quantify the value of the results; allocate resources proportional to the value of the results.

Constraints

The second type of requirement is called a constraint. *Constraints* are limitations on or boundaries around what you can do when you develop a solution for the system. Constraints can apply to virtually any aspect of your project and the resulting system.

Why do you care about constraints? Because constraints limit the options you have at virtually every phase of the development life cycle. Consider the constraints on each of these four development phases:

- **Requirements gathering:** Limitations on client skills and experience drive the type of solutions that you can offer. The application may need to offer substantially more help features for less-skilled users, whereas extremely skilled or experienced users might reject the same features as a hindrance.

- **Analysis:** Limitations imposed by policies and procedures, laws, contracts, and industry standards restrict the models that you develop to document the *problem domain*. You may not be able to be as creative as you'd like when the law or a contract says that it has to be done a particular way. For example, the inventory system must abide by generally accepted accounting principles. Failure to do so risks an audit, fines, or worse.

- **Design:** Programming languages, databases, middleware, and just about every technology impose specific limitations. These technologies often dictate field data types and sizes, data conversions, communication protocols, and more. This limits the options available to you to when you try to satisfy the system requirements. You might want to network the warehouse to the accounting office a few blocks away only to find the phone lines are over 30 years old and are currently tied up in a massive upgrade project that is running badly behind schedule.

- **Implementation:** Implementation technologies impose performance limitations that often conflict directly with the performance requirements for the business. This is, in fact, the motivation behind so much technological advancement (that is, removing these bottlenecks so that technological constraints don't sabotage business constraints). The warehouse may want to transition to radio frequency data entry, but the substation next door causes too much interference; the technology may be ideal, but to overcome the interference problem would cost twice what has been budgeted for the whole project.

Rules

Constraints are like mandates: It must be done this way! Rules are more like agreements: We've talked about it and agreed that the invoice needs to include these items and have these approvals. Rules need to be enforced, but if you find a better way to do it you can always talk about it again and choose to change it. In the meantime, you agree to implement and follow the decision consistently. Rules can be anything from the look of a form or screen, to a business process with checks and approvals, number of copies, and waiting periods. Constraining policies are typically upper-management decisions or directives from the business environment (legislation, regulations, and so on) and tend to be separate from the processes that implement them.

In the case study, the inventory control system requires you to complete the receiving documentation with the prescribed details about the shipper, products, shipping company, and time of arrival. Not all this information is necessarily essential to the business, but it does help management make decisions about shipping companies and suppliers based on their delivery performance.

During the analysis phase, rules are a major focus of discussion. They refocus your attention onto *why* the client is doing the job that particular way. For example, why do they need the extra shipment information? When you use this line of questioning, you bring the client back to that important question, "What is really needed to make this system work correctly?" And, "What is essential?" versus "What do you do because you want to, or because the old system didn't work, or because you are used to doing it that way?"

The UML diagrams provide places for you to capture these rules. In Sessions 5 through 8, you will use the Use Case model to describe how the users plan to use the system for filling orders, stocking products, and so on. Sessions 9 through 13 use the Class and Object diagrams to model rules and constraints for the resources the system manipulates like shipments, products, and orders. Sessions 14 and 15 model how the various processes are supposed to work using the Activity diagram. Sessions 16 through 23 explain how to use the Sequence, Collaboration, and Statechart diagrams to capture how objects behave when they are used in these processes.

Performance

Performance requirements define how well the system solution should perform when you use it. The challenge here is that the means to achieve the required performance may require choices at any or all the project phases. For example, the speed at which the product search window refreshes may reflect the volume of data being requested, bandwidth on the network, server memory or speed, the efficiency of the code, and so on. If you can identify the performance requirements, then you can use them at each phase of the project to evaluate how what you're deciding in that phase could affect the ultimate outcome.

Consider the impact on these design phases if the requirement is a specific response time threshold for all applications:

- **Requirements gathering:** Earlier, I said that the inventory control system users wanted to network the warehouse to the accounting office so that they can do inventory searches, but the phone lines would be so restrictive that this would interfere with the performance of the system. Addressing this requirement could require feasibility testing to determine exactly what performance levels could be achieved given the current limitations of the phone lines.

- **Analysis:** In the inventory system, users have defined product searches that bring the current system to its knees. You could restrict the allowed lookups to take advantage of the database configuration and guarantee the required response time.

- **Design:** The database in use is two versions behind and the current version promises to provide the speed that would satisfy the required performance level if we also put the restricted lookups in place. Unfortunately, the upgrade adds three months to the project and 15 percent to the project cost.

The most important point to remember here is that performance is not a concern to be left to the implementation phase. Performance should be addressed throughout the project.

An Inventory Control System

Now to the nitty-gritty part you've been waiting for! As a hands-on opportunity to explore the diagramming techniques, you'll work on modeling the inventory control system. Although you won't be able to build a complete model, you'll have ample opportunity to try the UML modeling notation in a reasonably realistic setting.

The goal of this course is to build at least one of each type of diagram to model the inventory control system. This should provide a representative sampling of how each type of diagram may be applied to understand and to solve a problem.

Beginning with user requirements and progressing through the logical modeling of classes and objects and their interactions, you will move on to process modeling, and finally implementation modeling. In each session, I explain the use of each diagram and the notation used to express the model fully.

Identifying requirements

There is a wealth of material in bookstores on gathering and documenting requirements. The variety is a reflection of the diversity of applications under development. Some of the techniques can be large and sophisticated. But because this book is intended as a crash course, I don't want you to get diverted from the focus, which is applying the UML modeling language to describe systems. So I take a simplified approach.

One approach to gathering requirements is to look for them by examining the problem statement and the supporting documents and interviews from different perspectives. Using these different perspectives also helps to validate the requirements by giving you the opportunity to compare and contrast what you find from three overlapping sources:

- **Users:** Users have expectations for the use of the system.
- **Resources:** Resources are represented as information that is created, used, and deleted by the system to support the system behavior.
- **Functionality:** Functionality refers to the behavior supported by the system.

While you're researching the problem from each unique perspective, be on the lookout for the four different types of requirements discussed earlier.

Users

Someone or something (another system or device) is going to communicate with your system. You need to know why and what they expect from their communication with the system. Consequently, the questions you ask should focus on the users' responsibilities that make them dependent upon the system or that make them an essential source of information for the system.

As you read through these questions, try to imagine the answers you may receive from the actors in the case study. You'll need that information to build the diagrams in the remaining chapters.

Business process requirements

- What are your job responsibilities? Do many people share the same set of responsibilities? If their jobs are different, then explain how and why.
- What does this system provide that ensures the success of your job or task? Is it information? Is it approval? Is it a specific output, like a report or form? What happens if you can't get the information?

Constraints

- Are there any regulations, contracts, or laws that dictate how you do your job?
- What authority, if any, do you need to access the features you use?

Rules

- What policies and procedures determine how you have to do your job?

Performance

- How many people will need to use the system? How many will use it concurrently?
- How slow can the system be before it interferes with your job?

Resources

What do I mean by a *resource* when talking about software systems? Information. Data. Typically, the sole purpose of a software system is to accumulate, manipulate, create, store, destroy, and retrieve information.

So how do you find these resources? One simple and very effective method is to examine the vocabulary of the users. Building a dictionary of the domain vocabulary is a good place to start. The terminology usually requires a bit of cleanup, but that too can be a healthy experience as you discuss the vocabulary with the users. Working from the vocabulary focuses your interview questions and makes better use of the client's time. In my experience, it also improves your relationship with the users when you seek to understand their world through their own words.

Business process requirements

- What resources do you acquire or dispose of? What resources/information do you rely on to do your job? What information are you responsible for (that is, what resources do you approve or requisition)?

Constraints

- What restrictions influence the acquisition, use, and disposal of each resource? Are there any legal or government regulations that dictate your use of this resource?

Rules

- What authority level is required to approve the acquisition, use, and disposal of each resource (that is, how do you determine who is and is not allowed to use it)? What policies govern the use of this resource within the company?

Performance

- How much time is allowed for each transaction involving this resource? Does the volume of resources affect your ability to process them effectively?

Functionality

Functionality simply means what you expect the system to do. The cleanest way I know to find out is to go back to the questions you asked the users. If you can find out what their jobs are, specifically what tasks they must perform, then you can identify the specific objectives that the system must support. Focusing on objectives is critical. Avoid getting caught up in how they achieve those objectives. Talking with users about their work without talking about how they do it is almost impossible. Most people operate on the level of process, how they do their job. That's okay as long as you always remember to ask, "Why?"

These questions keep you focused on the purpose of the function and away from processes that could be used to implement the function. This is a critical distinction when you get to Use Cases in Session 5.

Business Process Requirements

- Why do you do that? What do you expect to happen when you do that?
- What happens when it doesn't work? Is there more than one possible outcome?
- Do people with different jobs perform this same task? Do they do it for the same reason?

Constraints

- What regulations or laws govern how you are allowed to perform the task?

Rules

- What guidelines or policies dictate the way you perform the task?
- Does this task depend on other tasks?

Performance

- What factors influence or even determine how quickly you can complete the task?
- How quickly does the task have to be performed?

**10 Min.
To Go**

Avoiding early pitfalls

The UML gives us a reasonably precise language to communicate very effectively about challenging concepts. But the job of the analyst still boils down to good communication. So let's take a look at a few of the common pitfalls that can sabotage good communication.

Pitfall #1: Making assumptions

Every piece of information encountered during problem definition or analysis is under suspicion. I can't tell you how many shouting matches I've mediated between programmers and clients because one or the other assumed something in a conversation. The programmer assumed that the client spoke for everyone who does the same job, not realizing that nearly everyone had his own peculiar way of doing it. The client assumed that the programmer already knew most of the facts and only called the meeting to ask specific questions. So the client didn't volunteer any of the missing information and the programmer remained ignorant.

Confirm everything! When possible and reasonable, confirm it in multiple ways. Here again, the UML provides us the means to do exactly this type of verification. I'll provide examples of this cross checking as you learn about each of the UML diagrams.

Pitfall #2: Replicating existing implementations

This is probably the single most common and destructive pitfall. Most projects are under serious time pressure. Managers constantly ask the programmers, "Where is the code?" Analysis is all about critical thinking — asking why and challenging the status quo. What brought the approving managers to the point that they were willing to spend the company's money on this project? Something was viewed as an obstacle to the company. How can you remove the obstacle if you simply replace the existing system with a duplicate system in a different technology?

Pitfall #3: Mistaking preferences for requirements

Users are people. People have opinions — and not often the same opinions. Beware of people who have a vested interest in how things are done. One client may be the one who thought up the current process. Another client is the dragon slayer, seeking out anything and everything to change. Other clients simply refuse to reach a consensus.

Often, the most willing client to participate as the project liaison takes on one of the first two roles, champion or dragon slayer. Both bring a strong bias to the project requirements.

This situation challenges you to be the objective outsider. The modeling techniques I cover in the rest of the course provide you with a set of tools that will help objectify the issues and identify inconsistencies.

Done!

REVIEW

In this session, you began your evaluation of the problem statement, the description of the problem you are supposed to solve, or to be fair, an opportunity you are supposed to exploit. You identified four major types of requirements: business process, constraints, rules, and performance. You then used three different perspectives to investigate these requirements: users, resources, and functionality. The different perspectives help to guarantee that you don't miss anything and that you can validate the requirements by cross-checking them.

In the effort to understand a problem statement, you were cautioned to watch out for some common pitfalls:

- Avoid making assumptions of any kind. Always challenge and confirm.
- Be careful not to mistake user preferences for true requirements.
- Watch out for the possibility that you are simply replacing the old system with a duplicate in new attire (that is, a new platform or technology).

QUIZ YOURSELF

1. What is a problem statement? (See "The Case Study Problem Statement.")
2. What is a constraint? (See "Constraints.")
3. What is a rule? (See "Rules.")
4. When talking about requirements, what is a user? (See "Identifying requirements.")
5. When talking about requirements, what is functionality? (See "Identifying requirements.")
6. Why should you be skeptical of user preferences? (See "Avoiding early pitfalls.")

PART

I

Friday Evening Part Review

1. How would you describe the UML?
2. What was the source for the initial UML draft?
3. What did the Object-Oriented Analysis and Design Task Force RFP ask for?
4. How can the UML be extended?
5. What is included in the metamodel?
6. What are the three major elements of any methodology?
7. What key element of a methodology does the UML provide?
8. What are the hallmarks of the Rational Unified Process?
9. What are two of the most distinguishing features of the Shlaer-Mellor method?
10. What is a CRC card?
11. What resources make up the Use Case view?
12. Describe the static view.
13. What can be represented in the Activity diagram?
14. What is illustrated in the Collaboration diagram?
15. When would you use the Component diagram?
16. What should be your main focus when researching business processes?
17. Name three categories of requirements.
18. When talking about requirements, what is meant by a resource?
19. What are three common pitfalls in early analysis?
20. Give two examples of a dangerous assumption.
21. Why is replicating an existing system a pitfall?

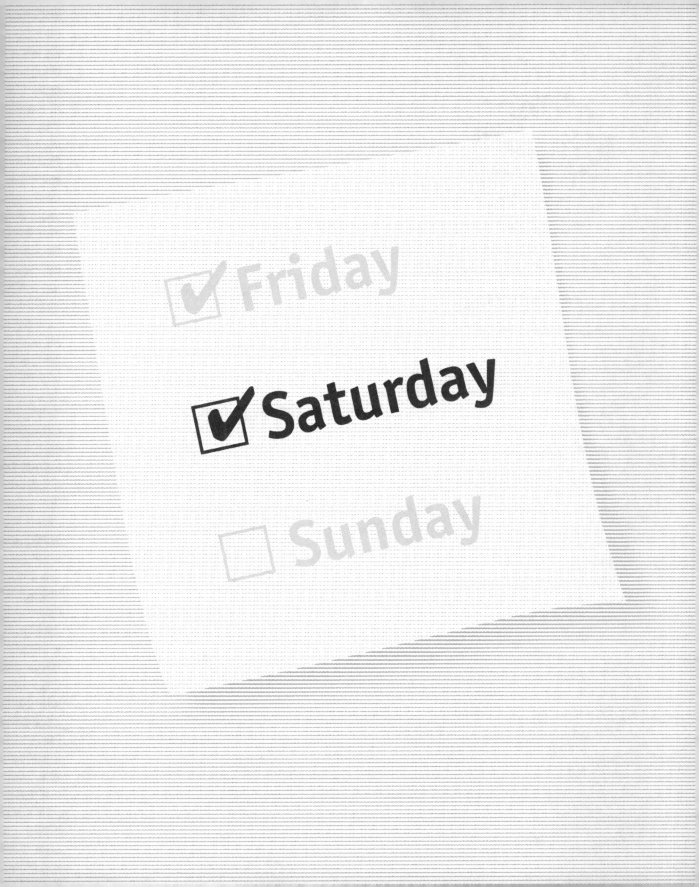

Part II — Saturday Morning

Part III — Saturday Afternoon

Part IV — Saturday Evening

PART

II

Saturday Morning

Understanding the Use Case Model

**30 Min.
To Go**

In 1992, Ivar Jacobson and his associates published a description of a process called Objectory that was successful for large-scale object-oriented projects at Ericsson, HP, and other telecommunications companies. They called the process a *Use Case driven* approach because it views the system from the perspective of how external entities (people and other systems) need to interact with the system.

The Use Case *model* is a collection of diagrams and text that together document how users expect to interact with the system. Figure 5-1 illustrates the Use Case diagram, the Use Case narrative, and the Use Case scenarios (using a flowchart or Activity diagram).

The Use Case model focuses on the critical success factors of the system, in terms of the functionality or features that the users need to interact with. By focusing on the system's features, you create a set of conceptual slots into which all the widely varied requirements can be placed.

Features can be tested, modeled, designed, and implemented. Users who require a particular feature become the audience for the modeling activities for that feature. By focusing on features, you also define the scope of the project (that is, which features will and will not be supported by the final solution and, typically, the list of features that will be implemented in each incremental release). In Session 6, you'll analyze the essential features of the case study problem statement.

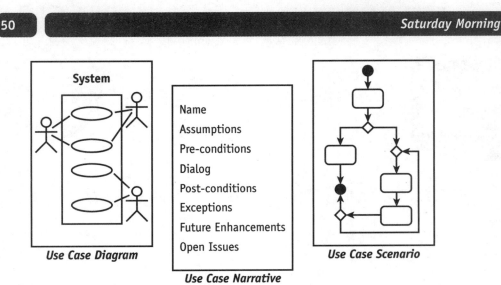

Figure 5-1   *Resources of the Use Case model*

The Purpose of the Use Case Model

The key difference between Use Cases and functional design is the focus. Functional design documents a process, but a Use Case focuses on the goal of a process. This change in mindset is essential in keeping us from jumping to solutions without first understanding why. Just think about how rapidly technology changes! A process that works today will likely become obsolete or inadequate very quickly. Furthermore, focusing on the process often leads to reproducing existing systems, rather than redesigning them, precisely because it focuses on "how" rather than "why."

Let me share a short story that I'm sure you can relate to. A husband was helping his wife prepare dinner. He noticed that before placing the ham in the oven, she carefully cut about three inches off the end of the ham. When he asked her why she did it, she simply stated that her mother always did it, so she assumed it was the right thing to do. Weeks later, they had occasion to ask his wife's mother about the ham. She said the same thing. Her mother had always done it, so she assumed it was correct. At a holiday dinner they asked Grandma why she cut the end off the ham. With a shocked look on her face she stated bluntly, "I never had a big enough pan!"

Goal-focused modeling keeps you focused on a target rather than the means of getting to the target (Figure 5-2). This keeps you open to a variety of solutions, allowing and possibly encouraging you to take advantage of technological advances.

Figure 5-2   *Focus on the target, the goal of the process.*

For example, in the case study, the Accounts Payable Department needs to be notified when products have been received. For years this has meant that the paperwork for the shipment was delivered to the warehouse supervisor who in turn delivered it to the Accounts Payable Department. If you document this process as a requirement, you miss the opportunity to automate the process and remove the physical problems and limitations of hand delivering documents.

The Resources of the Use Case Model

The Use Case Model takes advantage of three different viewpoints to fully describe each requirement. The first and simplest resource is the Use Case diagram. The Use Case narrative and Use Case scenarios make up the remainder of the model.

Use Case diagram

The Use Case diagram consists of five very simple graphics that represent the system, actors, Use Cases, associations, and dependencies of the project. The goal of the diagram is to provide a high-level explanation of the relationship between the system and the outside world. It is a very *flat* diagram (that is, it provides only a surface level, or black-box, view of the system).

The view represented by a Use Case diagram for an ATM application, for example, would correspond to the main screen of an ATM and the menu options available at that level. The ATM *system* offers the user a set of options such as withdraw, deposit, inquire on balance, and transfer funds. Each option can be represented by a separate Use Case. The customer (outside the system) is associated with each of the Use Cases (within the system) that he plans to use.

Use Case narrative

On the Use Case diagram, a Use Case is simply an ellipse with a simple label like "Receive Product." Although this label may provide a meaningful interface, it doesn't explain what you can expect from this system feature. For that, you need a textual description. The Use Case narrative provides a fairly standard (yet user-defined) set of information that is required to guide the analysis, design, and coding of the feature.

Use Case scenarios

A Use Case scenario is one logical path through a Use Case, one possible sequence of steps in the execution of the Use Case. A Use Case may include any number of scenarios. The set of scenarios for one Use Case identifies everything that can happen when that Use Case is used. Consequently, the set of scenarios becomes the basis for your test plan for the Use Case. As the application design deepens, the test plans are expanded to keep the tests focused on the original expectations for the Use Case expressed in the scenarios.

These three elements — the Use Case diagram, narrative, and scenarios — comprise the Use Case Model. The remainder of this session is devoted to the Use Case diagram. Session 7 covers the Use Case narrative, and Session 8 covers the Use Case scenarios.

Defining the Elements of the Use Case Diagram

Of the three elements that comprise the Use Case Model, the only one actually defined by the UML is the Use Case diagram (Figure 5-3).

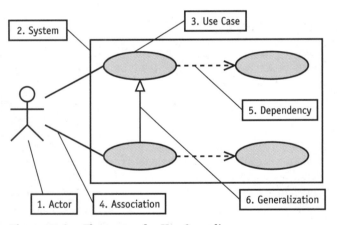

Figure 5-3   *Elements of a Use Case diagram*

Six modeling elements make up the Use Case diagram: systems, actors, Use Cases, associations, dependencies, and generalizations.

- **System:** Sets the boundary of the system in relation to the actors who use it (outside the system) and the features it must provide (inside the system).
- **Actor:** A role played by a person, system, or device that has a stake in the successful operation of the system.
- **Use Case:** Identifies a key feature of the system. Without these features, the system will not fulfill the user/actor requirements. Each Use Case expresses a goal that the system must achieve.
- **Association:** Identifies an interaction between actors and Use Cases. Each association becomes a dialog that must be explained in a Use Case narrative. Each narrative in turn provides a set of scenarios that function as test cases when evaluating the analysis, design, and implementation of the Use Case.

- **Dependency:** Identifies a communication relationship between two Use Cases.
- **Generalization:** Defines a relationship between two actors or two Use Cases where one Use Case inherits and adds to or overrides the properties of the other.

Now comes the fun part. It's finally time to learn the notation that will allow you to begin developing diagrams.

Use Case system

20 Min.
To Go

One of the first tasks in a project is to set the context and scope of the proposed application. You need to answer questions such as how much to include in the system, how this system relates to other systems in your architecture, and who plans to use this system.

All this could be described in a lengthy document. But, as the saying goes, a picture is worth a thousand words. This conviction helps explain the simplicity of the system notation, a mere rectangle with a name (Figure 5-4). The system icon simply provides a context into and around which you place all the elements that influence the construction of the system.

> **Having said that, I must tell you that the system icon is rarely used. It tends to be too restrictive and doesn't add substantial information to the diagram. Consequently, in most tools, you will only see Use Cases, actors, and their relationships.**

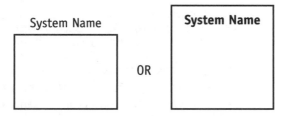

Figure 5-4 *System icon for the Use Case diagram*

Think of the system in terms of *encapsulation,* which asserts that to use an object, you need know only its interfaces, not its internal implementation. A system is like an object, in that each has a purpose and an interface. The internal implementations of the object or system may be replaced or enhanced without affecting other entities as long as the purpose and the interfaces remain unchanged.

So, the priority in defining the system is to define its purpose and the required interfaces. The purpose is the target of the project justification. The interfaces are the channels of communication between the actors outside the system and the features of the system itself, the Use Cases. Working inward from this fundamental requirement, you set the context for all subsequent modeling of the system's internal behavior.

Use Case actors

Systems always have users. Users in the classic sense are people who use the system. But users can also be other systems or devices that trade information.

In Use Case diagrams, people, systems, and devices are all referred to as *actors*. The icons to model them may vary, but the concept remains the same. An actor is a *role* that an external entity plays in relation to the system. To reiterate, an actor is a *role,* not necessarily a particular person or a specific system. Figure 5-5 shows some actor icons.

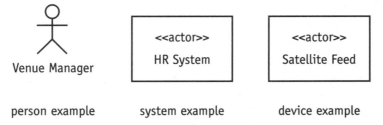

person example   system example   device example

Figure 5-5   *Actor icons for the Use Case diagram*

For example, an actor may be the role of a stock clerk placing products into inventory. Later that day the same person might work receiving products from a delivery truck. The same person played two roles. Likewise, many people can function in the same role. For example, warehouses have many stock clerks.

Using roles helps keep you focused on how the system is being used rather than on the current organization of the company into job titles and responsibilities. The things that people do must be separated from their current job titles for the system to be able to cope with the changes that are inevitable in any system.

How do you identify actors? Listen to descriptions of the system. Listen for the roles people perform when using the system. When multiple people perform the same function, try to name the role they all share when performing the particular function.

Throughout the modeling effort, the vocabulary of the user will reveal most of the key elements of the model. Watch for how parts of speech translate into model elements; actors typically show up as the subject in sentences describing how people use the systems.

Use Cases

Use Cases define the required features of the system. Without these features, the system cannot be used successfully.

Each Use Case is named using a verb phrase that expresses a goal the system must accomplish, for example, deposit money, withdraw money, and adjust account (see Figure 5-6). Although each Use Case implies a supporting process, the focus is on the goal, not the process.

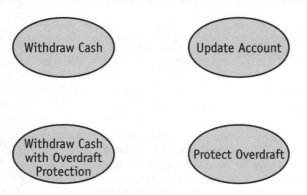

Figure 5-6   *Use Case notation for the Use Case diagram*

By defining Use Cases in this manner, the system is defined as a set of requirements rather than a solution. You do not describe how the system must work. You describe what the system must be able to do. The Use Cases describe only those features visible and meaningful to the actors who use the system. Keeping this in mind will help you avoid *functional decomposition,* the breaking down of procedures and tasks into smaller and smaller processes until you have described all the internal workings of the system. One of the pitfalls of systems development is going over budget, which happens when you don't limit the scope of each task or you make a model too inclusive. The UML provides seven diagrams, in addition to the Use Case Model, for fully describing the solution for the system, so remember that you can save some work for later.

One very common question about Use Cases is, "What requirements belong on the Use Case diagram and what requirements should be explained elsewhere?" The simplest answer I've found is, "Model only the features of the system that can be seen by an actor."

For example, the system must save data to a database, but the actor can't actually see this happening. The most they typically see is a message indicating that it did. In this situation, the Use Case level requirement is a message indicating success or failure on the save function, not the save function itself.

Use Case relationships

So far, I've defined the system, actors, and Use Cases, but now you need to associate each user with the system features they need to perform their jobs.

**10 Min.
To Go**

Association notation

A line connecting an actor to a Use Case represents an association, as shown in Figure 5-7. The association represents the fact that the actor communicates with the Use Case. In fact, in earlier versions of the UML spec, this was called a Communicates With relationship. This is the only relationship that exists between an actor and a Use Case. According to the UML spec, you may specify a directionality arrow on either end of the association line to denote the direction of the communication. Some associations are unidirectional (for example, the actor specifies information to the Use Case). Most associations are bidirectional (that is, the actor accesses the Use Case, and the Use Case provides functionality to the actor). For bidirectional associations, you may either place an arrowhead on both ends of the association line, or simply show no arrowheads at all. For simplification, most users tend to show no arrowheads at all. Most modeling tools provide the option to turn bidirectional arrows on or off. Just remember that the key is to identify which Use Cases the actors need to access. These connections will form the basis for the interfaces of the system and subsequent modeling efforts.

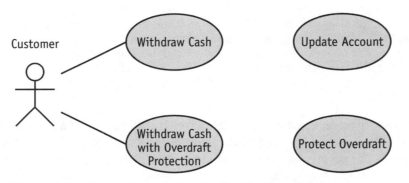

Figure 5-7   *Association notation for the Use Case diagram*

Stereotype notation

The stereotype notation is used throughout the UML, very commonly on Use Case dependencies, classes, and packages and other elements of the UML known as *classifiers*. The standard notation is to enclose the word in *guillemets* << >> (French quote marks), as in the <<include>> notation below. Stereotypes provide a means to extend the UML without modifying it. A stereotype functions as a qualifier on a model element, providing more information about the role of the element without dictating its implementation.

<<include>> dependency notation

Sometimes one Use Case may need to ask for help from another Use Case. For example, Use Cases titled Deposit Money and Withdraw Money may not actually update a bank account. They may delegate the changes to an existing Use Case called Update Account so that changes are controlled through a single feature that guarantees that all changes are done correctly.

When one Use Case delegates to another, the dependency is drawn as a dashed arrow from the "using" Use Case to the "used" Use Case and labeled with the <<include>> stereotype notation, as shown in figure 5-8. This conveys that executing the "using" (or calling) Use Case will include or incorporate the functionality of the "used" Use Case. If you have a programming background, you see right away the correlation with subroutine or function calls.

Delegation may occur for one of two reasons. First, another Use Case may already exist to perform the task that is needed. Second, a number of Use Cases may need to perform the same task. Rather than write the same logic multiple times, the common task is isolated into its own Use Case and reused by, or included into, each Use Case that needs it.

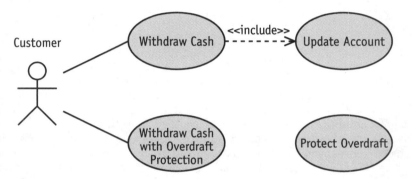

Figure 5-8   *<<include>> dependency notation for the Use Case diagram*

<<extend>> dependency notation

The <<extend>> dependency stereotype says that one Use Case *might* need help from another Use Case. In contrast, the <<include>> dependency stereotype says that one Use Case will *always* call the other Use Case. Somewhere in the logic of the Use Case that needs the help is an *extension point,* a condition test that determines whether or not the call should be made. There is no such condition in an include dependency.

The other contrast between the two dependency stereotypes is the direction of the dependency arrow. The <<include>> dependency arrow points from the main Use Case (the one currently executing) to the one that it needs help from. The <<extend>> dependency arrow points from the extension Use Case (the one providing the extra help) to the main Use Case that it is helping (see Figure 5-9).

If you read the basic definition of a dependency, the <<extend>> dependency arrow seems to be backwards. That is one reason I often put an "s" on the end of these stereotypes. For example, the Withdraw Cash Use Case <<includes>> Update Account (the Withdraw Cash Use Case will always update the account). Likewise, the Protect Overdraft Use Case <<extends>> Withdraw Cash (the Protect Overdraft Use Case will sometimes be called by the Withdraw Cash Use Case).

The extend dependency can be confusing for Java programmers who use "extends" to achieve inheritance. These two concepts have nothing in common. The UML provides a separate notation for inheritance (or generalization).

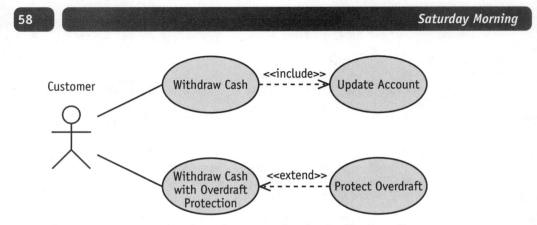

Figure 5-9 *<<extend>> dependency notation for the Use Case diagram*

Generalization

Inheritance is a key concept in object-oriented programming, and OO analysis and design. Inheritance tells us that one object has, at the time of its creation, access to all the properties of another class, besides its own class. Thus, the created object incorporates all those properties into its own definition. In layman's terms, we say things like, "A Ford Explorer is a car." A car is a well-defined general concept. When you create a Ford Explorer, rather than redefine all the car properties, you simply "inherit" or assimilate all the existing car properties, then override and/or add any new properties to complete the definition of your new Ford Explorer object.

The same idea, applied to actors and to Use Cases, is called *generalization,* and often goes by the nickname, an *"is a"* relationship. A Senior Bank Teller *is a* Bank Teller with additional authority and responsibilities. The "Withdraw Cash with Overdraft Protection" Use Case *is a* more extensive requirement than the "Withdraw Cash" Use Case.

To model generalization, the UML uses a solid line with a hollow triangle. It looks a bit like an arrow, but be careful not to confuse the two. The triangle is always on the end near the item that is being inherited. In the examples mentioned earlier, the triangle would be near "Bank Teller" and "Withdraw Cash," as shown in Figure 5-10.

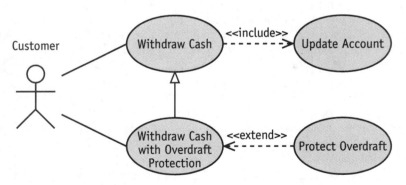

Figure 5-10 *Generalization notation for the Use Case diagram*

Done!

REVIEW

The Use Case model comprises a set of resources aimed at defining the goals of a system. The concept came from the work of Ivar Jacobson on a methodology called Objectory. The purpose of the model is to focus the development effort on the essential objectives of the system without getting lost in or driven by particular implementations or practices.

- The Use Case model consists of three primary resources: the Use Case diagram, the Use Case narrative, and Use Case scenarios.
- The Use Case diagram uses a system icon to define the boundaries of the system.
- Actors define entities outside the system that will use the system in some way.
- Associations indicate which actors will access which features (Use Cases) of the system.
- Dependencies describe the nature of the relationships between Use Cases.
- Generalization is used to illustrate inheritance relationships between Use Cases and between actors.

QUIZ YOURSELF

1. What is the relationship between people and roles in a Use Case diagram? (See "Use Case actors.")
2. Where do you use associations in a Use Case diagram? (See "Association notation.")
3. Why would you use the dependency stereotype <<include>>? (See "<<include>> dependency notation.")
4. When would you use the <<extends>> dependency stereotype? (See "<<extend>> dependency notation.")
5. Where can you use the generalization relationship on a Use Case diagram? (See "Generalization.")

Building the Use Case Diagram

Session Checklist

✔ Understanding the steps used to build a Use Case diagram

✔ Building the Use Case diagram for the case study

Session 5 introduced the notation for the Use Case diagram. In this session, you find out how to build a Use Case diagram by concentrating on the case study.

**30 Min.
To Go**

Building the Use Case Diagram for the Case Study

The following text makes up the description of the case study. I refer to this as the *problem statement*. Use this problem statement as your source for the information needed to build the Use Case diagram.

You will see the problem statement change from session to session. This is necessary within the book because I need to tailor the problem so that you will have an opportunity to use as many of the new concepts as possible in each session.

Receiving: The receiving clerks receive incoming shipments by matching purchase orders against the stock in the shipment. They inform the Accounts Payable department when the purchase order items have been received. The clients want the new system to handle the notification automatically.

Stocking: The products may come from cancelled orders, returned orders, or vendor shipments. The products are placed in the warehouse in predefined locations. The stock clerk looks up the correct location for the new products, places the products in that location, and updates the location inventory with the product quantity.

Order Fulfillment: Other staff members fill orders by locating the products required for the order. As they fill the order they update inventory to reflect the fact that they have taken the products. They also notify the Order Processing department that the order has been filled. The clients want the new system to handle the notification to Order Processing.

Shipping: When the orders are filled, they are then packed and prepared for shipping. The shipping folks contact the shippers to arrange delivery. They then update inventory after they ship the product. They also notify the Order Processing department that the order has shipped. The clients want the new system to handle the notification to Order Processing.

I don't for a second want to give the impression that this is the only way to build Use Case diagrams. But to get you started, I'm offering these steps as a guide. When you become comfortable with the Use Case concepts, you'll undoubtedly develop your own preferences and write me a wonderful letter full of ideas on how I can improve this book. I thank you in advance. For now, this should give you a solid start.

Step 1: Set the context of the target system

Context always comes first. Context provides the frame of reference for the information you're evaluating. Context defines the placement of the system within the business, including the work processes, business plans and objectives, other systems, people and their job duties, and constraints imposed by external entities like government and contractual agreements.

According to the problem statement, the participants:

- ". . . inform the Accounts Payable department"
- ". . . notify the Order Processing department"
- ". . . contact the shippers"

The context places the system within the warehouse operations, working closely with Order Processing and Accounts Payable, and with shippers.

 You can see also how establishing the context begs questions about the scope (for example, where exactly is the boundary of responsibility between Accounts Payable and Inventory Control?).

Step 2: Identify the actors

Find the people, systems, or devices that communicate with the system. The system-type actors are often easiest to spot as interfaces and external communication, such as notifications to the Accounts Payable and Order Processing systems. The other actors will be participants in the operation of the Inventory Control system. All these users will become your sources for finding and validating the required features of the system (that is, Use Cases).

The problem statement referred to two system-type actors, shown in Figure 6-1:

- "They inform the *Accounts Payable department* when the purchase order items have been received." The Accounts Payable System must know when the company has incurred a liability for a shipment.

- "They also notify the *Order Processing department* that the order has been filled." "They also notify the *Order Processing department* that the order has shipped." The Order Processing System needs to keep the customer informed of the status of its shipment.

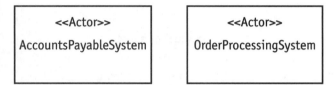

Figure 6-1 *System-type actors from the problem statement*

From the problem statement, you also find four human actors (shown in Figure 6-2):

- "The receiving clerks receive incoming shipments by . . . ." People receive products into inventory. I refer to this role as *Receiving*.

- "The shipping folks contact the shippers to . . . ." The people who ship the product, retain shippers, pack the product, and complete the shipping documents are referred to as *Shipping*.

- "Other staff members fill orders . . . ." The people responsible for filling orders, whether for samples, customer orders, wholesale, or retail, are referred to as *Order Fulfillment*.

- "The stock clerk looks up . . . ." The people responsible for putting the products into inventory are referred to as *Stock Clerk*.

Figure 6-2 *Human actors from the problem statement*

It is no accident that the naming so closely parallels the user's description of the system. Your abstractions should parallel the user's vocabulary. After all, you and the user are both representing the same real-world concepts.

Step 3: Identify the Use Cases

20 Min. To Go

Find the features or functionality that the system must provide by asking these and similar questions:

- **What does the system produce for the actor?** This question helps identify work products that the system must support, known as the *critical outputs*.

- **What does the actor help the system do?** This question helps us know the input facilities that the system needs to support, known as the *critical inputs.*

- **What does the system help the actor(s) do?** This question helps identify the rules that must be applied when the actors use the system.

The Use Cases identified in the problem statement text include:

- **ReceiveProduct:** ". . . receive incoming shipments . . . ."

  The goal is to record products into inventory, regardless of source.

- **ShipOrder:** ". . . they ship the product."

  The goal is to record shipments and ensure that the products they contain have left the premises.

- **StockProduct:** "The products are placed in the warehouse in predefined locations."

  The goal is to record that products have been placed into the designated locations within the inventory.

- **FillOrder:** "Other staff members fill orders . . . ."

  The goal is to allocate specific inventoried products exclusively to satisfy an order.

- **LocateProduct:** "The stock clerk looks up the correct location . . . ." "Other staff members fill orders by locating . . . ."

  The goal is to identify the location within the facility in which a specific product resides.

Your definitions at this time probably won't be final. A lot of information comes to light during the rigors of the analysis phase. But these preliminary definitions give you a lot of valuable research material to facilitate the analysis process.

Step 4: Define the associations between actors and Use Cases

Identify the actor(s) who need access to each Use Case/feature of the system. Each access relationship is a UML *association*. These associations are important because they tell you who the system *stakeholders* are (the people with a vested interest in the success of the system). For example, will the person at the order desk be able to do his job if he can't see the status of an order? As a stakeholder, what does he have to say about how the Use Case should work? You'll use that information in Session 7 when you write the Use Case narrative to explain what the stakeholders want the Use Case to do.

Watch how the vocabulary of the problem statement helps you identify the associations (shown in Figure 6-3):

- **An association between Receiving and ReceiveProduct.** "The receiving clerks receive incoming shipments . . . ."

- **An association between ReceiveProduct and AccountsPayableSystem.** "They inform the Accounts Payable department when the purchase order items have been received. The clients want the new system to handle the notification automatically."

- **An association between Shipping and ShipOrder.** "When the orders are filled, they are then packed and prepared for shipping. The shipping folks contact the shippers to arrange delivery. They then update inventory once they ship the product."

- **An association between ShipOrder and OrderProcessingSystem.** "They also notify the Order Processing department that the order has shipped. The clients want the new system to handle the notification to Order Processing."
- **An association between StockClerk and Stock Product.** "The stock clerk looks up the correct location for the new products, places the products in that location, and updates the location inventory with the product quantity."
- **An association between FillOrder and OrderProcessingSystem.** "They also notify the Order Processing department that the order has been filled. The clients want the new system to handle the notification to Order Processing."
- **An association between OrderFulfillment and LocateProduct.** "Other staff members fill orders by locating the products required for the order."

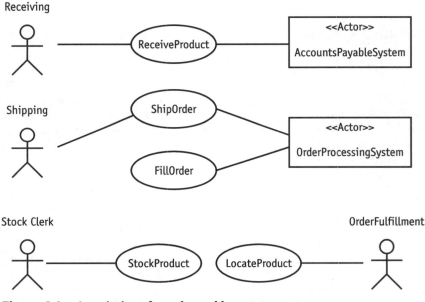

Figure 6-3 *Associations from the problem statement*

Step 5: Evaluate the actors and Use Cases to find opportunities for refinement

Rename, merge, and split actors and Use Cases as needed. When you build your diagrams based on interviews with users, it is easy to fall into the trap of replicating the current system (see Session 4). From your first draft of the descriptions of the actors and Use Cases, start asking critical questions, especially the simple but powerful question, "Why?" For example, ask, "Why is this actor responsible for these particular duties?" or "Why do these tasks have to be done together, separately, in this order, or done at all?" A system rewrite or major revision provides a great opportunity to clean house and address a lot of the legacy problems that have accumulated over time.

For example, the problem statement tells you that the receiving and stocking jobs are independent. Years ago they were, but now the staff unloads the trucks and places the products into inventory right away. Although the tasks may remain distinct, there is no longer a real distinction in the roles of the people doing the work. Perhaps the actor definitions should be merged, as illustrated in Figure 6-4.

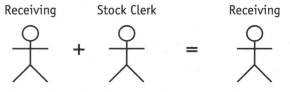

Figure 6-4   *Merging two roles into one role*

Step 6: Evaluate the Use Cases for <<include>> dependencies

Apply the <<include>> dependency stereotype between Use Cases when one Use Case always calls on another Use Case to help it with a task that the calling Use Case cannot handle. The included Use Case may already exist or it may recur in a number of Use Cases and need to be isolated. For example, updating inventory is one of the requirements for ShipOrder, StockProduct, and FillOrder. Figure 6-5 isolates the UpdateInventory requirement, defining it once rather than three times, and calls on it from the original three Use Cases.

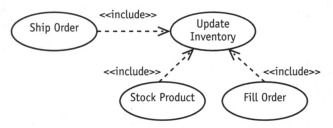

Figure 6-5   *<<include>> dependencies from the problem statement*

You can see right away that we place a high priority on reuse. Everything in a project has the potential for reuse. Use Cases, classes, work flows, analysis procedures, work products, analysis documents, design documents, and code make up only a short list of possible reusable resources.

Step 7: Evaluate the Use Cases for <<extend>> dependencies

10 Min. To Go

One Use Case may or may not use another Use Case depending upon a stated condition. When the condition is met, the call is made to the other Use Case. When the condition is not met, the call is not made.

This example does not have a reason to use the <<extend>> stereotype. But suppose that the users want the flexibility to add a product into inventory right off the truck, without placing it into one of the predefined locations. In essence, they would bypass the StockProduct Use Case. This bypass would only be used with manager-level authority. In this situation, ReceiveProduct would only call the Update Inventory extension if the manager approval were provided to do so. Figure 6-6 models the extend relationship.

Figure 6-6   *An example of <<extend>> dependency*

Watch out for the direction of the arrows; it is easy to get them reversed. Read the dependency in Figure 6-6 as "UpdateInventory extend(s) (is used with) ReceiveProduct if the extension point condition is met in ReceiveProduct."

Step 8: Evaluate the actors and Use Cases for generalization

In Session 5, you saw that generalization is a tool for organizing similarities and differences among a set of objects (like actors or Use Cases) that share the same purpose. Review the diagram for opportunities to apply the generalization concept.

The problem statement told us that, "The products may come from cancelled orders, returned orders, or vendor shipments." If the stocking rules are significantly different for the various types of incoming stock, you could use generalization on the StockProduct Use Case, as shown in Figure 6-7.

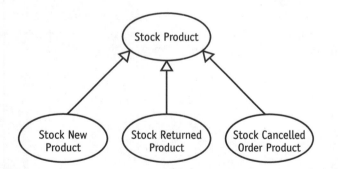

Figure 6-7   *Using generalization to identify differences within a type of Use Case*

Figure 6-7 shows that StockNewProduct inherits all the rules from StockProduct and then adds some variations unique to stocking new products. The same is true for StockReturnedProduct and StockCancelledOrderProduct.

Done!

REVIEW

The goal of the Use Case diagram is to define the expectations of the users. Those users may be people, systems, or devices that need to interact with the system. Their interactions may be to provide input, to receive output, or to dialog with the system in order to cooperate in the completion of a task. All these interactions are focused through a set of specific features of the system called Use Cases. Each Use Case defines one specific goal that the system can achieve.

The construction of a Use Case diagram requires the following steps:

1. Identifying the context of the system
2. Identifying the actors and their responsibilities
3. Identifying the Use Cases, the features of the system, in terms of specific goals
4. Evaluating the actors and Use Cases to find opportunities for refinement
5. Evaluating the Use Cases to find <<include>> type dependencies
6. Evaluating the Use Cases to find <<extend>> type dependency
7. Evaluating the actors and Use Cases for generalization (shared properties)

QUIZ YOURSELF

1. What is an actor? (See "Step 2: Identify the actors.")
2. How do you identify a Use Case? (See "Step 3: Identify the Use Cases.")
3. What is the notation for an <<include>> dependency? (See "Step 6: Evaluate the Use Cases for <<include>> dependencies.")
4. What is another name for a Use Case? (See "Step 3: Identify the Use Cases.")
5. What does it mean when you place the <<extend>> stereotype on a dependency? (See "Step 7: Evaluate the Use Cases for <<extend>> dependencies.")

Building the Use Case Narrative

Session Checklist

✔ Explaining the purpose of a Use Case narrative

✔ Explaining the elements of a typical Use Case narrative

✔ Writing a Use Case narrative for the case study

*30 Min.
To Go*

Although the Use Case diagram provides a convenient view of the main features of a system, it is too concise to completely describe what users are expecting. So, as with most diagrams, it must be supported by a narrative, a textual description that takes us to the next level of understanding.

There are many ways to write Use Case descriptions. Typically, each methodology will have its own set of elements and preferences. What I offer here is a set of common elements that you will find in most methodologies.

Elements of a Use Case Narrative

Describing a Use Case requires that you frame the context of the Use Case and describe the communication between the Use Case and the user, which could be an actor or another Use Case. With this in mind, most Use Case narratives include the following elements, or others very similar in meaning:

- Assumptions
- Pre-conditions
- Use Case initiation
- Process or dialog
- Use Case termination
- Post-conditions

Much of this language is borrowed from the "programming by contract" concept, developed and implemented by Bertrand Meyer in the creation of the Eiffel programming language. One chief goal of the programming by contract concept is to define each unit as autonomous, whether the unit is an object or a Use Case. Each unit should remain as independent from others as possible, also referred to as being *loosely coupled*. Unit independence allows each unit to be maintained without requiring corresponding changes in other units. This reduces the cost of development and maintenance of the system.

Assumptions

Typically, developers think of assumptions as bad, something to be avoided. Here, I'm applying the concept in a positive way. In order for the Use Case to work properly, certain conditions must be true within the system.

You agree, or you contract, never to invoke this Use Case unless you know that all the needed conditions have been met. In other words, assumptions describe a state of the system that must be true before you can use the Use Case. These conditions are *not* tested by the Use Case (contrast this later with the pre-conditions). For example, consider the tasks of performing authentication and authorization. A standard security check feature typically handles these functions. Each subsequent Use Case assumes that the user could not access the Use Case had he not made it past the security check. Consequently, you would rarely if ever include the security check in each Use Case.

So how does this help you with the design of the system? If one Use Case can't work and should not even be accessed unless another Use Case has first done its job, this condition dictates the order of execution. The assumptions give you explicit clues about the sequence of execution for Use Cases (that is, the workflow).

 Place common Use Case assumptions into a system-level document instead of including them in every Use Case narrative.

Pre-conditions

Pre-conditions are easily confused with assumptions. Like assumptions, pre-conditions describe a state of the system that must be true before you can use the Use Case. But unlike assumptions, these conditions *are* tested by the Use Case before doing anything else. If the conditions are not true, the actor is refused entry.

Most programmers have coded pre-conditions nearly every time they write a method or subroutine call that has parameters. When you write code, what are the first lines of code that you write in a function or method that has parameters? You validate the parameters. You test to make certain that the conditions are right to proceed with the rest of the code. Failure in these tests would mean problems for the subsequent code, so the call is refused and turned back to the requester. You established and tested the pre-conditions for execution of your method or function.

These rules or pre-conditions need to be published along with the interface to your Use Case. For example, a typical interface can only tell the client to provide two integer values and a character string. It can't tell them the rules that say that the first integer must be a value between 1 and 10, the second must be an integer greater than 100, and the character string can only be 30 characters in length. Without publishing these pre-conditions, anyone who wants to use your Use Case is forced into relying on trial and error to find the correct set of values.

Notice how rapidly we bring precision to the model from the simple beginnings of the Use Case diagram. You'll find the analysis process akin to pulling a thread on an old sweater. If you keep pulling, eventually you'll unravel the whole complex problem (while your mother yells at you for destroying a perfectly good sweater). Using simple checklists to remind you of the questions to ask can expedite the process and build a successful pattern of thought for problem solving. As you gain experience, modify the list of questions and tasks to improve the process and to make it your own.

The goal is not to become a disciple of a particular technique, but to find a technique that works for you.

Use Case initiation

A Use Case has to start somehow, but how? Some Use Cases start because an actor says, "Start." For example, you can select an option on a menu. The action tells the system to open the application. Time can also trigger a Use Case. Most software shops have scheduling software that kicks off programs at a preset time. Other Use Cases are implemented as objects themselves that watch for a point in time. A Use Case may be triggered by a system event like an error condition, a lost connection, or a signal from a device.

Use Case initiation provides a place to think through all the possible triggers that could launch the Use Case. This is critical when you start thinking about reusing Use Cases. If five actors and/or Use Cases plan on using the same Use Case, then you need to know how each user plans to kick it off. If each has different expectations, then you could be creating a problem. Multiple triggering mechanisms lead to high coupling and low independence. In other words, every time you change one of the triggers, you need to change the corresponding Use Case and make certain that you haven't created problems with the other triggering mechanisms. More triggers mean more complicated and costly maintenance.

Dialog

The *dialog* refers to a step-by-step description of the conversation between the Use Case (the system) and the user (an actor or another Use Case). Very often, it is helpful to model this sequence of events using an Activity diagram just as you might model a procedure for communication between two business units.

For example, you want to withdraw money, so you access the ATM at your local bank. The following dialog ensues:

You get past the security check Use Case, and you're presented with a menu of options.

You choose "Withdraw."

The system immediately asks you which account you want to withdraw the money from.

You reply that you want to withdraw from your primary checking account.

The system then asks you how much you want to withdraw.

You say that you want $47.

The system gives you a nasty error message saying it can't handle that number (because it's not a multiple of 20) and you need to try again.

Then you say you want $4,700.

The system again complains that you can't take that much money out in a 48-hour period.

"Okay, okay! Give me $100," you tell the system.

Now the system is happy and it gives you the money and a receipt.

When goals remain separate from implementation, you can evolve systems whose interface designs remain stable while their implementations take advantage of ever-improving user interface technologies. This conversation could just as easily have happened with any manufacturer's ATM even if it held different cash denominations (10's versus 20's), connected directly to a bank, or connected via a nationwide network. Also, you begin to see that some of the steps don't necessarily have to happen in the sequence presented here. The goal of the dialog is to uncover just what really needs to happen and what variations could be valid.

Even ATM interface designs vary. Have you ever seen an ATM designed for blind people? It performs the exact same conversation but with a different user interface. My home banking software accomplishes essentially the same function, too, but with still a different design for the interface. The system asks all the questions at once and I provide all the answers at once. Same design, different interface.

Use Case termination

Although there is usually only one triggering event to start a Use Case, there are often many ways to end one. You can pretty much count on some kind of normal termination where everything goes as planned and you get the result you anticipated. But things do go wrong. This could mean shutting down the Use Case with an error message, rolling back a transaction, or simply canceling. Each termination mechanism has to be addressed in the dialog.

The list of termination options is a bit redundant with the dialog, but just as was the case with pre-conditions, this redundancy provides some good checks and balances.

Post-conditions

Post-conditions describe a state of the system that must be true when the Use Case ends. You may never know what comes after the Use Case terminates, so you must guarantee that the system is in a stable state when it does end. In fact, some people use the term *guarantee* for just this reason. You guarantee certain things to be true when this Use Case completes its job. You might, for instance, guarantee to give the user a receipt at the end of the transaction, whether it succeeded or failed. You might promise to notify the user of the result of an attempted save to the database.

You may have noticed that some of the post-conditions above, such as giving the user a receipt at the end of the transaction, were already in the Use Case dialog and seem redundant. This may be true, but separating out post-conditions has proven to be an excellent check-and-balance mechanism. The added visibility has also proven to be very helpful in reviews with clients who want to know immediately what the system will do.

Additional narrative elements

20 Min. To Go

The narrative doesn't have to stop with just these elements. Some other common elements include future enhancements, unresolved issues, performance constraints, security requirements, shareholders, maintenance logs, and notes. And I'm certain that your compatriots can suggest more.

Workflow Requirements

A common question about Use Cases is "How do I show workflow or screen flow?" The short answer is that you don't. A more appropriate question would be, "How do I use the Use Case model to determine screen flow and workflow requirements?"

Workflow is often a difficult problem in system design. Personal opinion, personal preferences, and legacy workflows often get included as requirements. Remember the ham story from Session 5? Just like the cooks in the ham story, business practices are prone to faulty assumptions and unquestioned repetition. New systems often contain the same deficiencies that old ones had because they were not critically evaluated in the light of genuine requirements analysis.

To determine workflow requirements with Use Cases, first check out the pre-conditions and assumptions. If Use Case A requires the user to provide data that is obtained by Use Case B, or do something that Use Case B is responsible for, then logically Use Case B must come first.

These clues are a tremendous help when you recognize that many workflows were designed based on user preferences or experience. Because of this approach, they have not been checked against the rules and constraints that define the successful operation of the system. Here you have one means to do this verification.

Quite often, screen flow and workflows are far more flexible than you might think. Let the Use Case assumptions and pre-conditions tell you what the flow options are. Then design the workflows that are possible, letting the users decide what works best for them.

Writing a Use Case Narrative for the Case Study

To practice writing a narrative, you will use the Use Case Fill Order in the case study Use Case diagram from Session 6 presented in Figure 7-1. Given the description in the next paragraph, you can draft a narrative for the FillOrder Use Case. Use the narrative elements discussed earlier as a guide for organizing the narrative.

(From Session 6:)

FillOrder: This is basically your reason for being in business. Authorized personnel take Product from inventory according to the order specifications. They update the order and the inventory. If there are any items that can't be filled, they create a backorder.

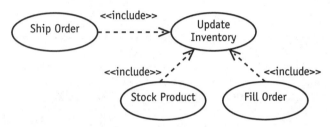

Figure 7-1   *Use Case diagram from Session 6*

The following section explains each of the fields of the narrative. The narrative begins in Table 7-1 with four common audit fields to track the narrative document: the name of the Use Case, a unique number (in case you need to change the name), the author of the narrative, and the last time it was updated. You typically want to keep track of who is changing the document, what they have changed, and when they changed it, to make certain that everyone is aware of the latest revisions and to prevent confusion and unnecessary delays due to misunderstandings.

Table 7-1   *The Fill Order Use Case Narrative: Audit Fields*

Field Name	Field Description
Name	Fill Order
Number	11
Author	Tom Pender
Last update	12/23/01

Your diagrams and documents will go through a lot of changes. Change control software is a very worthwhile investment.

Assumptions in the case study narrative

The FillOrder description says that only "authorized personnel" will use this Use Case. You could check security in this Use Case. But that approach leads to redundancy and the resulting high cost of maintenance. Instead you establish the assumption that security will be handled by another function, ValidateAccess. Furthermore, you'll trust that the security check was done correctly (see Table 7-2).

So what does that tell you about the relationship between the FillOrder and ValidateAccess Use Cases? It tells you the precedence. ValidateAccess must precede FillOrder in the workflow.

Table 7-2 *The Fill Order Use Case Narrative: Assumptions*

Field Name	Field Description
Assumptions	Valid user and has permission to use this feature

Pre-conditions in the case study narrative

Next, you establish the pre-conditions, the conditions that you will test to be sure that it's okay to proceed with the Use Case dialog. The Fill Order description said that the personnel "take Product from inventory *according to the order specifications*." That implies that they need to tell the system the Order that they plan to fill. Refer to the Pre-conditions row in Table 7-3. If the actor doesn't provide a valid order number, there isn't much you can do for him. If you look ahead to the dialog in Table 7-5, you'll see that the first few steps ask for the order number, get the order number, and try to find the order. Pre-conditions are always the first things tested in the dialog.

Table 7-3 *The Fill Order Use Case Narrative: Pre-conditions*

Field Name	Field Description
Pre-conditions	Provide a valid order number

**10 Min.
To Go**

Use Case initiation in the case study narrative

Next, referring to the Use Case initiation row in Table 7-4, you describe how the Use Case dialog is started. In this case, the actor simply asks to start the dialog, so you say that it's initiated on demand.

Table 7-4 *The Fill Order Use Case Narrative: Initiation*

Field Name	Field Description
Use Case initiation	This Use Case starts on demand

Use Case dialog in the case study narrative

Next, you describe the dialog between the actor and the Use Case (see Table 7-5). You see each action required by the actor and each response from the system. Some responses require a choice based on the progress so far, so you see the decision statements included in the dialog. This way, you know why the system gave the response it did. Other decision points are the result of an action, like attempting to find the order using the Find Order Use Case.

Table 7-5   *The Fill Order Use Case Narrative: Dialog*

Field Name	Field Description
Use Case dialog	The system asks the user for an order number
	The user provides the order number
	The system asks for the order (from FindOrder Use Case).
	If the Order is not found, Error, stop
	Else:
	The system provides the order to the user
	The user chooses an item
	Until the user indicates that he is done or there are no unfilled item quantities greater than 0:
	The system asks for the location of the item and
	unfilled quantity (from the LocateProduct Use Case)
	If the item is found (available):
	The user indicates the quantity of the item filled
	If there are any unfilled item quantities greater than 0:
	Create a backorder (using the CreateBackorder Use Case)

Based on the Use Case dialog, see if you can find an error or something missing from the Use Case diagram in Figure 7-1. Very often, taking a closer look at one aspect of the problem (like the narrative) will reveal new insights to update existing diagrams. This is a normal and desirable part of the modeling process.

Did you find the error in the Use Case diagram? In Table 7-5, the dialog said, "The system asks for the location of the item and unfilled quantity (from the LocateProduct Use Case)." You need to add an <<include>> dependency from the FillOrder Use Case to the LocateProduct Use Case.

Use Case termination in the case study narrative

In the termination row in Table 7-6, you list all the ways that this Use Case could end. Use Cases are not good at showing concurrency and interrupts, so this is often the only place to identify things such as a cancel event and timeouts. You'll need to use the Activity diagram or even the Sequence diagram a bit later to flesh out the concurrency and interrupt requirements. The termination section also provides you with a list of actions to consider when writing the post-conditions.

No one diagram can show everything. This is why it is so important to understand the purpose and features of each diagram. The diagrams are like tools in a toolbox. You have to know which one to use for each task.

Most business applications like FillOrder will let you cancel the session at specific points in the process. It is also usually wise to handle the condition where a user gets interrupted and leaves a session open. The timeout termination could watch for a specified period of inactivity before closing the transaction. And of course the user can actually complete the process of filling the order or simply indicate that he is done.

Table 7-6   *The Fill Order Use Case Narrative: Termination*

Field Name	Field Description
Use Case termination	The user may cancel
	The Use Case may timeout
	The user can indicate that he is done
	The user can fill all items on the Order

Post-conditions in the case study narrative

Finally, in the Post-conditions row in Table 7-7, you list the conditions that must be true when the Use Case ends. These conditions are especially important in that they reveal processing steps that may need to be added to the dialog to ensure that the system is stable when this Use Case is completed.

Table 7-7   *The Fill Order Use Case Narrative: Post-conditions*

Field Name	Field Description
Post-conditions	Normal termination: The changes to the Order must be saved (The backorder is handled by the CreateBackorder Use Case)
Cancel:	The Order must be saved unchanged If a backorder was being created, it must be cancelled

Note that the post-conditions include some items that go a bit beyond the scope of a Use Case, like saving the Order. A rule of thumb with Use Cases is that you include only what the user can see, and what can be inferred by what they can see. In this case, if the user gets a message indicating that the Order was updated, then you would include the messages in the Use Case dialog. You would not include the actual steps for updating the Order in the database. If your team feels that information is really needed, first make certain that users agree that your understanding, as documented in the narrative, was correct. Then you could take the Use Case description down a level to address the requirements you know have to be supported by the design. This rule is a little bit gray, but it comes with the territory.

Done!

REVIEW

The Use Case narrative describes, in user-level terms, what the users expect from the Use Case. The Use Case is a feature of the system with a beginning, a middle, and an end. As such, it needs to be explained in terms plain enough for the users to understand and verify, but precise enough for analysts and designers to rely on in order to build the system.

The features of a Use Case narrative aren't standardized, but this session provides a set of common elements in wide use:

- Use Case initiation describes how to start a Use Case.
- Assumptions define conditions that must be true, but are *not* tested in this Use Case.
- Pre-conditions define conditions that must be true, and *are* tested in this Use Case.
- The Use Case dialog explains how the user (whether an actor or another Use Case) interacts with the system during the execution of the Use Case.
- Use Case terminations define the different mechanisms that can cause the Use Case to stop execution.
- Post-conditions define the state of the system that must be true when the Use Case ends. This helps prevent Use Cases from leaving the system in an unstable condition for other Use Cases that follow.

Although these elements are valuable, they are by no means exclusive. Definitely look into other books and online resources on Use Cases, and augment the narrative to support your own method of development.

QUIZ YOURSELF

1. What is an assumption? (See "Assumptions.")
2. What is a pre-condition? (See "Pre-conditions.")
3. Who are the participants in the Use Case dialog? (See "Dialog.")
4. What is a Use Case termination? (See "Use Case termination.")
5. What are post-conditions? (See "Post-conditions.")

Identifying the Use Case Scenarios

Session Checklist

✔ Explaining the purpose and function of Use Case scenarios

✔ Finding Use Case scenarios for the case study

✔ Modeling the Use Case scenarios

**30 Min.
To Go**

A Use Case identifies a primary goal of the system. When an actor attempts to accomplish a goal using the system, there are usually decisions and rules that could influence the outcome. Exception conditions may also hinder the accomplishment of the goal.

Describing Use Case Scenarios

Each possible outcome of an attempt to accomplish a Use Case goal is called a *scenario*. A scenario is a single logical path through a Use Case. You could call a scenario an *instance* of a Use Case in that a scenario is one realization, or execution, of the conceptual Use Case. In other words, a Use Case defines what could happen, whereas a scenario defines what does happen under a given set of conditions.

The word *scenario* is used a number of ways. In the context of UML Use Cases, scenarios have a very specific meaning. Be careful not to confuse the more general usage of the term *scenario,* as an example or situation, with the explicit definition used here.

There are many ways to work with scenarios. You can simply read the narrative and extract each logic path from the text. Or you can draw out the logic with an Activity diagram so that the flow of logic can be visualized and more easily segmented. But whatever the means, the scenarios start to reveal the inner workings of the system and the expectations of the users in a way that the Use Case alone could not. This closer look will, as you'll see in subsequent sessions, open doors to further analysis of the system and ultimately to the design.

Probably the key lesson to learn here is the necessity of tackling the important questions and issues early, when you have the best chance to come up with the best possible solution. All too often, developers leave these questions until they're working on the code, when many of the big issues are easily lost in the mountain of details and the requirements are expressed in a form that is alien to most users.

Why you should care about Use Case scenarios

In some situations, a Use Case is simple enough that the narrative is more than ample to explain all the issues that define its proper execution. But in many other Use Cases, the logic can become troublesome. Many of the applications we work on are complex and require significant scrutiny. That is one reason why the UML provides a whole set of tools rather than just one.

In addition to addressing complexity, you need some way to test the accuracy and completeness of the Use Cases. Unfortunately, for many projects, developers often hold off testing until the end of the project, when they're short on time and focused on the solution rather than the requirements. Or worse yet, there is no time for testing at all, so final tweaking happens in production.

Speaking of requirements, did you know that the overwhelming majority of litigation regarding software projects is based on misunderstandings over requirements? In a recent abstract regarding his participation in litigation over software projects, Capers Jones of Software Productivity Research had this to say:

"The clients charge that the development group has failed to meet the terms of the contract and failed to deliver the software on time, fully operational, or with acceptable quality. The vendors charge that the clients have changed the terms of the agreement and expanded the original work requirements."

Furthermore, the problems that Mr. Jones refers to here are on projects where there is a contract. Consider how much worse the situation can become where the requirements process is less formal!

If you've ever worked in a quality-assurance group, or even worked with one, you know how frustrating the tester's role can be. Think about how the tester's challenge changes when she's able to create a test plan at the *beginning* of the project instead of waiting until the end. Then testing can take place in small increments *throughout* the project, instead of in a massive, difficult, and frustrating process at the end (if there is time to test at all).

This is why scenarios have taken on an increasingly important role in the requirements phase. But what happened to other tools like screen layouts and prototypes? They are still valuable, and in some cases provide a great way for users to visualize what you are trying to express in words and diagrams. The challenge is that the layouts themselves don't explain how they'll be used and why.

Another liability with prototypes is that they give the false impression that the application is nearly complete. This makes sense because the user only works with the interface. To users, the interface is the application. But you know that there is a lot more to it, including the logic expressed in the Use Case narrative and the scenarios; the places where you grapple with business objectives; and your plans to cope with all these issues to ensure the success of the system.

Having said this, I want to voice a caution: You can dissect Use Cases endlessly looking for anything and everything possible. But you want to avoid analysis paralysis by recognizing that you won't get everything right the first time through. It just isn't possible. Allow for a number of passes through the problem with limited time frames. Move on to other diagrams and revisit the Use Cases and scenarios after looking at the problem from the unique perspectives that the other diagrams provide. Let the diagrams reveal information and inconsistencies, or prove you right. Above all, allow time for practice. Trial and error can be excellent teachers.

How to find Use Case scenarios

So how do you find these scenarios? Reading a narrative and following every possible path can be difficult sometimes. One very simple and practical tool to use to find the scenarios visually is an Activity diagram. I almost always draw Activity diagrams rather than rely solely on text. Visual models provide a valuable complement to text. Together, the two perspectives can reveal insights not visible from only one perspective. Given that people learn in different ways, having different tools to explain the problem can help everyone grasp the important issues more easily.

One major benefit of an Activity diagram is its ability to quickly reveal dead-end segments and incomplete paths. The Activity diagram is still grounded in textual description for each activity, so there is significant overlap that helps ensure that your information is consistent.

If you aren't comfortable with flowcharts or Activity diagrams, you may want to skip ahead to Sessions 14 and 15 before finishing this chapter.

To find a scenario, start at the beginning. It usually works best to follow the path of the successful scenario first since it will usually be the most comprehensive. Trace the steps until you come to a decision, represented by a diamond. Now you have to make a choice. Select one of the possible paths leading out of the diamond, preferably the path that leads to the successful completion of the scenario, and continue to trace the steps. Continue the process until you reach an end point. That is Scenario 1. Now return to the top and retrace the first scenario to the first branching point (decision). Start the second scenario at the branch, but follow a different path leading out of the decision. Continue tracing the steps as before. If you loop back to a place you have already been, then stop. Avoid creating redundant segments.

Repeat the process until you have traced a path through every segment of the diagram. You should now have a set of segments that together account for every element of the Activity diagram.

Finding Use Case scenarios for the case study

Now that you have an understanding of what a scenario is and how to find one, I want to walk you through the case study Use Case "FillOrder." Table 8-1 contains the dialog portion of the Use Case narrative for FillOrder (created in Session 7) that will be the basis for the Activity diagram to follow.

Table 8-1 *Use Case Narrative for FillOrder*

Field Name	Field Description

Use Case dialog	The system asks the user for an order number.
	The user provides the order number.
	The system asks for the order (from LocateOrder Use Case).
	If the Order is not found, Error, stop.
	Else:
	    The system provides the order to the user.
	    The user chooses an item.
	Until the user indicates that she is done or there are no unfilled item quantities greater than 0:
	    The system asks for the location of the item and unfilled quantity (from the LocateProduct Use Case).
	    If the item is found (available):
	    The user indicates the quantity of the item filled.
	If there are any unfilled item quantities greater than 0:
	    Create a backorder (using the CreateBackorder Use Case).

For the FillOrder Use Case, I have drawn an Activity diagram (Figure 8-1) so that you can more easily see the logical steps involved in the execution of the Use Case.

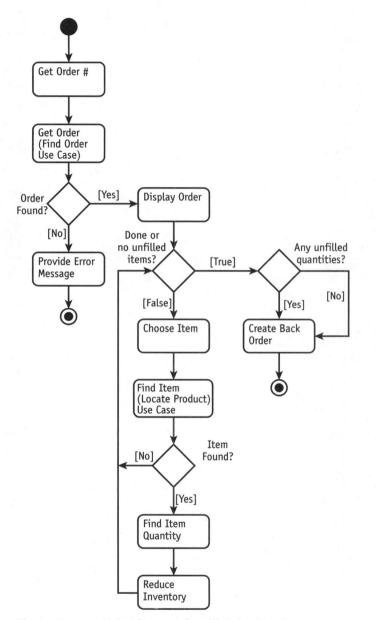

Figure 8-1　*Activity diagram for Fill Order Use Case*

In Figure 8-2, trace the logic for the successful scenario first. Trace each step until you reach a decision point where the logic splits into multiple paths. Now you are faced with a choice.

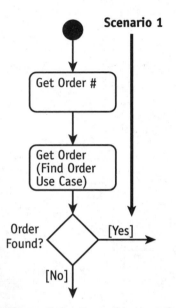

Figure 8-2   *Trace the scenario to the first decision point.*

In Figure 8-3, you select the [Yes] path out of the "Order found?" decision and follow it to the next decision point, "Done or no unfilled items?" Continue to the end of the successful scenario by choosing one path to follow at each decision.

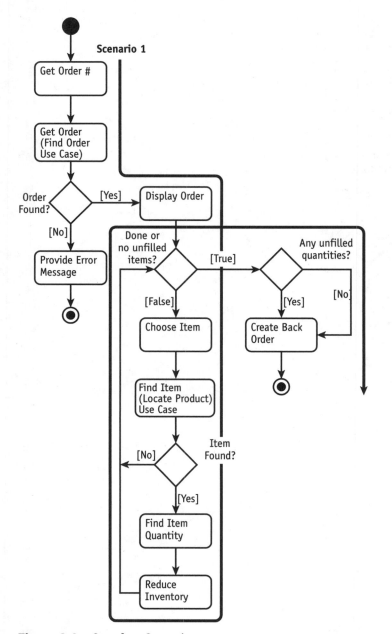

Figure 8-3 *Complete Scenario 1.*

In Figure 8-4, you start identifying alternative scenarios. Start at the first decision point of the first scenario. Select one of the other paths out of the decision. In this case, you take the [False] path and continue to the end point. This marks the second scenario segment.

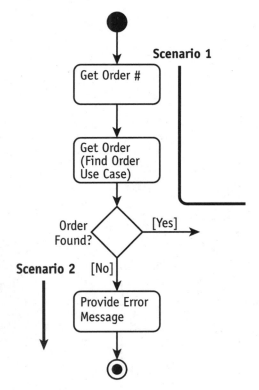

Figure 8-4   *Scenario 2*

In Figure 8-5, you identify the third scenario by continuing from the "Item Found?" decision of Scenario 1 (near the bottom of Figure 8-5). But this time choose the path where the item was not found. Following this path leads you back to the top of the loop at the decision "Done or no unfilled items?" Both of the paths out of this decision are already handled by Scenario 1, so you stop. This segment is Scenario 3.

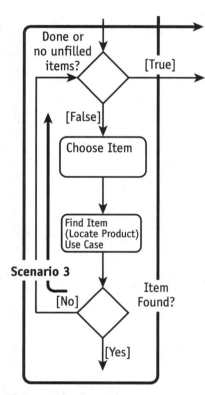

Scenario 1

Figure 8-5   Scenario 3

In Figure 8-6, you identify the fourth scenario by continuing from the "Any unfilled quantities?" decision of Scenario 1. But this time choose the path where there are unfilled quantities. Following this path tells you to create a backorder before the scenario ends. This segment is Scenario 4.

Scenario 1

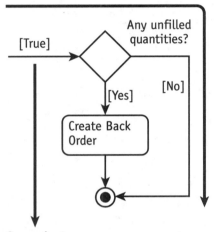

Scenario 4

Figure 8-6   *Scenario 4*

The goal of developing scenarios is to account for every logical possibility in the flow of the Use Case. Every segment identifies a unique line of logic within the total Use Case.

But you're not done yet.

Applying Use Case scenarios

**10 Min.
To Go**

Technically, the definition of a Use Case scenario says that each scenario describes a single logical path through a Use Case. Using the Activity diagram, you can visually identify each path simply by following the connecting lines in the diagram. But in the Fill Order Use Case example, each individual arrow traces a separate logical segment, not necessarily a complete logical path, from the beginning of the Use Case to the end of the Use Case. For example, alternative Scenario 3 only identified the steps that were unique from those already identified by Scenario 1.

I did not show repeated segments of paths already singled out by a previous scenario. This convention is a common one employed to avoid redundancy and extra work. When I write the formal scenarios, or test cases, I simply build the test case from the scenario segments. By doing a little mixing and matching, I can provide comprehensive coverage of every combination. For example, to fully specify Scenario 2, I would include the first two steps and the decision from Scenario 1 plus the unique steps of Scenario 2.

Note too that, whenever you encounter a loop, the scenario maps out only a single pass through the loop. To test the loop thoroughly, run the scenario segment multiple times, remembering to test the boundary conditions.

The result of completing the description of all the scenarios should be a reasonably complete test plan for each Use Case. Remember, though, that you have only modeled the system at the Use Case level. That means that the test plan you have so far is really only acceptance-level testing, not full system or integration testing. But the Use Case level test plan provides the framework for all the test plans for successive phases in the project.

Done!

REVIEW

Use Cases express what the users expect the system to provide.

- Use Case narratives explain in detail how the users expect to interact with the system when they invoke the Use Case.

- Scenarios break down the narrative explanation to provide a detailed examination of every possible outcome of the Use Case, why each outcome happens, and how the system is supposed to respond.

- The Activity diagram provides a visual evaluation of the Use Case narrative. Although it isn't necessary to use an Activity diagram, it can be very helpful, especially for complex Use Cases.

- A scenario is a single logical path through a Use Case, expressing one possible outcome. Finding Use Case scenarios requires you to follow each unique series of activities and decisions from the beginning of the Use Case to a single end point. Together, the scenarios should account for every possible way that a Use Case could execute.

- When the scenarios have been identified, they may be used to develop a comprehensive acceptance-level test plan. They may also be used to test the results of subsequent analysis and design efforts.

QUIZ YOURSELF

1. What is a Use Case scenario? (See "Describing Use Case Scenarios.")
2. How many scenarios are in a Use Case? (See "Describing Use Case Scenarios.")
3. What two methods can you use to describe the logical flow of a Use Case? (See "Describing Use Case Scenarios" and "How to find Use Case scenarios.")
4. If a scenario is a single logical path, how do you handle looping logic? (See "Applying Use Case scenarios.")
5. How will the scenarios be used later in the project? (See "Applying Use Case scenarios.")

Modeling the Static View: The Class Diagram

Session Checklist

**30 Min.
To Go**

The Class diagram is by far the most used and best known of the object-oriented diagrams. It is the source for generating code and the target for reverse engineering code. Because the Class diagram is the primary source for code generation, the other diagrams tend to serve as tools of discovery that add to your knowledge about how to build the Class diagram. Use Cases identify the need for the objects as resources used by the system to achieve its goals. The Sequence and Collaboration diagrams are excellent tools for discovering object interactions and, by inference, defining interfaces. The Activity diagram is very good for discovering the behavior implemented by objects and so helps to define the logic of operations on the objects.

The Object Model

The phrase *object model* has been the source of some confusion. Object Model is often used as a synonym for Class diagram. In this book, *object model* is used to mean the set of diagrams used to model objects, namely the Class and Object diagrams. The Class diagram is the more recognized and used of the two diagrams. The Object diagram is often implemented within the Class diagram, not as a separate diagram. In fact, the UML specification does not actually define the Object diagram. It is simply a Class diagram that contains only objects.

The Class diagram

The Class diagram represents classes, their component parts, and the way in which classes of objects are related to one another. A class is a definition for a *type of object*. It's really not much different from what you find in a dictionary. If you want to find out what a widget is, you look up the word *widget*. You would find a description of what a widget looks like, its purpose, and any other pertinent information for understanding widgets. There are no actual widgets in the dictionary, only descriptions. There are no real objects in a class, only descriptions of what a particular type of object looks like, what it can do, and what other objects it may be related to in some way.

To document this information, the Class diagram includes attributes, operations, stereotypes, properties, associations, and inheritance.

- **Attributes** describe the appearance and knowledge of a class of objects.
- **Operations** define the behavior that a class of objects can manifest.
- **Stereotypes** help you understand this type of object in the context of other classes of objects with similar roles within the system's design.
- **Properties** provide a way to track the maintenance and status of the class definition.
- **Association** is just a formal term for a type of relationship that this type of object may participate in. Associations may come in many variations, including simple, aggregate and composite, qualified, and reflexive.
- **Inheritance** allows you to organize the class definitions to simplify and facilitate their implementation.

Together, these elements provide a rich set of tools for modeling business problems and software. However, the Class diagram is still limited in what it can show you. Generally speaking, it is a static view of the elements that make up the business or software. It's like a blueprint for a building or a piece of machinery. You can see the parts used to make it and how they are assembled, but you cannot see how the parts will behave when you set them into motion. This is why we need other diagrams to model behavior and interactions over time (that is, modeling the objects in motion). Figure 9-1 shows how all the other diagrams support the Class diagram.

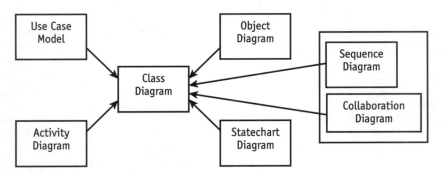

Figure 9-1 *All diagrams support the Class diagram.*

Although other diagrams are necessary, remember that their primary purpose is to support the construction and testing of the Class diagram. Whenever another diagram reveals new or modified information about a class, the Class diagram must be updated to include the new information. If this new information is not passed on to the Class diagram, it will not be reflected in your code.

The Object diagram

- The class defines the *rules;* the objects express the *facts.*
- The class defines what *can be;* the object describes *what is.*

If the Class diagram says, "This is the way things should be," but the Object diagram graphically demonstrates that "it just ain't so," then you have a very specific problem to track down. The reverse is true, too. The Object diagram can confirm that everything is working as it should. Session 13 walks you through an example of applying the Object diagram for just this purpose.

Elements of the Class Definition

The *class symbol* is comprised of three *compartments* (rectangular spaces) that contain distinct information needed to describe the properties of a single type of object.

- The *name compartment* uniquely defines a class (a type of object) within a package. Consequently, classes may have the same name if they reside in different packages.
- The *attribute compartment* contains all the data definitions.
- The *operations compartment* contains a definition for each behavior supported by this type of object.

 Technically, the UML allows for user-defined compartments as well as the three standard ones, but I'll leave that as an advanced topic for another book or for your own personal study of the UML specification.

Sessions 10 and 11 present the rest of the notations that make up the Class diagram.

Modeling an Attribute

**20 Min.
To Go**

An attribute describes a piece of information that an object owns or knows about itself. To use that information, you must assign a name and then specify the kind of information, or data type. Data types may be primitive data types supplied by a language, or abstract data types (types defined by the developer). In addition, each attribute may have rules constraining the values assigned to it. Often a default value helps to ensure that the attribute always contains valid, meaningful data.

Attribute visibility

Each attribute definition must also specify what other objects are allowed to see the attribute — that is its *visibility*. Visibility is defined as follows:

- Public (+) visibility allows access to objects of all other classes.
- Private (-) visibility limits access to within the class itself. For example, only operations of the class have access to a private attribute.
- Protected (#) visibility allows access by subclasses. In the case of *generalizations* (inheritance), subclasses must have access to the attributes and operations of the superclass or they cannot be inherited.
- Package (~) visibility allows access to other objects in the same package.

Note the symbols for each type of visibility. The symbols provide a convenient shorthand and tend to be used instead of the full name.

The rules for protected visibility vary a little among programming languages. Check the rules for your particular implementation environment. For example, protected in Java allows objects of classes within the same package to see the value as well.

Given these requirements, the following notation is a common way of defining an attribute:

<u>**visibility / attribute name : data type = default value {constraints}**</u>

Writing this down as a kind of cheat sheet isn't a bad idea. It will help you remember all the issues you need to address when defining data. Here's the run-down on each element in this expression.

- **Visibility (+, -, #, ~):** Required before code generation. The programming language will typically specify the valid options. The minus sign represents the visibility "private" meaning only members of the class that defines the attribute may see the attribute.
- **Slash (/):** The derived attribute indicator is optional. Derived values may be computed or figured out using other data and a set of rules or formulas. Consequently, there are more design decisions that need to be addressed regarding the handling of this data. Often this flag is used as a placeholder until the design decisions resolve the handling of the data.
- **Attribute name:** Required. Must be unique within the class.
- **Data type:** Required. This is a big subject. During analysis, the data type should reflect how the client sees the data. You could think of this as the external view. During design, the data type will need to represent the programming language data type for the environment in which the class will be coded. These two pieces of information can give the programmer some very specific insights for the coding of get and set methods to support access to the attribute value.
- **Assignment operator and default value:** Optional. Default values serve two valuable purposes. First, default values can provide significant ease-of-use improvements for the client. Second and more importantly, they protect the integrity of the system from being corrupted by missing or invalid values. A common example is the

tendency to let numeric attributes default to zero. If the application ever attempts to divide using this value, you will have to handle resulting errors that could have been avoided easily with the use of a default.

- **Constraints:** Constraints express all the rules required to guarantee the integrity of this piece of information. Any time another object tries to alter the attribute value, it must pass the rules established in the constraints. The constraints are typically implemented/enforced in any method that attempts to set the attribute value.

 The constraint notation brackets appear throughout UML diagrams to identify any and all additional information that helps clarify the intent of the modeling element. Place any text in the constraint brackets that is required to explain the limitations to be imposed on the implementation of the modeling element.

- **Class level attribute (underlined attribute declaration):** Optional. Denotes that all objects of the class share a single value for the attribute. (This is called a *static* value in Java.)

Creating an attribute specification

Table 9-1 shows you how to create a sample attribute definition for a company name. The field has to handle characters and punctuation marks commonly found in company names, but you're limited to 30 positions. There is a no default value, but you want valid display data, so you must initialize the field to spaces.

Table 9-1 *Creating an Attribute Specification*

Attribute Element Description	Attribute Element Example
Create an attribute name	**company**
Add the attribute data type	company:**character**
Add the attribute's default value, if any	company:character **= spaces**
Set the constraints on the attribute value. For this example, first identify the field length.	company:character = spaces **{1 to 30 characters}**
Next identify the types of data that can be used in the attribute. Add this information within the brackets.	company:character = spaces {1 to 30 characters **including alphabetic, spaces, and punctuation characters; no special characters allowed}**
Set the attribute visibility (designate private visibility with a minus (-) sign in front of the attribute).	- company:character = spaces {1 to 30 characters including alphabetic, spaces, and punctuation characters; no special characters allowed}

In a modeling tool, an attribute definition may appear as a set of fields on a specification window, or the single line format, or a combination of the two. Regardless of the tool interface, this set of fields can be a good tool for remembering the types of questions you need to answer for each piece of information in your model. This data forms the foundation for your databases, your user interfaces, reporting, and nearly every aspect of your design. Thoroughness here pays big dividends later.

Modeling an Operation

Objects have behaviors, things they can do and things that can be done to them. These behaviors are modeled as operations. By way of clarification, the UML distinguishes between operation and method, whereas many people use them interchangeably. In the UML, an operation is the declaration of the signature or interface, the minimum information required to invoke the behavior on an object. A method is the implementation of an operation and must conform to the signature of the operation that it implements.

Elements of an operation specification

Operations require a name, arguments, and sometimes a return. Arguments, or input parameters, are simply attributes, so they are specified using the attribute notation (name, data type, constraints, and default), although it is very common to use the abbreviated form of name and data type only.

Note that if you use constraints on an argument, you are constraining the input value, not the value of the attribute as it resides in the source object. The value in the source object was constrained in the attribute definition within the class.

The return is an attribute data type. You can specify the visibility of the operation: private (-) limits access to objects of the same class, public (+) allows access by any object, protected (#) limits access to objects of subclasses within the inheritance hierarchy (and sometimes the same package), and package (~) limits access to objects within the same package. Given these requirements, the following notation is used to define an operation:

visibility operationName (argname : data type {constraints}, ...) :

 return data type {constraints}

Once again, writing this down as a kind of cheat sheet isn't a bad idea. It will help you remember all the issues you need to address when defining operations. Here's the run-down on each element in this expression.

- **Operation name:** Required. Does not have to be unique, but the combination of name and parameters does need to be unique within a class.

- **Arguments/parameters:** Any number of arguments is allowed. Each argument requires an identifier and a data type. Constraints may be used to define the valid set of values that may be passed in the argument. But constraints are not supported in many tools and will not be reflected in the code for the operation, at least not at this point.

- **Return data type:** Required for a return value, but return values are optional. The UML only allows for the type, not the name, which is consistent with most programming languages. There may only be one return data type, which again is consistent with most programming languages.

- **Visibility (+, -, #, ~):** Required before code generation. The visibility values are defined by the programming language, but typically include public (+), private (-), protected (#), and package (~).

- **Class level operation (underlined operation declaration):** Optional. Denoted as an operation accessible at the class level; requires an instance (object) reference.

- **Argument name:** Required for each parameter, but parameters are optional. Any number of arguments is allowed.

- **Argument data type:** Required for each parameter, but parameters are optional.

- **Constraints:** Optional. In general, constraints express rules that must be enforced in the execution of the operation. In the case of parameters, they express criteria that the values must satisfy before they may be used by the operation. You can think of them as operation level pre-conditions.

**10 Min.
To Go**

Creating an operation specification

Table 9-2 shows you how to create a sample operation to determine the total amount due on an order. The total is the sum of all line items less the volume discount. Each line item amount is the product of the unit price and discount. You need the answer back as a dollar amount.

Table 9-2   *Creating an Operation Specification*

Operation Element Description	Operation Element Example
Name the operation.	**totalOrderAmount**
Define the arguments/parameters: All the input information is on the Order object, so an instance of Order is the only argument. Name the argument and data type and separate them with a colon. Try to use argument names that match the argument type; this makes referring to the value within the method easier. The data type in this example is the user-defined class "Order." Enclose the arguments in parentheses.	totalOrderAmount **(order : Order)**

Continued

Table 9-2   *Continued*

Define the return data type: The result returned by the operation must be a dollar amount, simply a number with two decimal positions. Often we create a user-defined data type (or *abstract* data type) to contain dollar values. Place a colon and the return data type after the arguments.	totalOrderAmount (order : Order) : **Dollar**
Identify and describe any constraints: You can use the all-purpose constraint notation {} to hold the text that describes the computation. As an alternative, you can put the rule in the data dictionary under the derived attribute "total_order_amount."	totalOrderAmount (order : Order) : Dollar **{The total is the sum of all line items less the volume discount. Each line item is the product of the unit price and quantity.}**
Set the visibility of the operation: The UML notation for public is a plus (+) sign.	+ totalOrderAmount (order : Order) : Dollar {The total is the sum of all line items less the volume discount. Each line item is the product of the unit price and quantity.}

Modeling the Class Compartments

Now you need to put all this together in a class symbol. The class notation consists of the three compartments mentioned earlier. You've just seen the contents of the second and third compartments for attributes and operations, respectively. The first compartment — the name compartment — gives the class its identity.

Figure 9-2 shows a UML class symbol with all three compartments and all the elements needed to define a class with UML notation. The text addresses each compartment of the class and refers back to Figure 9-2.

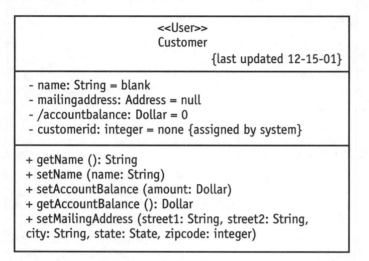

Figure 9-2   *Complete class specification with all three compartments*

Name compartment

In Figure 9-2, the name compartment occupies the top section of the class box. The name compartment holds the class name, an optional stereotype, and optional properties. The name is located in the center of the compartment. The stereotype (<< >>) may be used to limit the role of the class in the model and is placed at the top of the compartment. Common examples of class stereotypes include <<Factory>>, based on the Factory design pattern, and <<Interface>>, for Java interfaces or for user interfaces.

Properties use the constraint notation { } and are placed in the bottom-right corner of the compartment. Properties are basically constraints used to clarify the intent in defining the model element. Properties can be used to document the status of a class under development or for designations such as *abstract* and *concrete*.

Attribute compartment

In Figure 9-2, the attribute compartment occupies the middle section of the class box. The attribute compartment simply lists the attribute specifications for the class using the notation presented earlier in "Modeling an Attribute." The order of the attributes does not matter.

Operation compartment

In Figure 9-2, the operations compartment occupies the bottom section of the class box. Operations are simply listed in the operation compartment using the notation presented in "Modeling an Operation." The order does not matter. The operation compartment is placed below the name compartment, and below the attribute compartment when all compartments are visible.

Creating Different Views of a Class

The completed class definition can be shown with all three compartments visible or as just the name compartment. This form is often used in the early stages of analysis when the focus is on object definitions and relationships. As more information is discovered about the attributes and operations, the other two compartments can be revealed as well.

Some tools also give the option to show some or all of the operation specifications. For example, one view may show only the operation names. Another view may reveal the names and the arguments, while yet another may show the entire signature with argument data types and return data types. Figure 9-3 illustrates two ways of drawing the class symbol. This facility helps focus evaluation of the diagram to the interests of the audience.

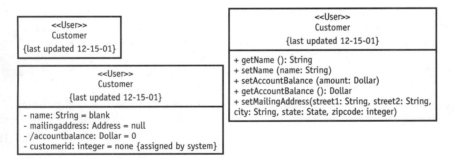

Figure 9-3 *Alternative views of a class symbol for different audiences and purposes*

Done!

REVIEW

The Class diagram is the primary diagram for code generation and for reverse engineering. Consequently, it tends to be the focus of most modeling efforts, with all the other diagrams playing a supporting role. The term object model is actually a reference to two diagrams, the Class diagram and the Object diagram, although when the term is used it most often refers to a Class diagram.

- The Class diagram represents all the *rules* regarding the construction and use of objects. The Object diagram describes the *facts* about objects that actually exist. Consequently, the Object diagram provides a valuable testing tool to verify the Class diagram.

- The class symbol consists of three compartments: the name compartment, the attribute compartment, and the operations compartment. The UML supports the definition of additional compartments. The UML also supports a number of views of the class that allow the analyst to focus attention on particular features of the class.

- Attributes must be specified with all the information needed to protect the integrity of the data they describe. To do so, the attribute declaration includes visibility, a unique name (within the class), a data type, possibly a default value, possibly constraints, and, when appropriate, a class-level designation.

- Operations must be specified with all the information needed to guarantee the proper use and execution of the behavior. To do so, the operation declaration includes visibility, a name, the list of arguments/parameters and their required data types, a return data type when needed, and, when appropriate, a class-level designation.

QUIZ YOURSELF

1. What diagram is used to generate code? (See "The Object Model.")
2. What are the three parts of a class in a UML class symbol? (See "Elements of the Class Definition.")
3. How do you fully define an attribute? (See "Modeling an Attribute.")
4. Name two ways to use the Object diagram. (See "The Object diagram.")
5. What element defines the level of access that is required by an operation? (See "Elements of an operation specification.")

The Class Diagram: Associations

✔ Explaining and illustrating the basic notation for all associations

✔ Explaining and illustrating the notations for association classes, reflexive associations, and qualified associations

**30 Min.
To Go**

Associations between objects are similar to associations between people. In order for me to work with you, I need to communicate with you. This requires that I have some way to contact you, such as a phone number or an e-mail address. Further, it is often necessary to identify why we are associated in order to clarify why we do and do not participate in certain kinds of communication. For example, if we are associated because you are a programmer and I am a database administrator, we probably will not discuss employee benefits as part of our duties.

There would also probably be some limitations placed on our interactions:

- We would want to limit the number of participants in the relationship to ensure efficiency.

- We would want to check the qualifications of the participants to ensure we have the right participants.

- We would want to define the roles of the participants so that everyone knows how to behave.

All these requirements apply equally to objects. The UML provides notations to address them all. I'll start with the basics and then add a few twists.

Modeling Basic Association Notations

The following notations appear on almost every association you will model. Most of these elements are similar to those you find in data modeling or database design. In fact, most of the concepts come from these fields. The concepts worked well in data modeling, so they were simply brought forward into object modeling as a form of "best practices." I suggest you memorize them because you will spend a lot of time working with them.

Association name

The purpose of the association can be expressed in a *name,* a verb or verb phrase that describes how objects of one type (class) relate to objects of another type (class). For example, a person owns a car, a person drives a car, and a person rents a car. Even though the participants are the same in each association, the purpose of each association is unique, and as such they imply different rules and interactions.

To draw the UML associations for these three examples, you need to start with four basic elements.

- The *participating classes,* Person and Car. In this session I show only the name compartment so that your attention remains focused on the classes and their associations.

- The *association,* represented by a line between the two classes (pretty technical huh?).

- The *name* of the association, represented by a verb or verb phrase on the association line. Don't worry about the exact position of the name. As long as the name appears somewhere in the middle of the line, you're okay. Just leave room at both ends of the association for all the other things you'll learn about later in this session.

- The *direction* to read the name (indicating the direction is optional).

The first two examples in Figure 10-1 read pretty much the way I described them in the text — Person owns Car and Person drives Car. Note that if these two statements are true, then the reverse would be equally true — Car is owned by Person and Car is driven by Person. Associations may be read in both directions as long as you remember to reverse the meaning of the association name from active to passive.

But in the third example in Figure 10-1, the association name would not make sense if you read it in the typical left to right fashion — Car rents Person. This is a case where the direction indicator is particularly appropriate, even required, to make sense of the association by reversing the normal reading order so that it reads from right to left — Person rents Car.

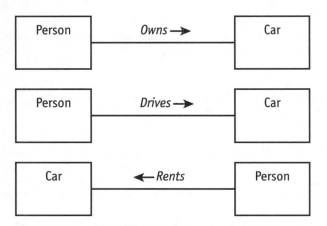

Figure 10-1   *Directional notation for association names*

 Remember the direction indicator when you're making a lot of changes to a diagram where you have to rearrange the classes. It is easy for classes to reverse position on the diagram, resulting in nonsensical association names. The indicators can prevent unnecessary confusion.

**20 Min.
To Go**

Association multiplicity

The UML allows you to handle some other important questions about associations: "How many Cars may a Person own?" "How many can they rent?" "How many people can drive a given Car?" Associations define the rules for *how* objects in each class may be related. So how do you specify exactly *how many* objects may participate in the relationship?

Multiplicity is the UML term for the rule that defines the number of participating objects. A multiplicity value *must* be assigned to each of the participating classes in an association. As illustrated in Figure 10-2, you need to ask two separate questions.

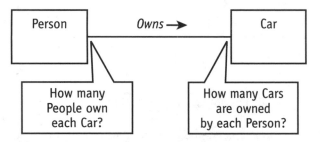

Figure 10-2   *Assigning multiplicity to each end of an association*

The answer to each question goes next to the class that describes the objects that the question is counting. The answer to "How many People . . ." goes on the end of the association near the Person class. The answer to "How many Cars . . ." goes on the end of the association next to the Car class.

Multiplicity is expressed in a couple of ways. The most common is a range defining the minimum number of objects allowed and the maximum number of objects allowed in the format

Minimum . . Maximum

You must use integer values for the minimum and maximum. But, as you have probably found in your own applications, sometimes you don't know the upper limit or there is no actual upper limit. The UML suggests the use of an asterisk to mean *no upper limit*. Used by itself, the asterisk can also mean the minimum is zero *and* there is no upper limit, or *zero or more*.

You may also encounter a situation when a range is not appropriate. If you had to define how many cylinders are in the engines you service, you might want to say, "I only work on 4-, 6-, and 8-cylinder engines." For these situations, the UML suggests a comma-separated list (for example, 4,6,8).

You can simplify the notation when the minimum and maximum values are the same by using a single value. So instead of writing 4..4, you can just write 4. This is a nice shortcut, but beware! The most common place to use this shortcut is when the multiplicity is 1..1. Unfortunately, the shortcut encourages people to overlook or ignore the possibility that the minimum is zero, that is, the relationship is optional.

I'll use the example of a car and an engine. That's easy! Each car has one engine, right? Well, what about cars on an assembly line? During the first *n* stages of assembly, there is no engine in the car. In this case, the multiplicity should be 0..1 to allow the car to exist before it has an engine installed. Frankly, I have found very few instances when the minimum multiplicity should be 1. My rule of thumb is to set the minimum to 0 until I have positive proof that the one object cannot exist with the other object.

Most software failures are because of small, difficult-to-find errors like the difference between 0 and 1. Most of those errors are caused by assumptions or failures to think critically about the details. I once witnessed an explosion in a power plant caused by a one-character mistake in a program. Like they say, "The devil is in the details."

Here's a summary list of the options for specifying multiplicity followed by some examples.

- Values separated by two periods (..) mean a range. For example, 1..3 means between 1 and 3 inclusively; 5..10 means between 5 and 10 inclusively.

- Values separated by commas mean an enumerated list of possibilities. For example, 4,6,8 means you may have 4 objects or 6 objects or 8 objects of this type in the association.

- Asterisk (*) when used alone means zero or more, no lower or upper limit.

- Asterisk (*) when used in a range (1..*) means no upper limit — you must have at least one but you can have as many more as you want.

Association roles

Sometimes the association name is a bit hard to determine. For example, what English word could you use for the association name between parents and children? The UML provides an alternative that may be used in place of the name or along with it to help make the reason for the association as clear as possible. This alternative is called a *role* because it describes *how an object participates* in the association.

For example, many employees contribute to a project. But you know from experience that they participate in different ways. Figure 10-3 shows how you can draw multiple associations and label them to differentiate the types of participation. Each role is placed at the end of the association next to the type of object that plays the role. You may use them on one, both, or neither end of each association.

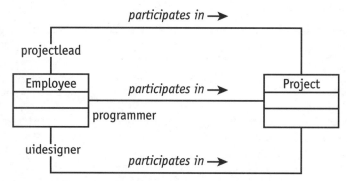

Figure 10-3 *Role names on an association*

There is one other thing worth noting about roles and names. Role names generate code. Association names *do not* generate code. The role name can be used to name the attribute that holds the reference to the object that plays the role. In Figure 10-3, the Project object could have an attribute named programmer that holds a reference to an Employee object that plays the role of programmer, and another attribute called projectlead that holds reference to another Employee object that plays the role of project lead.

Association constraints

Constraints appear throughout the UML notation. You used them in Session 9 when you declared attributes and operations. Constraints fulfill much the same function for associations. First take a look at Figure 10-4, in which no constraints are specified.

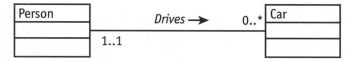

Figure 10-4 *An association without constraints*

Is it really true that *any* Person object can drive a Car? Legally, only people with valid driver's licenses are allowed to drive. You can add this information to the model using a pair of curly braces {} containing the text that describes the rule you want to enforce (for example, {must have a valid driver's license}). In Figure 10-5, you place the constraint at the end of the association near Person, the type of object that must conform to the rule before it can participate in the relationship.

{must have valid driver's license}

Figure 10-5   *An association with a constraint on the Person objects' participation*

Constraints may appear on both ends, either ends, or neither end of the association. It really depends on the problem you're trying to describe. Don't worry too much about placement. You can place the constraint anywhere near the end of the association.

But what if there is more than one constraint? Simple. Just add more text between the braces. *Don't create more braces.*

The UML also defines a constraint language for a more rigorous constraint specification. For more information, check out UML 1.4 chapter 6 Object Constraint Language (OCL) Specification.

Modeling Extended Association Notations

10 Min.
To Go

Now that you have the basics down, you're ready for a few, more-exotic concepts. Actually, some or all of these concepts may be familiar to you from database design or personal programming experience.

Association class

An association class encapsulates *information about an association*. Let me say that again, because this one often proves difficult to understand. An association class encapsulates *information about an association*.

In Figure 10-6, you know that Customers order Products. But when customers order products there is usually more that you need to know, like when did they order the products? How many did they order? What were the terms of the sale? All the answers to these questions are simply data. All data in an object-oriented system must be contained in (encapsulated in) an object. There must be a class to define each type of object. So, define all this data in a class. Then to show that the data describes the association, attach the new class to the association with a *dashed line*.

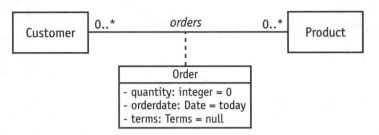

Figure 10-6　*Association class notation*

Be on the lookout for association classes when you see a multiplicity of more than one on *both* ends of the association. You don't always need an association class on these *many-to-many* associations, but it is a common place to find them.

Reflexive association

Reflexive association is a fancy expression that says objects in the same class can be related to one another. The entire association notation you've learned so far remains exactly the same, except that both ends of the association line point to the same class. This is where the reflexive association gets its name. The association line leaves a class and *reflects back onto* the same class.

Both examples in Figure 10-7 are equivalent expressions. The only difference is that one uses roles and the other uses an association name.

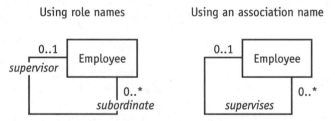

Figure 10-7　*Two ways to model a reflexive association*

A reflexive association is a very common way to express hierarchies. The example in Figure 10-7 models a hierarchical reporting structure. I could use the same technique for companies owned by other companies.

Qualified association

Qualified associations provide approximately the same functionality as indexes, but the notation has a bit of a twist. To indicate that a customer can look up an order using the order's *ordernumber* attribute, place the *ordernumber* attribute name and data type in a rectangular box on the *Customer* end of the association. The rest of the association notation remains intact but is pushed out to the edge of the rectangle.

The placement of the qualifier is sometimes confusing. The best way I have found to remember it is to think of it like this (refer to Figure 10-8):

"The Customer *uses* the ordernbr to look up an Order."

or

"One type of object uses the qualifier to access the other (qualified) type of object."

The qualifier goes next to the class of objects that will *use* the value to do the look up. It is not exactly intuitive but it works.

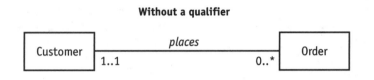

Figure 10-8   Qualified association

 Typically the qualifier is an attribute of the class on the opposite end of the association, so make certain that the two names and data types agree.

Use qualifiers to reduce the multiplicity in the same way you would use indexes in a database to reduce the search time for a specific row or subset of rows. For example, in Figure 10-8, note how the multiplicity for the Order end of the association changed from 0..* to 1..1. This is because the qualifier provided a unique key for Order objects. Before the qualifier was established, navigation across the association would result in a list of all orders associated with that Customer, because the Customer relationship was the only reference available to select the Orders.

Done!

REVIEW

Associations define how objects will be allowed to work together.

- An association is named to describe the purpose of the relationship.
- Role names may be used with or in place of the association name to describe how the objects participate in the relationship.

- Multiplicity defines the number of objects that may participate. Ranges are specified as minimum value..maximum value. When the minimum and maximum are the same, you may simplify the range to a single value (but watch out!). A comma-separated list represents an enumeration of options. An asterisk may be used to indicate that there is no defined upper limit to the number of objects. By itself, an asterisk means *zero or more* objects.

- Constraints are rules that must be enforced to ensure the integrity of the relationship. The constraints may be placed on each end of the association. Constraints are always enclosed in a single pair of curly braces {}.

- An association class encapsulates information about an association. The most common types of data include when the relationship began, when it ended, and the current state of the relationship. But there can be any number of data items. Apart from its origin, an association class is a class like any other class.

- The phrase *reflexive association* describes an association in which all the participating objects are of the same type (class). The association line goes out of a class and turns right back to the same class so that both ends of the association touch the same class. All the other notations and rules for defining associations apply to reflexive associations. One of the most common uses for reflexive associations is for defining hierarchies.

- Qualified associations simplify the navigation across complex associations by providing keys to narrow the selection of objects.

- All these notations may appear on the same diagram.

Quiz Yourself

1. What should the association name describe? (See "Association name.")
2. When would you want to use role names and where do you place them? (See "Association roles.")
3. What is a constraint? (See "Association constraints.")
4. Where do you most often find opportunities to use an association class? (See "Association class.")
5. Why would you use a qualified association? (See "Qualified association.")

PART

II

Saturday Morning
Part Review

1. What is the relationship between people and roles in a Use Case diagram?
2. Where do you use associations in a Use Case diagram?
3. Why would you use the <<include>> dependency stereotype?
4. When would you use the <<extend>> dependency stereotype?
5. Where can you use the generalization relationship on a Use Case diagram?
6. Why is it so important to set the context of the system first?
7. How do you find associations?
8. How do you model the fact that one Use Case always uses the help of another Use Case?
9. How do you model the fact that one Use Case sometimes uses the help of another Use Case, but only under a specified condition?
10. How do you know that you can use generalization?
11. What is the purpose of defining the Use Case initiation?
12. What is the fundamental difference between assumptions and pre-conditions?
13. What is the Use Case dialog?
14. Why do we define the termination options separately from the dialog?
15. How do you know how detailed the dialog should be?
16. What is the relationship between a Use Case and a scenario?
17. Why are scenarios important to a project?
18. What two sources can you use to find scenarios?
19. How should you handle segments of logic that are repeated, as in loops?
20. How can you apply scenarios to aid in the quality of your project?
21. What is the primary difference between the Class diagram and the Object diagram?
22. What does a constraint mean in an attribute specification?
23. What does a constraint mean in an operation specification?

24. What appears in the name compartment of a class?

25. Do you always have to display all the information about a class?

26. What should the association name describe?

27. When would you want to use role names and where do you place them?

28. What is a constraint?

29. Where do you most often find opportunities to use an association class?

30. Why would you use a qualified association?

PART

III

Saturday Afternoon

The Class Diagram: Aggregation and Generalization

Session Checklist

✔ Explaining the concepts of aggregation and composition

✔ Illustrating the use of the notation for aggregation and composition

✔ Explaining the concepts of generalization and inheritance

✔ Illustrating the use of generalization

**30 Min.
To Go**

In Session 10, you learned about associations. An association describes a set of rules regarding how objects may be related to one another. But associations can be a bit more restrictive. In this session, I describe two common subtypes of association, called aggregation and composition. Then I explain how you can refactor your design using generalization (inheritance).

Modeling Aggregation and Composition

Figure 11-1 outlines the relationships among the concepts of association, aggregation, and composition.

Later in this session, I explain the contents of this graphic more fully. But right now I want to make two points as clear and strong as possible:

- Every aggregation relationship *is a type of association*. So every aggregation relationship has all the properties of an association relationship, plus some rules of its own.
- Every composition relationship *is a form of aggregation*. So every composition relationship has all the properties of an aggregation, plus some rules of its own.

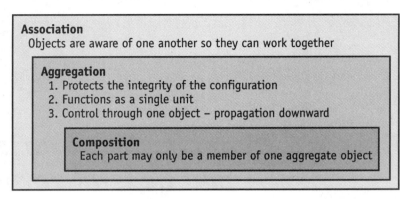

Figure 11-1 *The relationship between association, aggregation, and composition*

Elements of aggregation

Aggregation is a special type of association used to indicate that the participating objects are not just independent objects that know about each other. Instead, they are *assembled* or *configured* together to create a new, more complex object. For example, a number of different parts are assembled to create a car, a boat, or a plane. You could even create a logical assembly like a team where the parts are not physically connected to one another but they still operate as a unit.

To model aggregation on a Class diagram:

1. Draw an association (a line) between the class that represents the member and the class that represents the assembly or aggregation. In Figure 11-2, that would mean a line between the Team class and the Player class.

2. Draw a *diamond* on the end of the association that is attached to the assembly or aggregate class. In Figure 11-2, the diamond is next to the Team class that represents a group of players.

3. Assign the appropriate multiplicities to *each end* of the association, and add any roles and/or constraints that may be needed to define the rules for the relationship. Figure 11-2 shows that a Player may be a member of no more than one Team, but a Player does not have to be on a Team all the time (0..1). The Team is always comprised of exactly nine Players (9..9 or just 9). A Player is considered a *member* (role name) of a Team. Every Player is constrained by the fact that she must have a current contract in order to be a member of a Team.

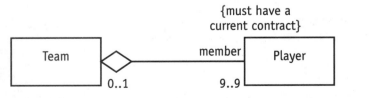

Figure 11-2 *How to represent an aggregation relationship in the UML*

What makes aggregation unique? More importantly, what makes aggregation beneficial? Aggregation describes a group of objects in a way that changes how you interact with them. The concept is aimed at protecting the integrity of a configuration of objects in two specific ways.

First, aggregation defines a single point of control in the object that represents the assembly. This ensures that no matter what others might want to do to the members of the assembly, the control object has the final word on whether the actions are allowed. This assignment of control may be at many levels within the aggregation hierarchy. For example, an engine might be the controller of its parts, but the car is the controller of the engine.

Second, when an instruction is given that might effect the entire collection of objects, the control object dictates how the members will respond. So for all intentions, the assembly appears to function like a single object. When I push the gas pedal, telling the car I want to accelerate, the entire car assembly (with its thousands of parts) accelerates, not just the gas pedal.

Elements of composition

Composition is used for aggregations where the life span of the part depends on the life span of the aggregate. The aggregate has control over the creation and destruction of the part. In other words, the member object cannot exist apart from the aggregation. Draw this stronger form of aggregation simply by making the aggregation diamond solid (black).

In Figure 11-3, the team example uses aggregation, the hollow diamond. Players are assembled into a team. But if the Team is disbanded, the players live on (depending of course on how well they performed). The Book example uses composition, the solid diamond. A Book is composed of Chapters. The Chapters would not continue to exist elsewhere on their own. They would cease to exist along with the Book.

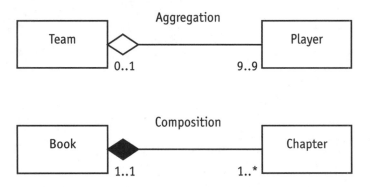

Figure 11-3   *How to represent a composition relationship in the UML*

Note how the multiplicity provides some clues on the distinction between aggregation and composition. On the Team example in Figure 11-3, each Player may or may not be a member of a Team (0..1). This tells me that a Player may exist independent from the Team. The Book example says that a Chapter must be associated with one and only one Book (1..1). This tells me that a Chapter cannot exist independent of the Book, so it must be a composition relationship.

Composition does have a coding equivalent in Java using the *inner class* construct. Although the UML and Java implementations differ slightly, they are close enough to perhaps help you understand the concept if you are already familiar with Java.

Creating aggregation and composition relationships

Problem statement: "Our Company maintains a group of race cars. Our cars use some of our new 8-cylinder engines and new transmissions. Once the engines are assembled, the pistons, carburetor, and plugs cannot be swapped between engines due to changes caused by the high temperatures.

"We want to keep records of the performance achieved by each engine in each car and each transmission in combination with each engine. Our drivers evaluate each car to give us their assessment of the handling. We need a system to track the configurations and the drivers' assessments."

Figure 11-4 shows that each car can be configured with different engine and transmission combinations. The configuration is built using an engine and a transmission (aggregation). The drivers test the car configurations. The association class ConfigurationAssessment contains the details of the drivers' evaluations for each configuration.

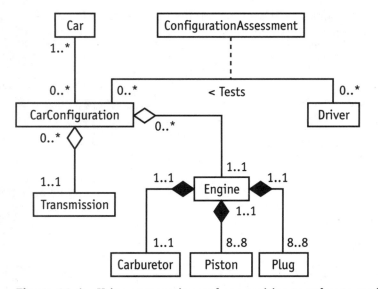

Figure 11-4   *Using aggregation and composition together to model racecar performance*

The engine is composed of the carburetor, pistons, and plugs (along with other unnamed parts). However, these parts become permanent parts of the engine once installed, so they are modeled with composition instead of aggregation.

It is common practice not to show the multiplicity on the composite end of the associations whenever it is 1..1. There are rare exceptions when the multiplicity could be different or you simply want to show it for clarity or consistency.

Modeling Generalization

20 Min. To Go

Generalization is the process of organizing the properties of a set of objects that share the same purpose. People use this process routinely to organize large amounts of information. Walk through a grocery store and you will find foods located in areas of the store depending upon their properties. Dry goods are located in one area, fruits and vegetables in another, meat in yet another. All these items are foods, but they are different kinds of foods or types of foods. Words such as *kind of* or *type of* are often used to describe a generalization relationship between classes (for example, an apple is a type of fruit that is in turn a kind of food and so on).

You might also hear this type of relationship called *inheritance*. Many times the terms *generalization* and *inheritance* are used synonymously. If an apple is a kind of fruit, then it *inherits* all the properties of fruit. Likewise, an apple is a *specialization* of fruit because it inherits all the generalized properties of fruit and adds some unique properties that only apply to apples. In the reverse, I could say that the concept fruit is a *generalization* of the facts that are true for watermelons, apples, peaches, and all types of objects in the group.

A generalization is *not* an association. I'll repeat that so you won't forget it. A generalization is *not* an association. In fact, association and generalization are treated as separate model elements in the UML metamodel. Associations define the rules for how *objects* may relate to one another. Generalization relates *classes* together where each class contains a subset of the elements needed to define a type of object. Instantiating all the element subsets from each of the classes in a single inheritance path of the generalization results in one object. In the Fruit illustration in Figure 11-5, to create a Red Delicious Apple, I would need to combine the RedDelicious class, the Apple class, and the Fruit class to get all the attributes and operations that define a Red Delicious Apple. From the combined class I could create (instantiate) an object of type RedDelicious (apple).

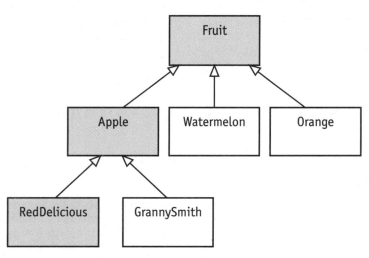

Figure 11-5 *Modeling generalization*

To express the same thing in words, I might say, "A 'Red Delicious' is a type of apple, and an apple is a type of fruit." For this reason, you sometimes hear generalization called the "is a" relationship (that is, every red delicious object "is an" apple object and every apple object "is a" fruit object).

This unique relationship between classes in a generalization raises an interesting problem. In Session 9, I described the concept of visibility. Visibility determines which other objects can see the attribute or operation. Normally, attributes are set to private so that only objects of the same class may see them. But what would happen to the RedDelicious class in Figure 11-5 if the attributes of the Apple class were set as private? RedDelicious would not have access to them so inheritance is in essence short-circuited. Another visibility, called *protected visibility,* is defined to handle just this situation. The protected visibility allows only objects of the same class *or subclasses* to see the element.

 There are variations in the implementation of the protected visibility between programming languages. Be sure to check the language manual for the correct interpretation.

Elements of generalization

Because the generalization (also called an *inheritance*) relationship is *not* a form of association, there is no need for multiplicity, roles, and constraints. These elements are simply irrelevant.

To draw a generalization relationship, we first need to define *superclass, subclass,* abstract class, concrete class, and *discriminator*. A superclass is a class that contains some combination of attributes, operations, and associations that are common to two or more types of objects that share the same purpose. Fruit and Apple are examples of superclasses. The term *superclass* reflects the concept of superset. The superset or superclass in this case contains the traits that are common to every object in the set.

A *subclass* is a class that contains some combination of attributes, operations, and associations that are unique to a type of object that is partially defined by a superclass. In Figure 11-5, Apple, Watermelon, Orange, RedDelicious and GrannySmith are all examples of subclasses. Note that a class may be both a superclass and a subclass.

The term *subclass* reflects the concept of subset. The subset, or subclass, contains a unique set of properties for only certain objects within the set. The GrannySmith class in Figure 11-5 would only contain the properties that are unique to GrannySmith apples. A GrannySmith object would get the rest of the information about the properties it shares with all apples from the Apple superclass, and all the properties it has in common with all fruits from the Fruit superclass. In other words, it actually takes three classes to generate a single object representing a GrannySmith apple.

An *abstract* class is a class that cannot create objects (cannot be instantiated). Any superclass that defines at least one operation that does not have a method is said to be abstract, or lacking a complete definition. Only a superclass can be abstract.

A *concrete* class is a class that has a method for every operation, so it can create objects. The methods may be defined in the class or inherited from a superclass. All classes at the bottom of a generalization hierarchy *must* be concrete. Any superclass *may* be concrete.

A *discriminator* is an attribute or rule that describes how I choose to identify the set of subclasses for a superclass. If I wanted to organize the information about types of cars, I could discriminate based on price range, manufacturer, engine size, fuel type, usage, or any number of other criteria. The discriminator I choose depends on the problem I am trying to solve. In Figure 11-6, I use a very common practice. I identify a set of predefined types (that is, type of fruit and varieties within types). Other times I might use a property of the objects themselves like size, price range, capacity, or age.

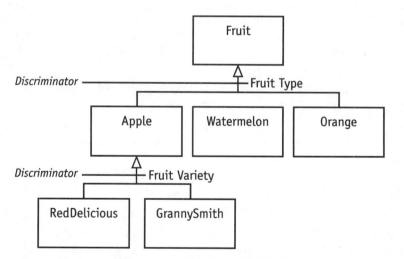

Figure 11-6   *Modeling generalization with discriminators*

The composition of a class reveals the possible discriminating properties. Classes define properties of objects such as attributes, operations, and association. These are the first three possible discriminating properties. If objects of the class share the same attributes, like age and address, they might be in the same subgroup. However, objects might have the same attribute (like age), but the values allowed for age in some of the objects are different from those allowed in others. For example, every Person has an age value assigned. However, minors would have age values less than 21 (in some states) and adults would have ages greater than 20.

The same concept applies to operations. Objects might have the same operation, that is, the same interface, like "accelerate." But different objects might implement that interface in very different ways. A car accelerates very differently from a rocket. Even different cars accelerate using different combinations of parts and fuels.

In summary, there are at least five objective criteria I can use to discriminate between objects within the same class (superclass):

- Attribute type
- Attribute values allowed
- Operation (interface)
- Method (implementation)
- Associations

Proper use of the discriminator facilitates the use of design patterns such as abstract factory and state.

There are actually two ways to draw a generalization. Figure 11-5 showed separate lines from each subclass to its superclass. Figure 11-6 merged the lines from all the subclasses of a superclass. In either form, draw a triangle at the superclass end of the generalization line (pointing to the superclass). (Note that you draw a triangle, not an arrow.) Connect the other end of the generalization to the subclass. Add the discriminator on the generalization line in simple text.

An illustration: How to model generalization

**10 Min.
To Go**

Building a generalization hierarchy can work in two directions, from the most general class down to the most specialized classes (specialization), and from the most specialized classes to the most generalized class (generalization).

The following example builds from general concept down to specifics, using the class Dog. I need to keep track of various breeds in a dog obedience school in order to understand and anticipate their unique training requirements.

Step 1: Draw the starting superclass, as in Figure 11-7. It is a class like any other class. The only thing that makes it a superclass is the fact that I plan to break it down.

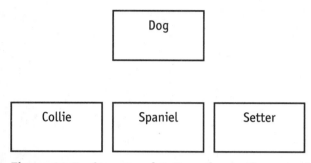

Figure 11-7 *Steps 1 and 2: Draw the starting superclass and the first set of specialized classes (subclasses).*

Step 2: Identify the discriminator for the first level of differentiation or specialization. In this example I chose *breed*. List the possible values for the discriminator. Identify what distinguishes the values from one another using the five objective criteria I described earlier in "Elements of generalization." Then create a class for each value. In Figure 11-7, I broke Dog down into the breeds (discriminator) Collie, Spaniel, and Setter.

Step 3: Connect all the Breed subclasses to the Dog superclass using the generalization relationship, a line with the triangle at the superclass end of the line (see Figure 11-8). Place the discriminator label on the line. It doesn't really matter where exactly, as long as it is between the superclass and subclasses. Other analysts are going to look at my diagram and wonder why I chose this set of subclasses. In any given problem there might be quite a few different ways to organize the information.

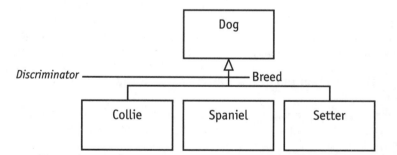

Figure 11-8 *Step 3: Draw the generalization relationship.*

Step 4: The process continues by repeating the steps for each new subclass I create. In Figure 11-9, I have expanded only the Spaniel subclass.

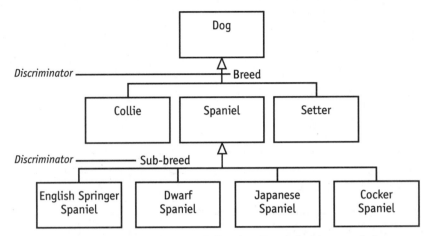

Figure 11-9   Step 4: Further specialization — subclassing a subclass

Done!

REVIEW

Associations identify the fact that types of objects can work together. Two specialized forms of association, aggregation and composition, tighten the rules about how the objects work together.

- Aggregation models assemblies or configurations of objects. You identify an aggregation association with a hollow diamond on the end of the association.

- Composition is a form of aggregation. Composition says that the member objects may not exist outside of the assembly. You identify a composition association with a solid diamond on the end of the association.

- Generalization is *not* a form of association. It is often called the "is a" relationship. Generalization allows you to break apart a class definition according to the similarities and differences in the objects that the class represents. You identify an inheritance or generalization relationship with a hollow triangle at the superclass end of the relationship.

- A superclass contains shared properties, common to many types of objects within the same class. A subclass contains only the properties unique to one type of object within the class.

- Abstract classes cannot create objects because their definition is missing a method for at least one operation. Concrete classes can create objects because they have access to a method for every operation.

- The discriminator describes the attribute(s) or rule that you used to choose the subclasses. You place the discriminator on the relationship line between the superclass and the subclasses.

QUIZ YOURSELF

1. What is the relationship between association and aggregation? (See "Modeling Aggregation and Composition.")

2. What is the relationship between composition and aggregation? (See "Modeling Aggregation and Composition.")

3. What symbol should you use to draw an aggregation association? (See "Modeling Aggregation and Composition.")

4. What symbol should you use to draw a composition association? (See "Modeling Aggregation and Composition.")

5. What is a superclass? (See "Elements of generalization.")

6. What is a subclass? (See "Elements of generalization.")

7. What is a discriminator? (See "Elements of generalization.")

Applying the Class Diagram to the Case Study

Session Checklist

✔ Applying the Class diagram notation to the case study

✔ Introducing the UML notation for design patterns

✔ Applying design patterns

S essions 9 through 11 covered the most commonly used elements of the Class diagram. Now that you know the individual elements of the Class diagram, it's time to put it all together in relation to the case study.

*30 Min.
To Go*

Modeling the Inventory Control System for the Case Study

I have taken a portion of the problem statement and expanded it so that you'll have the opportunity to use most of the notations that you've learned so far. This portion of the problem description will be your source for the modeling effort.

> **In a real project, you would also use the Use Case narratives. But for the narrow scope of this course (to learn the UML notation), I chose to use this abbreviated text.**

Problem statement: for the inventory control system

"Our system is designed to inventory and ship uniquely identified products. These products may be purchased directly from vendors and resold as is, or we can package vendor products together to make our own custom product. Customers place orders for one or more items, but we acknowledge interested customers in the system whether they have purchased yet or not. Each item corresponds to a product. We identify each product using a unique serial number. The Customer may inquire on the status of his Orders using the order number."

"Shipments of products from vendors are received and placed into inventory. Each product is assigned to a location so that we can easily find it later when filling orders. Each location has a unique location identifier. Customer orders are shipped as the products become available, so there may be more than one shipment to satisfy a single customer order. But a single shipment may contain products from multiple orders. Any items that have not been shipped are placed on a backorder with a reference to the original order."

Building the Class diagram

To build the Class diagram, follow the steps described in Sessions 9 through 11:

1. Identify the classes, name them, and define them so you know why they are part of the model. Turn to Session 9 for a reminder if you get stuck.

2. Identify, name, and define the associations between pairs of classes. Watch out for reflexive associations as well. Assign multiplicity and constraints where needed. If naming an association is difficult, try role names. Session 10 provides an explanation of each of these model elements.

3. Evaluate each association to determine whether it should be defined as aggregation. If it is aggregation, then could it be composition? If you need help remembering the distinction between aggregation and composition, turn to Session 11.

4. Evaluate the classes for possible specialization or generalization. Check out Session 11 if you get stuck.

Figure 12-1 illustrates the completed Class diagram. You can try building the diagram on your own, then compare your results with Figure 12-1, or you can go ahead and examine the diagram. In the numbered list that accompanies the figure, I explain each of the model elements.

1. *"Customers place orders for one or more items, but we acknowledge interested customers in the system whether they have purchased yet or not."*

    On the "places" association between Customer and Order, the multiplicity of 1..1 means that every Order must be placed by a Customer. An Order cannot exist on its own.

This sounds kind of like composition, doesn't it? But it can't be composition if it doesn't first satisfy the rules for aggregation. That is, the order would have to be part of the customer. Because the order is not part of the customer, the relationship is a simple association.

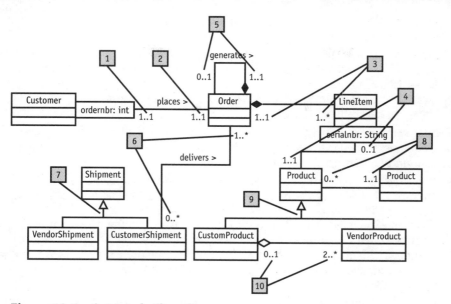

Figure 12-1 *Case study Class diagram*

2. *"Customers place orders for one or more items, but we acknowledge interested customers in the system whether they have purchased yet or not. The Customer may inquire on the status of his Orders using the order number."*

On the "places" association between Customer and Order, some customers may not yet have placed any orders while others may have been doing business with us for a long time. The Order multiplicity should be 0..*. But a Customer can use the order number as a qualifier to look up a specific Order (qualified association), so the multiplicity with the qualifier is 1..1.

3. *"Customers place orders for one or more items. . . ."*

An Order is constructed using one or more Line Items. Each Line Item includes information like a price and any applicable discount. But every Line Item exists only as part of an Order represented by composition and a multiplicity of 1..1 on the Order. There must be at least one item on the Order so the LineItem multiplicity is 1..*.

4. *"Each item corresponds to a product. We identify each product using a unique serial number."*

Each Line Item is associated with a specific Product (1..1). The Line Item refers to the Product using a serial number as a qualifier (qualified association). A Product might not ever be ordered, so the multiplicity on the Line Item end is zero to one (0..1). In other words, a Product might not yet be associated with a Line Item.

5. *"Any items that have not been shipped are placed on a backorder with a reference to the original order."*

> An Order that is not filled completely will generate another Order that it refers to as a backorder (role name) and that backorder is associated with the Order that generated it (reflexive composition). Each backorder refers to exactly one other Order, its source (1..1). But each Order may or may not generate backorders (0..*).

6. *"Customer orders are shipped as the products become available, so there may be more than one shipment to satisfy a single customer order. But a single shipment may contain products from multiple orders."*

> The Order is shipped to the Customer via a Customer Shipment. When the Order has not yet been shipped, the multiplicity on the Customer Shipment is zero (that is, there is no Shipment associated with the Order). When more than one Shipment is needed to fill the Order (for example, the items are being shipped from multiple locations or are restricted by shipping requirements), the multiplicity is "many." Hence the complete multiplicity range is 0..*. A shipment may contain products from many orders, resulting in an Order multiplicity of 1..*.

7. *"Shipments of products from vendors are received and placed into stock. . . . Customer orders are shipped as the products become available."*

> Customer Shipment is just one *type* of Shipment (generalization). Another *type* of Shipment is the incoming Vendor Shipment referred to in the receiving process. CustomerShipment and VendorShipment are specializations of Shipment and so inherit all the properties of Shipment.

8. *"Each product is assigned to a location so that we can easily find it later when filling orders. Each location has a unique location identifier."*

> Many Products or no Products may be in a given Location (0..*). But in order for you to record a Product into inventory, you have to assign it to a Location. So there will never be a Product that is not associated with a Location. This requires a multiplicity of 1..1 on the Location end of the association.

9. *"These products may be purchased directly from vendors and resold as is, or we can package vendor products together to make our own custom product."*

> VendorProduct and CustomProduct are both *types* of Product (generalization), specializations of the class Product. Both can be ordered and shipped. But CustomProducts are configurations of VendorProducts and VendorProducts are standalone items that are ordered and shipped independently, not in a configuration of other Products.

10. *". . . we can package vendor products together to make our own custom product."*

> We can create custom products using VendorProducts; for example, a home entertainment system might consist of a receiver, CD player, speakers, TV, and so on (aggregation). Why is it aggregation and not composition? Because the VendorProducts, like the CD player, may exist and be sold separately from the entertainment system. The multiplicity on VendorProduct is 2..* because a CustomProduct is only a logic entity made up of a combination of at least two VendorProducts. A VendorProduct may be sold individually and does not have to be part of any CustomProduct configuration (0..1).

Remember to pay close attention to the vocabulary of the problem description. The people who work every day with this information have already created and refined their own verbal abstractions to describe their environment. When you write software, you're only copying their abstractions into another form (software) by applying the rigor and precision of a disciplined analytical approach.

Understanding UML Notation for Design Patterns

20 Min. To Go

After a short time working with Class diagrams you will begin to see the same structures appear in many of your diagrams. You will see *patterns* in the way a problem or a solution is defined. The UML provides a notation to represent common software patterns in your Class diagram to make creating your diagrams easier and to make the diagrams easier to understand.

Software design patterns have created a lot of interest in the past few years. They have also generated some misconceptions. So what exactly is a software design pattern? The software version of the pattern concept was actually borrowed from other disciplines like building architecture where patterns help architects work more easily with complex structures. In fact, you use patterns all the time. For example, when I say the word *kitchen,* what comes to mind? You probably envision counters, cupboards, a refrigerator, a stove, maybe a microwave, and various types of food. Now, if everyone knows what a kitchen is, does that mean that all kitchens are identical? No, the concept of *kitchen* can be implemented in literally thousands of different ways.

Kitchen is only a pattern, an idea that allows people to share a common vision without limiting how they each want to implement that vision. So how do you define a pattern? Table 12-1 identifies and describes four basic elements for defining a pattern.

Table 12-1   *Elements of a Pattern Definition for Kitchen*

Pattern Element	Element Example for Kitchen
A problem to solve	We need a place to store and prepare food.
The resources to solve it	We can use appliances, counters and cupboards, food, utensils, and so on.
The set of rules about how the resources could be used to solve the problem	The refrigerator stores perishable items prior to preparation, the oven is used to heat food, and so on.
Guidelines to know when the pattern works well and when it does not	It works well within the context of a house. It does not work well outside the house (for example, while camping or picnicking).

Formal definitions for software patterns include a bit more, but for an introduction this is more than adequate.

One important thing to remember about patterns is that they define a *concept,* not *code.* You can find books that provide code examples for patterns so that you can see how you might apply the pattern in your own code. But a pattern is not the code. It is a concept designed to help developers communicate common solutions to common problems. In fact, because communication and problem solving are parts of nearly every occupation, you can find patterns in almost every discipline of software development. There are analysis level patterns, business patterns, architectural patterns, and many more, all developed to facilitate communication about solutions that are used consistently to solve similar recurring problems in each area of endeavor.

One software design pattern, called the *observer design pattern,* addresses the problem where one object needs to know when something happens to another object so that it can respond immediately to the change. The example in Table 12-2 uses the Order and the Shipment from the Inventory Control case study to illustrate the pattern. Using the four elements from Table 12-1 as a guide, Table 12-2 describes how the observer design pattern allows you to immediately update the Order when the Shipment leaves the building.

Table 12-2 *The Observer Design Pattern Example*

Pattern Element	Element Description for Observer Pattern
A problem to solve	The Order needs to be updated to a status of "shipped" when the Shipment has left the premises. The "shipped" status is the condition that kicks off the Accounts Receivable and tracking processes.
The resources to solve it	The observer pattern identifies two resources, an *observer* object and an *observable* (observed) object. The observable object is responsible for notifying the observers. This eliminates the need for the observer to constantly ask the observable (observed) object what is happening.
The set of rules about how the resources could be used to solve the problem	The rules for the observer pattern dictate two roles: The Shipment object that is being observed assumes the role of the *observable* object, and the Order takes on the role of the *observer.* The Order tells the Shipment object that it wants to be notified when something happens. The Shipment places the Order on its list of observers to be notified. When the Shipment is shipped, the Shipment sends a standard notification to all the observers in the list. When the Order receives the notification, it can then respond as it needs to.
Guidelines to know when the pattern works well and when it does not	The observer pattern can be overused, causing performance problems that result from the volume of notifications sent to all observers for every change in the observable object. It works best when a few very specific immediate responses are essential to the application, as in a user interface, embedded application, or automation.

The next question is how to model the use of a pattern in the UML. The UML refers to a pattern as a *collaboration* (not to be confused with a Collaboration diagram). In Figure 12-2, the collaboration is rendered as an oval shape containing the pattern name. The classes are drawn around it. Then you draw dashed lines from the collaboration to the classes that implement the pattern. At the end of the dashed lines next to the classes, you place the role that the class plays in the implementation of the pattern. In Figure 12-2, the Shipment plays the role of observable and the Order plays the role of observer.

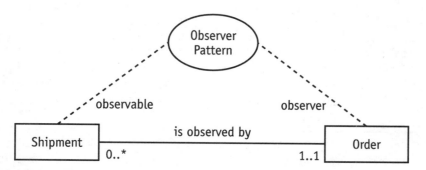

Figure 12-2   *Observer pattern example in a Class diagram*

Using Design Patterns in the Class Diagram

*10 Min.
To Go*

Another common problem in applications is managing complex *state-specific behavior*. If you haven't worked much with states, that may sound complicated. But you may have worked around this problem without realizing it. Have you ever written a method in which you found you had to use a lot of conditional logic like *if* statements or *case* statements? You couldn't determine how the method should work until you first checked on the condition of various attributes in the object. Well, an object's state is nothing more than the current values of its attributes. So when you checked the attribute values in the conditional logic, you were actually checking the object's state.

When the implementation of the methods depends on changes in the attribute values (state changes), the code can quickly become very complicated to write and difficult to maintain. The state design pattern offers a solution that both makes the initial writing easier and substantially reduces the maintenance costs.

Table 12-3 describes the state design pattern.

Table 12-3 *The State Design Pattern Example*

Pattern Element	Element Description for State Pattern
A problem to solve	You need to create a Product class for the Inventory Control System. The Product will be used in a number of different steps within the system. Depending on where a Product is in the workflow, each method on the Product may or may not be valid. Also, some methods might need to behave differently during different steps in the workflow.
The resources to solve it	The state design pattern has two resources, in this example they are the Product, which provides the *context,* and the Product State (*state*), which defines the state-specific implementations for each method. Figure 12-3 illustrates the Class diagram for this relationship.
The set of rules about how the resources could be used to solve the problem	The rules for the state design pattern dictate two roles: the *context*, which is provided by the Product class, and the *state*, which is provided by the Product State class. The Product State is actually a generalization of classes that define the individual states for Product and their state-specific implementations for each operation. The Product receives requests in the course of normal business. But rather than implement the requested operations, it delegates or forwards each request to an instance of a ProductState subclass that represents the current state of the Product. The ProductState instance performs the implementation that it owns for the operation and returns control to the Product. As the state of the Product changes, each new request is actually forwarded to an instance of a different ProductState subclass that represents the current condition of the Product.
Guidelines to know when the pattern works well and when it does not	Many objects simply don't have a significant number of states, or their behavior doesn't vary significantly from state to state.

Figure 12-3 shows the association "delegates to" between Product and ProductState. If that were all the Class diagram showed you, then you wouldn't really be able to tell *why* they were associated. After all, Products are also associated with LineItems and Locations. The association name may give you a clue, but when you add the pattern notation, you immediately bring in all the information about how the pattern tells you to use these two classes in this relationship. The pattern notation explains their communication, the methods they need to support, and the attributes they will need in order to support the relationship and the communication.

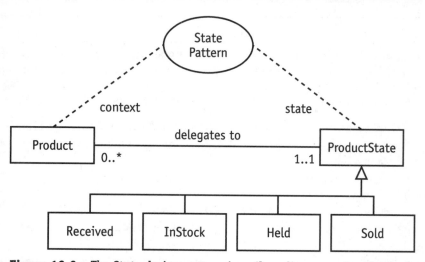

Figure 12-3 *The State design pattern in a Class diagram using the Product example*

Using the design pattern notation in the Class diagram can streamline the review process. If all the reviewers know that portions of your design have been addressed using proven techniques, then the trust level can rise above the level associated with a homegrown design that has never been tried. Although all the design needs to be tested, the creation and review of the design can be streamlined.

There are many more documented patterns, and more are being developed all the time. To learn patterns, you may want to keep in mind the four elements listed in this session. First, learn to identify the problems that the patterns are designed to address. If you know the problems, then as you go to work on your next project you'll recognize the problem when it appears. You'll see objects that transition through many states and say, "Ah ha! Maybe I can use the state pattern to make this easier to work with." Now you have a handle to an existing, proven resource (a pattern), and you can find out how it works and apply it to your design. Second, know when not to use a pattern. Think back to the kitchen example. A kitchen pattern was designed to address the need to store and prepare food. But do you really want a kitchen implementation when you go backpacking?

I want to share one parting caution about patterns. Patterns are helpful insofar as they improve your ability to share common solutions with your teammates. But that implies that you *and* your teammates know, understand, and use the same patterns consistently. If you throw lots of new patterns into your design and your teammates have no idea what you're doing, then what have you gained? You still have to explain every detail of your design. In fact, some patterns are refined so much that they aren't very easy to understand. You may actually make your application more abstract and difficult to test and maintain, because the testers and maintenance programmers can't figure out your code.

Done!

REVIEW

The Class diagram models the resources of the problem domain. Associations represent the rules that govern the relationships between the resources. Multiplicity defines the allowable combinations of objects in a relationship. Qualified associations provide a means to access one or more objects with an identifier, thus reducing search time and complexity.

- To build the Class diagram, follow the steps described in Sessions 9 through 11:
    1. Identify the classes, name them, and define them so you know why they are part of the model.
    2. Identify, name, and define the associations between pairs of classes. Watch out for reflexive associations as well. Assign multiplicity and constraints where needed. If naming an association is difficult, try role names.
    3. Evaluate each association to determine whether it should be defined as aggregation. If it is aggregation, then could it be composition?
    4. Evaluate the classes for possible specialization or generalization.
- Patterns define a common solution to a common problem. Patterns identify the problem needing a solution, the resources to solve the problem, the rules for how the resources should be used to solve the problem, and when it is and is not appropriate to apply the pattern. Patterns are *not* code.
- The notation for applying patterns to a Class diagram is an oval collaboration icon with the pattern name. Dashed lines connect the pattern to the participating classes. The role names are placed at the ends of the dashed lines near the class that plays the role.

QUIZ YOURSELF

1. How would you use multiplicity to say that a Shipment must contain at least one Product but can contain as many Products as you like? (See "Modeling the Inventory Control System for the Case Study.")
2. What notation would you use to indicate that there are two different types of Shipments? (See "Modeling the Inventory Control System for the Case Study.")
3. What is a pattern? (See "Understanding UML Notation for Design Patterns.")
4. What is the notation for a pattern? (See "Understanding UML Notation for Design Patterns.")
5. How do you indicate the way in which a class participates in a pattern? (See "Understanding UML Notation for Design Patterns.")

Modeling the Static View:
The Object Diagram

Session Checklist

✔ Explaining the purpose and notation of the Object diagram

✔ Comparing and contrasting the Object and Class diagrams

✔ Explaining how to use the Object diagram to test a Class diagram

The Object diagram is primarily a tool for research and testing. It can be used to understand a problem by documenting examples from the problem domain. It can also be used during analysis and design to verify the accuracy of Class diagrams.

Understanding the Object Diagram

**30 Min.
To Go**

The Object diagram models *facts* about specific entities, whereas the Class diagram models the *rules* for types of entities. Objects are real things, like you and me, this book, and the chair you're sitting in. So an Object diagram would represent, for example, the *fact* that you own this copy of *UML Weekend Crash Course*. In contrast, a Class diagram would describe the *rule* that people can own books.

To come up with a set of rules that describe objects and their relationships, you must have real things on which to base the rules. The qualities of each real object are compared to identify common properties that support a common description. If an object is encountered that does not fit the description, either the current description must change or a new description must be created to support the new facts.

Earlier in this book, you started with a problem domain that you described using the Use Case view. Use Cases described interactions between the actors and the system. From those Use Cases, you found scenarios. Now scenarios become your source for test cases to verify every behavior that your system needs to support. Scenarios are also the source for the facts you'll use to build your Object diagrams.

Introducing Elements of the Object Diagram Notation

The Object diagram consists of just two elements: objects and links. You know already that an object is a real entity created from a class, a definition of a type of object. In the same way, a link is created from an association, the definition of a type of relationship. A link represents a relationship between two objects. An association defines a type of relationship and the rules that govern it.

Figure 13-1 shows an object called Tom. Like the Class notation, the Object notation has a name compartment at the top of the box. The name includes the name of the object *and* the name of the class to which the object conforms: "Customer." This helps distinguish the object Tom of type Customer from the object Tom of type Employee. This notation also allows you to model an example or test case in which many objects of the same class participate (for example, one employee supervises another employee).

Tom: Customer
custID = 123456 name = Tom Pender address = 1234 UML Ave

Figure 13-1   *UML Object notation*

Use the format *object name : class name* to fully define the object name. Then the entire expression is underlined. You may also use the abbreviated form, *: class name,* without the object name. This form is called an *anonymous object.* It is used when you want to draw an example where it doesn't really matter which specific object participates in the example because any object of the named class would behave in exactly the same way.

The second compartment in the object box contains facts about the attributes. Each attribute is named and assigned a value. In Figure 13-1, you see name = Tom Pender. An object is real. It exists. So it can have values assigned to each attribute. Even a value of blank or null is a value that distinguishes the condition of the object from other possibilities. Note how different this is from the class attribute compartment. The class contained definitions for each attribute and contained no values. Again, the class is a set of *rules* where the object is a set of *facts.* The class says that an Employee object *may* have a name attribute that contains a String value 20 characters long. The object says that the name attribute *does* contain the value "Tom Pender."

Comparing the Object Diagram and the Class Diagram Notations

**20 Min.
To Go**

Figure 13-2 contains a Class diagram showing the rules regarding Shipment and Product and the relationship between the two objects. The Class diagram defines the attributes that must be used to define each type of object and the behaviors that each type of object must support.

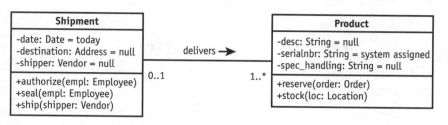

Figure 13-2 *UML Class notation for the Shipment and Product*

The Object diagram in Figure 13-3 shows that the object 4321 of type Shipment has two Products. Each attribute for the three objects is assigned a value. Note that the special handling attribute on one Product is blank. This can be a valid value. It is the class definition for the attribute that determines the valid values that may be assigned to the attribute when it appears within an object.

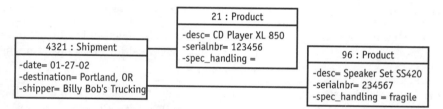

Figure 13-3 *UML Object notation for a Shipment with two Products*

Note what is missing from the object notation that was required in every class. The third compartment, containing the operations, was omitted. But why leave it out of the object if the class sets the rules that an object must follow? When you included the attributes, it was because each object potentially possessed different values for the attributes defined by the class. But the class defines an operation that does *not* have multiple interpretations or values. Every object of the same class possesses the *same operations*. To model the operations again on the Object diagram would add redundancy without adding new information. So you leave the operations off of the Object diagram.

Having seen examples of the differences between the Class and Object diagrams, you can now refer to Table 13-1 for a side-by-side comparison of their features. A working knowledge of the relationship between these two types of diagrams will help you understand how to use them both to facilitate analysis and test the results of your analysis and design efforts.

Table 13-1   *Comparison of the Class and Object Diagrams*

Class Diagram	Object Diagram
The class has three compartments: name, attribute, and operation.	The object has only two compartments: name and attribute.
The class name stands alone in the class name compartment.	The format for an object name is object-name, colon, class-name (<u>1234:Order</u>), with the entire expression underlined. You will encounter this notation in other diagrams that model objects rather than classes. Sometimes the object name is left off and only the colon and class-name are used. This is referred to as an anonymous object.
The class attribute compartment defines the properties of the attributes.	The object defines only the current value of each attribute for the test or example being modeled.
Operations are listed in the class.	Operations are not included in the object because they would be identical for every object of the same class.
The classes are connected with an *association* with a name, multiplicity, constraints, and roles. Classes represent a "classification" of objects, so it is necessary to specify how many may participate in the association.	The objects are connected with a *link* that has a name and no multiplicity. Objects represent single entities. All links are one-to-one, so multiplicity is irrelevant. Roles may be used on links.

Applying Object Diagrams to Test Class Diagrams

Drawing a Class diagram and incorrectly assuming that it's correct is very easy to do. That's why you need to use additional diagrams to test the Class diagram. For example, if I brought you the Class diagram in Figure 13-4, which models the products for the Inventory Control application (sure that it's too simple to be wrong), you could test my diagram with an Object diagram. If you did, you would find four different problems and be able to provide *objective proof* that the Class diagram needs to be changed.

 If errors can be made on such a simple model, think of how valuable such a testing method is for very complex models.

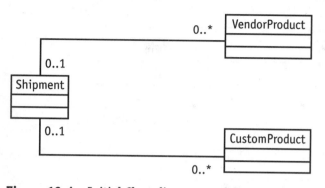

Figure 13-4 *Initial Class diagram modeling products*

Figure 13-4 tells you that each Shipment may have zero or more VendorProducts and zero or more CustomProducts. Each type of Product may or may not have been shipped.

The rest of this session steps through the construction of an Object diagram that models the set of test cases for the Product Class diagram in Figure 13-4. The construction process demonstrates the model elements of the Object diagram and how the Object diagram illustrates test cases.

I'm going to go through this one step at a time. You may spot more problems with the original Class diagram than the current test case reveals. By the time I cover all the test cases, we should have found all the problems. If we don't, just send me a nice letter with the corrections.

**10 Min.
To Go**

Test case 1

A CustomProduct is created by assembling VendorProducts. VendorProducts 28, 38, and 72 create CustomProduct 425.

Figure 13-5 shows how the Class diagram is changed to include the aggregation relationship between CustomProduct and VendorProduct.

The change shows that a CustomProduct is created from one or more VendorProducts. But a VendorProduct doesn't have to be used in a CustomProduct.

Test case 2

What is the minimum number of objects that make up a CustomProduct configuration? After reviewing all the test data, we find that a CustomProduct must consist of at least two VendorProducts. Otherwise, there is no way to distinguish a CustomProduct from a VendorProduct.

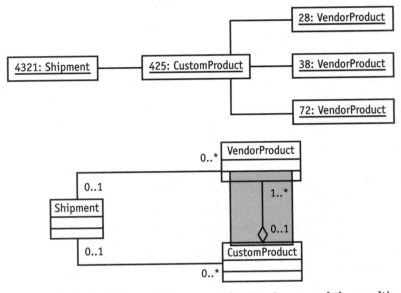

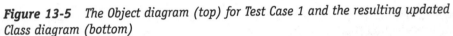

Figure 13-5 *The Object diagram (top) for Test Case 1 and the resulting updated Class diagram (bottom)*

Figure 13-6 shows that the test case revealed the need to alter the minimum multiplicity for VendorProducts used to assemble a CustomProduct from 1 to 2.

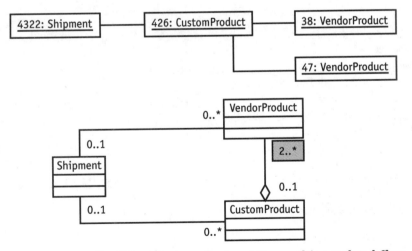

Figure 13-6 *The Object diagram (top) and the resulting updated Class diagram (bottom)*

Test case 3

Is there evidence that a CustomProduct may be configured into another CustomProduct?

Figure 13-7 shows that the test case revealed the need to support aggregation between one CustomProduct and other CustomProducts. For example, a component stereo system, consisting of five VendorProducts, could become part of a home entertainment center.

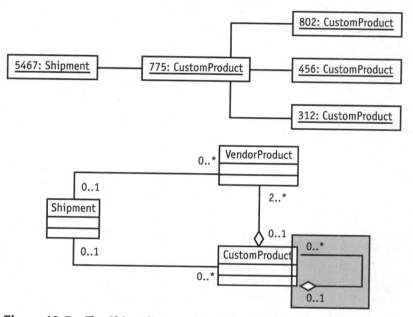

Figure 13-7 *The Object diagram (top) and the resulting updated Class diagram (bottom)*

Test case 4

Are there any common characteristics among the objects used to configure CustomProduct?

Figure 13-8 shows that both CustomProducts and VendorProducts can be part of a CustomProduct. This common property can be generalized. That is, you can create a generalized class to contain what the two types of products have in common. The new aggregation association says that any type of Product (VendorProduct or CustomProduct) may participate in the assembly of a CustomProduct.

Both classes also define the same type of association with Shipment. This too can be moved up to the generalized class. A single association from Shipment to Product says that any type of Product (VendorProduct or CustomProduct) may be shipped.

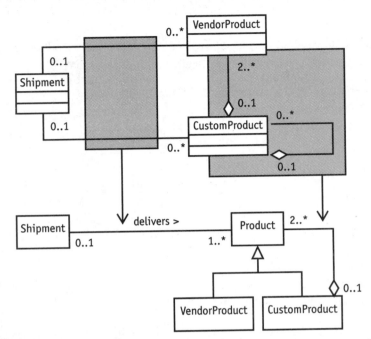

Figure 13-8 *Identifying common properties to create a generalization*

 By the way, the Product generalization combined with the aggregation between the subclass CustomProduct and the superclass Product is an example of the software design pattern called the Composite design pattern (not to be confused with composition).

Use the Object diagram on an as-needed basis to model specific examples or test cases. Compare the representation of the *facts* against the representation of the *rules* set forth in the Class diagram. Adjust the Class diagram to address errors and missed requirements.

REVIEW

Done!

In this session, you learned the notation for the Object diagram.

- The Object diagram is used to analyze the objects in the problem domain to determine the class definition requirements.
- After the Class diagram has been developed, the Object diagram is used to test the Class diagram.
- Objects are identified with a name in the form *object-name: class-name*. The object name can be left off to indicate an anonymous object.
- The object icon consists of two compartments, one for the name and one for the attributes. Attributes are described with a name and the current value.

- Operations are not defined on objects because every object of the same class would have identical operations, creating redundancy in the model.
- Objects are connected using links. Classes are connected using associations. Links are defined with a name and optional roles. Multiplicity and constraints are not relevant with a link.

QUIZ YOURSELF

1. Name two reasons for using an Object diagram. (See "Understanding the Object Diagram.")
2. Name the two elements of the Object diagram. (See "Introducing Elements of the Object Diagram Notation.")
3. How do you write the name of an object? (See "Introducing Elements of the Object Diagram Notation.")
4. What is a link? (See "Introducing Elements of the Object Diagram Notation.")
5. Why don't you represent operations in an object? (See "Introducing Elements of the Object Diagram Notation.")

Modeling the Functional View:
The Activity Diagram

Session Checklist

✔ Explaining the purpose and use of the Activity diagram

✔ Explaining the Activity diagram notation

**30 Min.
To Go**

The Activity diagram is part of the Functional view because it describes logical processes, or functions, implemented using code. Each process describes a sequence of tasks and the decisions that govern when and how they are done. You must understand these processes in order to write correct code.

Functional modeling has acquired a poor reputation with the onset of object-oriented (OO) modeling. But both functional modeling and data modeling provide valuable insight into software development. OO development methods simply bring the two concepts together. Functional modeling is still a very basic part of any application design.

Introducing the Activity Diagram

In the past, you used flowcharts, a simple technique with a wide range of applications. The UML offers an enhanced version of flowcharts in the form of the Activity diagram, the focus of this session.

Where might you use the Activity diagram? There are at least three places in the UML where an Activity diagram provides valuable insight: workflow, Use Cases, and operations.

Modeling workflow and Use Cases

When modeling a Use Case, you're attempting to understand the goal that the system must achieve in order to be successful. Use the Activity diagram to follow the user through a procedure, noting the decisions made and tasks performed at each step. The procedure may incorporate many Use Cases (workflow), a single Use Case, or only part of a Use Case as you have currently modeled it. It's all part of the validation process. Each diagram lends a new perspective to the information about the system.

A workflow-level Activity diagram represents the order in which a set of Use Cases is executed. An Activity diagram for one Use Case would explain how the actor interacts with the system to accomplish the goal of the Use Case, including rules, information exchanged, decisions made, and work products created.

Modeling the user's work this way does not bind you to that particular version of the process. Remember that for each goal (Use Case), there may be any number of valid processes. But creating such a model will likely reveal the essential elements of the process in a way that is familiar to the users. The new presentation then facilitates the interview to clarify the tasks and the reasons behind them. This is your opportunity to ask those all-important "why" questions to get at the goal of the process and each task used to perform the process.

Defining methods

The Activity diagram can also be used to model the implementation of complex methods. When defining the implementation for an operation, you need to model the sequence of data manipulation, looping, and decision logic. Modeling complex functions can prevent problems later when you write the code by revealing all the requirements explicitly in the diagram. Models make most, if not all, of your assumptions visible and consequently easier to review and correct.

That last statement is worth emphasizing. It is very tempting to shortcut the modeling process, but the true value of modeling is in revealing what you know so that it can be challenged and verified. Making assumptions sabotages this very valuable benefit of modeling.

The Activity diagram contains all the logical constructs you find in most programming languages. In fact, it can translate quite well into pseudo-code or even native code.

I should offer one clarification here regarding the vocabulary of the UML. The word *operation* in the UML refers to the declaration portion of a behavior defined by a class. This typically means the name, parameters, and possibly the return type. This is also often called the *interface,* the information you use to tell the object what you want it to do.

In contrast, the word *method* is used to refer to the implementation of an operation, the code that is executed when you invoke the interface. The Activity diagram may be used to design the requirements for a method. Because the UML does not provide a place to model the methods in a Class diagram, or anywhere else, the Activity diagram can fill in this missing piece.

Not everyone has accepted or uses the definitions for operation and method as they are used in the UML.

To be sure, not every operation is complicated enough to warrant drawing an Activity diagram. The point is that the Activity diagram is well suited to the task when it is needed.

Taking a Look at Activity Diagram Notation

In this section, I give you a quick tour of the notation. A lot of this may be familiar if you've used flowcharts, so feel free to skim over the session until you spot something that looks new.

Activities and transitions

An *activity* is a step in a process where some work is getting done. It can be a calculation, finding some data, manipulating information, or verifying data. The activity is represented by a rounded rectangle containing freeform text. An *Activity diagram* is a series of activities linked by *transitions,* arrows connecting each activity. Typically, the transition takes place because the activity is completed. For example, you're currently in the activity "reading a page." When you finish this activity, you switch to the activity "turning page." When you are done turning the page . . . well, you get the idea. Figure 14-1 shows this idea graphically.

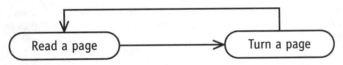

Figure 14-1 *Activities and transitions*

This notation starts to show the overlap between the Activity diagram and the Statechart diagram. In fact, the Activity diagram is a subset of the Statechart diagram. Each Activity is an *action state* where the object is busy doing something (as opposed to waiting). Each transition is a change in state, a change from one activity or active state to the next. So as you learn the Activity diagram, you are well on your way toward understanding the Statechart diagram as well. You'll see and use the Statechart diagram in Sessions 20 through 23.

You may sometimes see the word "Do:" preceding the name of an activity. This is a common and valid notation to distinguish an activity from other state-related behaviors defined by the UML.

Guard condition

Sometimes the transition should only be used when certain things have happened. A *guard condition* can be assigned to a transition to restrict use of the transition. Place the condition within square brackets somewhere near the transition arrow. The condition must test true before you may follow the associated transition to the next activity. The Activity diagram segment in Figure 14-2 tells you that you can't leave the table when you've finished your dinner unless you have finished your vegetables.

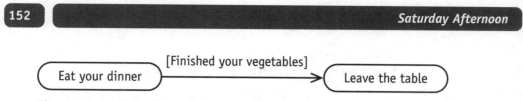

Figure 14-2 *A guard condition on a transition*

Decisions

The Activity diagram diamond is a decision icon, just as it is in flowcharts. In either diagram, one arrow exits the diamond for each possible value of the tested condition. The decision may be as simple as a true/false test (for example, the left-hand illustration in Figure 14-3 asks, "Are there sufficient funds in the customer's account to cover the withdrawal?"). The decision may involve a choice between a set of options. For example, the right-hand illustration in Figure 14-3 asks, "Would you like chocolate, vanilla, strawberry, or rocky road ice cream?"

Each option is identified using a guard condition. Each guard condition must be mutually exclusive so that only one option is possible at any decision point. The guard is placed on the transition that shows the direction that the logic follows if that condition is true. If you write code, then you have probably used a case statement to handle this same type of problem.

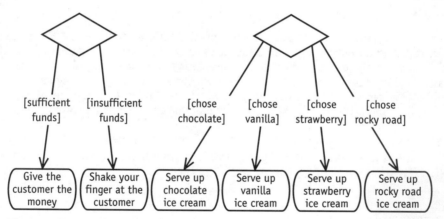

Figure 14-3 *Making a decision*

Because every choice at a decision point is modeled with a guard condition, it is possible to use the conditional logic on transitions leaving an activity as well. For example, in Figure 14-4 the activity of computing the new account balance reveals whether the account is overdrawn. All the information needed to make the choice is provided by the activity. To show the choices resulting from an activity, simply model the transitions exiting the activity, each with a different guard condition.

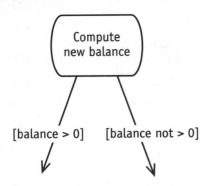

Figure 14-4 *Making a decision in an activity*

Use the decision diamond form from Figure 14-3 when no processing is included in the step. This usually means that the needed information has been accumulated from a number of previous steps or the decision is an explicit choice by an actor. Use the form in Figure 14-4 when the completion of the activity provides all the required information to support the decision.

Merge point

The diamond icon is also used to model a *merge point,* the place where two alternative paths come together and continue as one. The two paths in this case are mutually exclusive routes. For example, you and I might each walk from your house to the store. I choose to walk down the left side of the street while you walk down the right. But two blocks before the store we both have to turn right and walk on the right side of that street to the store's front door. Neither of us could take both routes at the same time. But whichever route we take we have to walk the last two blocks in exactly the same manner.

You can also think of the merge point as a labor-saving device. The alternative would be to model the same sequence of steps for each of the paths that share them.

Figure 14-5 shows alternative paths merging and continuing along a single path. The diamond represents the point at which the paths converge.

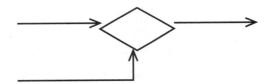

Figure 14-5 *The diamond as a merge point*

10 Min. To Go

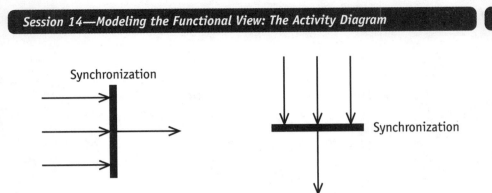

Figure 14-8 *Merging control using the synchronization bar*

I should point out that identifying a concurrency *opportunity* does not necessarily dictate a concurrency *requirement*. It simply models the fact that sequential processing is not required, and if the implementation environment supports it, there may be a chance to optimize the performance of the application by exploiting the concurrency opportunity.

Done!

REVIEW

The Activity diagram is the UML version of the classic flowchart. It may be applied to any process, large or small. Three common applications of flowcharts are to explain workflow (a series of Use Cases), to explain a single Use Case, and to explain a method.

- The Activity diagram represents a task as an activity drawn as a rounded rectangle containing a freeform text description of the task. The transition from one activity to the next is shown as an arrow. The notation provides for start and end points, using a dot and a bull's-eye, respectively.

- Model decisions with a diamond. Each transition exiting the decision must be labeled with a guard condition and the conditions must be mutually exclusive. The diamond may also be used to represent a merge point, joining two alternative paths in the sequence.

- Guard conditions may also be used on transitions leaving an activity, where the result of the activity provides all the information needed to meet one of the conditions.

- Concurrency allows multiple threads or processes to execute simultaneously. The fork bar shows one transition initiating multiple transitions. The synchronization bar shows multiple transitions coming to an end and one new transition taking over.

QUIZ YOURSELF

1. Name two situations in which the Activity diagram is typically applied. (See "Introducing the Activity Diagram.")

2. What notations indicate the start and end points in an Activity diagram? (See "Start and end.")

3. What symbol is used to show the start of concurrent processes? (See "Concurrency.")

4. How do you indicate the direction to follow out of a decision point? (See "Decisions.")

5. What is a transition? (See "Activities and transitions.")

SESSION

15

Applying the Activity Diagram to the Case Study

Session Checklist

✔ Explaining the steps for building an Activity diagram

✔ Building an Activity diagram for the case study

**30 Min.
To Go**

The narrative for the Use Case tells you the rules and the logic required to accomplish that goal. But text can be difficult to test, so you may want to draw the logic in an Activity diagram.

Building an Activity Diagram for the Case Study

The problem statement for the Inventory Control system included the Use Case Receive Product. You can use the text from the Use Case narrative (Table 15-1) as a guide while we build the Activity diagram for the case study.

If you are struggling with this new notation, you might try drawing the old-style flowchart first and then add the new concurrency features of the Activity diagram as needed.

Table 15-1   *The Use Case Narrative for Receive Product*

Field Name	Field Description
Name	Receive Product
Number	2.0
Author	Joe Analyst
Last update	12/31/01 (working over New Year's Day to make points with the boss)
Assumptions	The user has authority to use this transaction
Pre-conditions	Shipment is from a valid Shipping company
Use Case initiation	This Use Case starts on demand
Use Case dialog	The user enters the Shipper identification number (ShipperID)
	If not found, display the "Shipper not found" error message Prompt to re-enter or cancel
	Else (found) proceed
	Display the Shipper details
	Enter the Shipment details (date, sender, number of pieces)

	For each product in the Shipment
	    Find the Purchase Order using the PO_nbr
	    If not found, display "invalid P.O." error message and set the item aside
	    Else (P.O. found)
	        Match the product to an item on the Purchase Order
	        If not matched, display "invalid item" error message and set the item aside
	        Else check off the item and qty on the Purchase Order

	Notify Accounts Payable of the updated Purchase Order
	Display the "Accounts Payable notified" message
	And
	Update inventory for the items Products received

Field Name	Field Description
	Display "inventory updated successfully" message
	Print the receiving confirmation
Use Case termination	This Use Case ends when:
	The system displays the message that it could not find the Shipping company and the user cancels
	Accounts Payable has been notified and the inventory has been updated
	The user cancels the transaction

Post-conditions	Upon successful completion of the transaction:
	    Update inventory
	    Notify Accounts Payable
	    Print a confirmation to go with the receiving documents

	Upon receiving the Cancel option: Return to its initial state prior to this Use Case

One way to proceed with the Activity diagram is to follow the Use Case narrative. First, identify the pre-conditions. The pre-conditions must be tested before you allow the Use Case to execute. Table 15-1 identifies a pre-condition that the "Shipment is from a valid Shipping company." Figure 15-1 shows the start symbol followed by the activities to enter the Shipper_ID and find the Shipper in your system. The result of the find is either successful or not. The two possible results give you the guard conditions to direct the flow to either of the next two activities, prompt to re-enter or cancel, and display Shipper details.

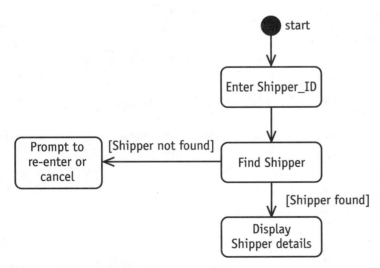

Figure 15-1 *Modeling the pre-conditions*

**20 Min.
To Go**

Figure 15-1 implies that you would let them try again or cancel. To do that, you need to loop back to the beginning and offer them a choice. Figure 15-2 illustrates the needed changes. To loop back to a previous place in the logic, use a merge point diamond. To provide a choice, use the decision diamond. Then each path out of the decision diamond must be labeled with a guard condition. In this case, you offer them two choices: proceed to Enter Shipper_ID or cancel.

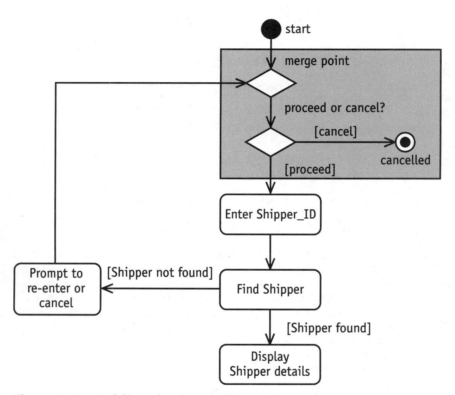

Figure 15-2 *Modeling a looping condition and merge point*

Next identify the post-conditions and terminations. (I do these together because there is often a great deal of overlap.) The narrative told you that the Use Case terminates when:

- The system displays the message that it could not find the Shipping company and the user cancels
- Accounts Payable has been notified and the inventory has been updated
- The user cancels the transaction

The narrative also told you that the system must:

- Update inventory
- Notify Accounts Payable
- Print a confirmation to go with the receiving documents
- Return to its initial state (prior to this Use Case) upon receiving the Cancel option

Figure 15-3 shows the activities to notify accounts payable, update inventory, and print the confirmation. I added an activity to display a message for each action so that the user knows that his requirement was met. Right now it looks like you just have fragments, but you'll tie all these pieces together further into the session.

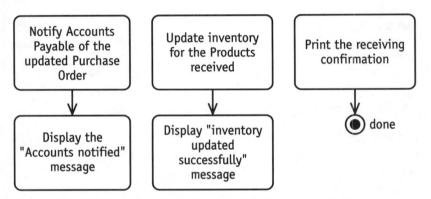

Figure 15-3   *Modeling the post-conditions and terminations*

Next, you need to model the processing for each piece in the shipment. Figure 15-4 sets up the loop "for each product" with a decision diamond that asks whether there are "more pieces to receive."

For each product in the Shipment:

1. Find the Purchase Order using the PO_nbr
2. If not found, display "invalid P.O." error message and set the item aside
3. Else (P.O. found)

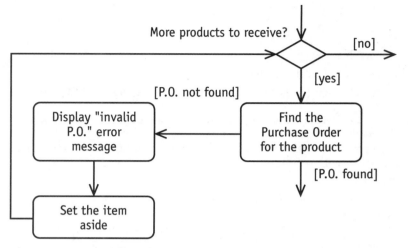

Figure 15-4 *Modeling the Use Case dialog, "For each piece find the Purchase Order"*

Figure 15-5 continues the flow for items where the P.O. was found.

10 Min. To Go

4. Match the product to an item on the Purchase Order
5. If not matched, display "invalid item" error message and set the item aside
6. Else check off the item and qty on the Purchase Order

After these steps are completed, they loop back to the *"more products to receive"* decision.

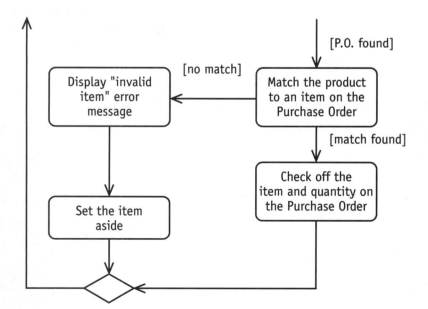

Figure 15-5 *Modeling the Use Case dialog, "matching the items to the P.O."*

Now you have all the pieces you need to do a bit of organizing. One opportunity to watch for is concurrency. Identify tasks that may be done at the same time because they don't depend on one another. For example, Figure 15-6 shows that notifying accounts payable and updating inventory don't overlap or depend on one another so they can be modeled as concurrent activities. Use the fork bar to show that you want to follow both logical paths at the same time. Use the synchronization bar to show that you're done with the concurrent tasks and want to continue on a single logical path. In this example, after all the updates and notifications are done, you can print the confirmation.

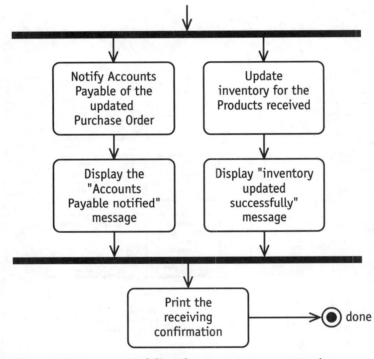

Figure 15-6   *Modeling the concurrency opportunity*

Figure 15-7 puts all the segments together. Notice in the bottom left below the activity labeled "Display "invalid item" error message" I added another merge point to bring together the segments from Figures 15-4 and 15-5.

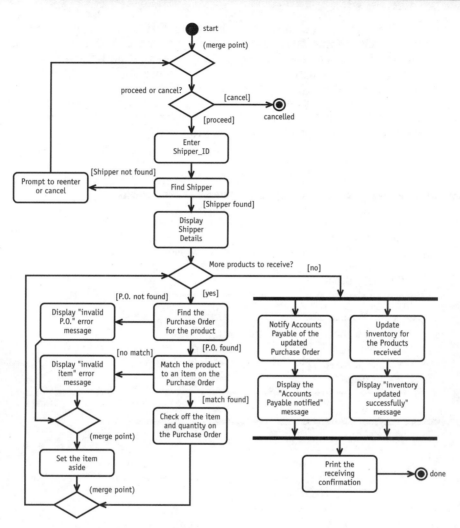

Figure 15-7   *The complete Activity diagram*

As you can see from the example, all the old flowchart elements are still there. UML has added concurrency to keep pace with technology.

Done!

REVIEW

Often, text can be a bit too ambiguous for defining a complex process. The Activity diagram offers a visual alternative that also supports common programming constructs. As such, it bridges the gap nicely between user requirements and programming requirements.

- To translate the user description into an Activity diagram, isolate each task as an activity. Indicate the sequence of the tasks by drawing the transition arrow from one activity to the next activity in the sequence.

- Multiple processes may take place at the same time. Model them using the fork bar and the synchronization bar. The fork initiates multiple processes and the synchronization bar shows the completion of the multiple processes and the continuation of activity as a single process.

- To model decisions in the process, you have two options. A decision that results from the completion of an activity is drawn using guard conditions. Each transition out of the activity is labeled with a unique (mutually exclusive) conditional expression enclosed in square brackets [ ]. For a decision that is not the result of one specific activity, use the diamond icon. Each transition out of the diamond decision point is also labeled with a unique conditional expression enclosed in square brackets [ ].

- When the logical flow of the process needs to return to a previous point in the flow, use the diamond icon as a merge point diamond. There may be two or more arrows entering the merge point, but only one exiting the merge point.

- End points are drawn using a bull's-eye symbol. There may be as many end points as the logic requires. In practice, there should be one transition to an end point for each Use Case termination option.

Quiz Yourself

1. What part of the Use Case narrative provides the start for your Activity diagram? (See "Building an Activity Diagram for the Case Study.")

2. What notation do you use to return to a previous place in the Activity diagram? (See "Building an Activity Diagram for the Case Study.")

3. The Activity diagram offers two ways to handle decisions. When do you use the diamond symbol for a decision? (See "Building an Activity Diagram for the Case Study.")

4. What notation do you use to show that a transition triggers multiple processes? (See "Building an Activity Diagram for the Case Study.")

5. What notation do you use to show that multiple, concurrent paths end and become one logical path? (See "Building an Activity Diagram for the Case Study.")

Start and end

The UML also provides icons to begin and end an Activity diagram (see Figure 14-6). A solid dot indicates the beginning of the flow of activity. A bull's-eye indicates the end point. There may be more than one end point in an Activity diagram. Even the simplest Activity diagram typically has some decision logic that would result in alternative paths, each with its own unique outcome. If you really want to, you can draw all your arrows to the same end point, but there is no need to do so. Every end point means the same thing: Stop here.

Figure 14-6   *Begin and end notation for the Activity diagram*

Concurrency

The UML notation for the Activity diagram also supports concurrency. This allows you to model the features of languages that have been introduced since the flowchart was invented, like Java, C++, and even Smalltalk, on hardware capable of true concurrency. To show that a single process starts multiple concurrent threads or processes, the UML uses a simple bar called a *fork*. In the examples in Figure 14-7, you see one transition pointing at the bar and multiple transitions pointing away from the bar. Each outgoing transition is a new thread or process.

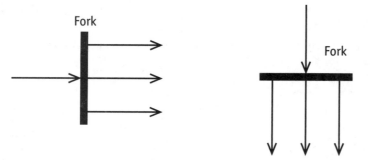

Figure 14-7   *Split of control using a fork: initiating multiple threads or processes*

Synchronization or merging of the concurrent threads or processes is shown in much the same way. Figure 14-8 shows multiple transitions pointing at the bar, this time called a *synchronization bar,* and one pointing out of the bar. This indicates that the concurrent processing has ended and the process continues as a single thread or process.

Modeling the Dynamic View: The Sequence Diagram

**30 Min.
To Go**

The static view (Class and Object diagrams) represents how the objects are defined and arranged into a structure. It does not tell you how the objects behave when you put them to work. In contrast, the dynamic view represents the interactions of the objects in a system. The dynamic view contains diagrams specifically designed to model how the objects work together. It can represent how the system will respond to actions from the users, how it maintains internal integrity, how data is moved from storage to a user view, and how objects are created and manipulated.

Understanding the Dynamic View

Because system behaviors can be complex, the dynamic view tends to look at small, discrete pieces of the system like individual scenarios or operations. You may not see the dynamic view used as extensively as the Class diagram, simply because not all behaviors are complicated enough to warrant the extra work involved. Even so, the Class diagram and the diagrams of the dynamic view are the most often used diagrams in projects because they most directly reveal the specific features required in the final code.

Knowing the purpose of Sequence and Collaboration diagrams

There are actually three UML diagrams in the dynamic view: the Sequence diagram, the Collaboration diagram, and the Statechart diagram. Sessions 16 through 19 cover the Sequence and Collaboration diagrams, their notation and usage, and their similarities and differences. Sessions 20 through 23 deal with the Statechart diagram.

The Sequence and Collaboration diagrams both illustrate the *interactions between objects*. Interactions show us how objects talk to each other. Each time that one object talks to another it talks to an interface (that is, it invokes an operation). So if you can model the interactions, you can find the interfaces/operations that the object requires.

 You may think it's odd that the UML has two diagrams that do the same thing. In a way, you're right. The reason is that they came from two different methodologies and they each offer a slightly different perspective that can be quite valuable. (You can find more on this in Session 18.)

In the Use Case view, you modeled the features of the system and developed scenarios describing how the system should behave when those features are used. The Sequence diagram provides a path from the textual descriptions of behaviors in the scenarios to operations/interfaces in the Class diagram.

Mapping interactions to objects

Everything in an object-oriented system is accomplished by objects. Objects take on the responsibility for things like managing data, moving data around in the system, responding to inquiries, and protecting the system. Objects work together by communicating or interacting with one another. Figure 16-1 shows a Sequence diagram with three participating objects: Bill the Customer, Bill's Order, and the Inventory. Without even knowing the notation formally, you can probably get a pretty good idea of what is going on.

> Steps 1 and 2: Bill creates an order.
>
> Step 3: Bill tries to add items to the order.
>
> Step 4 and 5: Each item is checked for availability in inventory.
>
> Step 6 and 7: If the product is available, it is added to the order.
>
> Step 8: He finds out that everything worked.

Building the Sequence diagram is easier if you have completed at least a first draft of the Use Case model and the Class diagram. From these two resources, you get sets of interactions (scenarios) and a pool of candidate objects to take responsibility for the interactions.

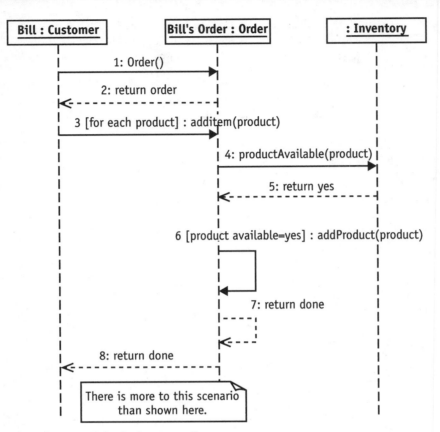

Figure 16-1   *A basic Sequence diagram*

Defining the basic notation of the Sequence diagram

**20 Min.
To Go**

All Sequence diagrams are modeled at the object level rather than the class level to allow for scenarios that use more than one instance of the same class and to work at the level of facts, test data, and examples. The Sequence diagram uses three fundamental notation elements: objects, messages/stimuli, and object lifeline.

In the Sequence diagram, the *objects* use the same notation as in the Object diagram. In Figure 16-1, you see the three participating objects lined up across the top of the diagram. The object lifeline (identified by reference #1 in Figure 16-2) is a vertical dashed line below each object. The object lifeline always runs from the beginning at the top to the end at the bottom. The amount of time represented depends on the scenario or other behavior you're modeling.

A message or stimulus is usually a call, a signal, or a response. A message is represented by an arrow. The type of arrow visually describes the type of message. The solid line and solid arrowhead style represent a message that requires a response. The dashed arrows are the responses. (I cover more arrow types later in this session.) The messages are placed horizontally onto the timelines in relative vertical position to one another to represent the order in which they happen. This arrangement allows you to read the diagram from beginning to end by reading the messages from top to bottom.

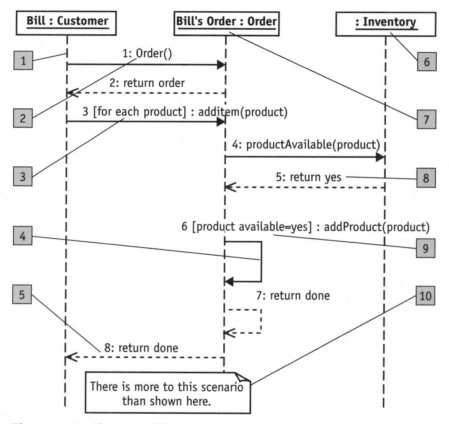

Figure 16-2 *Elements of the Sequence diagram notation*

The reference numbers on Figure 16-2 denote these items:

1. Object lifeline
2. Message/Stimulus
3. Iteration
4. Self-reference

5. Return

6. Anonymous object

7. Object name

8. Sequence number

9. Condition

10. Basic comment

The sequence numbers are optional but are very helpful when you need to discuss the diagram and make changes. Each message arrow describes an interface/operation on the object it is pointing to. Consequently, the message contains the operation signature, that is, the name, arguments, and optionally the return, such as addItem(product):boolean.

The dashed return arrows pointed to by references #2 and #5 each contain only the answer to a message. Some folks leave these off. But the purpose of modeling is to reveal information, not make assumptions. Showing the returns can help ensure that what you're getting back is consistent with what you asked for in the message.

Figure 16-2, reference #3, shows how you can indicate that an operation should be performed repeatedly. Use the square condition brackets to enclose either the number of times or the condition that controls the repetitions, for example [for each product].

The same condition brackets may be used to control whether a message is even sent. Reference #9 points to step 6, which uses the test [product available = yes] to make certain that the previous step succeeded before performing the operation in step 6.

Reference #10 shows how you may use a UML comment to add information that is not explicitly part of the notation.

Defining the extended notation for the Sequence diagram

Sequence diagrams can be enhanced to illustrate object *activation* and object *termination* and to customize messages.

10 Min. To Go

Figure 16-3 includes some changes to the original Sequence diagram in order to illustrate these new features. To show that an object is active, the notation is to widen the vertical object lifeline to a narrow rectangle, as shown in Figure 16-3. The narrow rectangle is called an "activation bar" or "focus of control." Reference #1 shows when the object becomes active at the top of the rectangle. Note that the object becomes active when it begins to do work. Reference #2 shows when the object is deactivated or finishes its work and waits for the next request. Using this notation, we can see that the Inventory object is only active while it is responding to the "productAvailable" inquiry, and the Order is activated more than once: once to create the Order object and once each time it is asked by Bill to perform "addItem."

To show that an object is terminated, place an X at the point in the object lifeline when the termination occurs. This is usually in response to a message such as delete or cancel. See message 10: cancel() followed by the X at reference #5. The absence of the X on an object lifeline means that the object lives on after this sequence of events is ended.

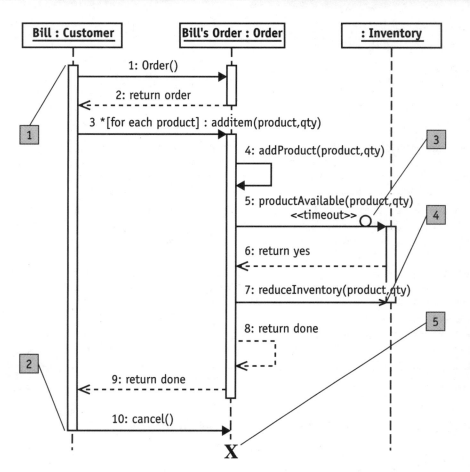

Figure 16-3   *Extended elements of the Sequence diagram notation*

Observe these notations in Figure 16-3:

1. Activation: The start of the vertical rectangle, the activation bar
2. Deactivation: The end of the vertical rectangle, the activation bar
3. Timeout event: Typically signified by a full arrowhead with a small clock face or circle on the line
4. Asynchronous event: Typically signified by a stick arrowhead
5. Object termination symbolized by an X

Figure 16-3 also introduces some new types of messages. Reference #3 points to a message with a circle on the line and the stereotype <<timeout>>. This is called a *timed event*. Often there is also a condition or a constraint on the message that expresses the timing parameters for the event, for example, {if we don't get a response from inventory within 2 seconds we will bypass the item and check later}. The timeout is an example of a UML extension. It is not a part of the core UML notation, but represents a valid usage.

Reference #4 points to an *asynchronous event*. Typically, you see events that require some type of response like addItem (did it work or not?) or productAvailable (is there any product in stock?). But there are times when the event is simply a signal to another object to do something. For example, just a moment ago my wife told me that dinner was ready. Knowing my work habits, she knows better than to expect a response. In Figure 16-3, message 7, you send a message to inventory to reduce the count on the product by the quantity supplied. It is up to inventory to queue the request and take care of it. The place order process is not going to wait. (This makes a good illustration but it is probably not very good design.)

Note the difference in the arrows. An asynchronous message uses a stick arrowhead instead of the solid arrowhead used for simple or synchronous messages.

Now, take a look at messages 4 and 8. Message 4 starts the operation "addProduct" but the return doesn't come until message 8. All the messages between 4 and 8 are the messages sent by the Order object while performing the operation "addProduct." This is another good reason to show the returns. Without the returns explicitly shown in Figure 16-3, it would be possible to interpret the diagram to say that the system first adds the product before it even checks to see if the product is available.

Finally, to model object creation, you have a few options. In Figure 16-3, message 1, you see the message Order() pointing to the object lifeline. This is a common coding convention for a constructor (an operation with the same name as the Class), an operation that creates an object. But the Sequence diagram uses an object lifeline that should allow us to represent object creation visually. Figure 16-4 shows two variations using the object lifeline.

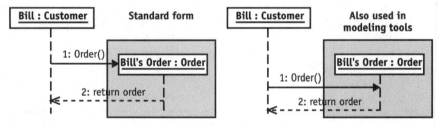

Figure 16-4   *Two ways of modeling object creation*

The example on the left is the form explicitly defined by the UML. The creation message (constructor) points directly at the Object. This means that the object icon has to be placed somewhere down the page where the creation actually happens instead of at the top. Using this technique implies that objects at the top of the page already existed when the scenario started.

The example on the right is a minor variation where the constructor points to the object lifeline just below the object. But the object is still placed on the diagram at the point in time when it is created, rather than at the top.

The goal is to represent the fact that the object did not exist prior to the creation message. The object lifeline literally comes into existence when the creation message is sent, so there is no object lifeline before (above) the creation message.

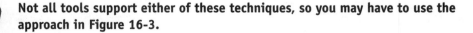

Not all tools support either of these techniques, so you may have to use the approach in Figure 16-3.

Done!

REVIEW

The dynamic view includes diagrams designed to illustrate how objects work together. The Sequence and Collaboration diagrams specifically show how objects talk to one another to accomplish a goal of the system, one scenario in a Use Case, or one operation.

- The Sequence diagram is built around three fundamental elements: the objects, messages, and the object lifeline. The objects represent the participants. The messages represent the communication that they send to one another. The object lifelines allow us to arrange the messages in the proper relative sequence.

- Messages may be synchronous (requiring a response) or asynchronous (not requiring a response). A simple or synchronous message uses a solid line with a solid arrowhead. The asynchronous message uses a solid line with a stick arrowhead. Both of these message types represent the invocation of an operation on the object they are pointing to. So the name of the message becomes an operation signature with the name, arguments, and return type.

- The return from or answer to a message uses a dashed line and a line-style arrowhead. The return is simply information, so it is written on the return arrow.

- A message may be conditional on some prior result. This can be shown using the guard condition notation placed in front of the operation name.

- An object may be active or inactive at various times in the Sequence diagram. To show that an object is busy, use a narrow vertical rectangle, called an activation bar, on the object lifeline from the time the object becomes active to the time that it stops. An object usually becomes active because it has been asked to do something. It becomes inactive when it is finished with the current task.

- When an object is deleted or destroyed, the timeline ends and an X marks the termination.

QUIZ YOURSELF

1. What does the dynamic view represent? (See "Knowing the purpose of Sequence and Collaboration diagrams.")

2. Where do you place the participating objects in a Sequence diagram? (See "Defining the basic notation of the Sequence diagram.")

3. How does the Sequence diagram show that one object tells another object to do something? (See "Defining the basic notation of the Sequence diagram.")

4. How does the Sequence diagram show that an object is busy? (See "Defining the extended notation for the Sequence diagram.")

5. How does the Sequence diagram show that an object no longer exists? (See "Defining the extended notation for the Sequence diagram.")

PART

III

Saturday Afternoon Part Review

1. Describe two key characteristics of aggregation.
2. Describe the distinguishing characteristic of composition.
3. How can multiplicity give you a clue as to whether the association should be aggregation or composition?
4. What is the difference between specialization and generalization?
5. What is the effect on the application when you choose between 0..1 and 1..1 multiplicity?
6. What is the benefit of using qualified associations?
7. If a design pattern is not code, how does it help you solve a problem?
8. How would the pattern notation help in a development project?
9. How does the role notation aid in the description of the pattern in the Class diagram?
10. If the Class diagram models all the rules for creating and using objects, why do you need to use an Object diagram?
11. Why does the object name notation have both the object name and the class name?
12. How do the attribute descriptions differ between the Class and Object diagrams, and why?
13. How is a link different from an association?
14. Why aren't the operations shown in an Object diagram?
15. The Activity diagram is used primarily for modeling logic. But when in the development process would you encounter the need to model logic?
16. Two of the Activity diagram symbols are used for dual purposes. Can you describe them?
17. How do you indicate that a transition may occur only if a condition has been satisfied?

18. Is a diamond the only way to indicate a decision?

19. True or false: An Activity diagram may have only one start and one end.

20. How many end points should there be in an Activity diagram?

21. How do you decide whether to use a diamond or an activity as a decision point?

22. How do you model looping logic in an Activity diagram?

23. How do you model processes that do not need to be done sequentially?

24. How do you indicate the condition under which the logic should follow a specific transition?

25. What are the three fundamental elements of the Sequence diagram?

26. How does the Sequence diagram describe an event where one object tells the other to do something?

27. How does the Sequence diagram show that an object invokes one of its own operations?

28. How do you know where to start the object activation bar symbol?

29. What is the difference between the solid line with a solid arrowhead and the dashed line with a line style arrowhead?

PART

IV

Saturday Evening

Applying the Sequence Diagram to the Case Study

Session Checklist

✔ Explaining the steps to build a Sequence diagram

✔ Reinforcing the Sequence diagram notation

**30 Min.
To Go**

I n Session 16, you learned the notation for the Sequence diagram. In this session, you use the notation to build a complete set of Sequence diagrams for a Use Case.

Building a Sequence Diagram from a Scenario

To build the Sequence diagram, you'll use the Use Case from Session 8 called Fill Order. The flowchart in Figure 17-1 identifies all the scenarios.

You'll draw a total of four Sequence diagrams: one diagram for each scenario. When a scenario includes steps already defined in a previous scenario/Sequence diagram, simply refer to the other diagram in a comment and add the messages that are unique for the new scenario/Sequence diagram. This approach saves a lot of time in the creation and maintenance of the diagrams.

Begin by identifying all the participating objects. Each object is placed at the top of the diagram, as in Figure 17-2. The order doesn't really matter. However, when the diagram is finished, it sometimes helps to move them around to improve the readability of the messages on the diagram. This Use Case includes the Order Fulfillment Clerk, the System itself, the Orders database, two Orders (the primary and the backorder), and the Inventory.

Figure 17-2   *Sequence diagram with objects and timelines*

The first Sequence diagram models Scenario 1. The first, or primary, scenario should be the successful path. The success path is almost always the most comprehensive. The other scenarios are then just deviations from the main scenario.

Each step of the flowchart becomes a message and/or a return on the Sequence diagram (depending on how the step is described). The first step is "Get Order #." On the Sequence diagram (Figure 17-3) this appears as a procedure call (step 1) and a response (step 2). Note the format of the procedure call (message):

- Sequence number (optional)
- A colon
- Condition (optional)
- Operation signature, which is made up of:
  - Visibility, (+ means public, - private, # protected)
  - Operation name (getOrderNbr)
  - Arguments () – no arguments for this call
  - A colon
  - Return data type (int – meaning integer value).

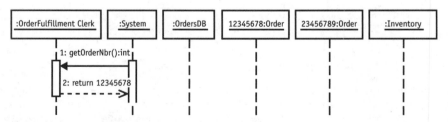

Figure 17-3   *Add steps 1 and 2; get the order number*

The next step is "getOrder" from the database. In the flowchart, I stated that this was a call to the Find Order Use Case. In order to keep the focus on the Sequence diagram construction, I model it here as a procedure call with a response. In Figure 17-4, steps 3 and 4 show the call and response.

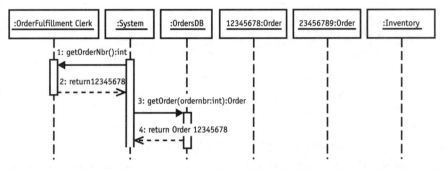

Figure 17-4   *Add steps 3 and 4; get the Order using the order number*

The return is simply the data (the Order) being sent back as a result of performing the operation. Remember that the Sequence diagram is modeling a test case, so the return should be a value. Sometimes you'll model a rule, in which case you would show the return data type rather than a specific value.

The next step is "display Order." Because this message does not require a response, Figure 17-5 shows the use of an asynchronous communication using a line-style arrow. There is no corresponding return arrow.

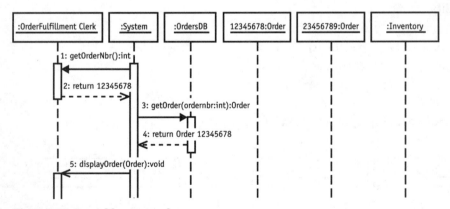

Figure 17-5   *Add an asynchronous message.*

The rest of the steps are modeled in Figure 17-6. After the Order is displayed in step 5, the system asks the user for the first item to look up (step 6, getItem():int). The system is expecting to get an integer representing the number of the item on the Order to look up. It gets the reply "item #1" in step 7. The system uses the item number in step 8 to ask the Order for the corresponding product serial number. The Order returns the product serial number in step 9.

The system uses this item number to ask Inventory if the product is available in step 10. Inventory replies that it is available (true) in step 11. Since the product is available, the system tells the Order to mark the item "filled", in step 12, and to return the actual Product in step 13. The system uses the Product to tell Inventory to remove this Product from the Inventory records because it has been allocated to the Order. The Inventory responds saying that the operation succeeded (return true in step 15).

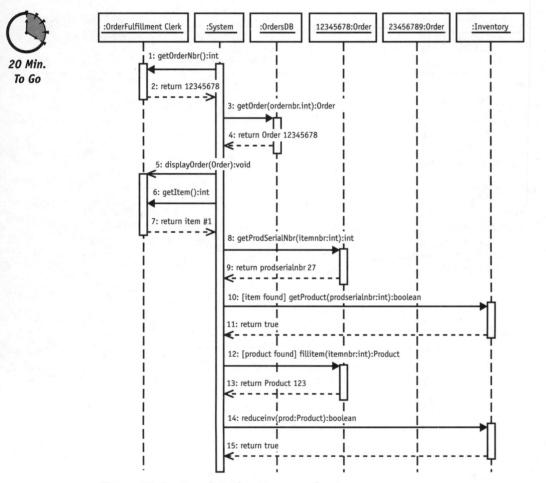

20 Min. To Go

Figure 17-6   *Complete the sequence of messages.*

In Figure 17-6, you can also see the object activations, the narrow vertical rectangles on the timelines. The object activations indicate when each object is busy. Typically the activation begins when a message hits the timeline and ends when the response is sent back. In the case of the system object, the activation runs the entire length showing that the system is overseeing the entire set of interactions. This is sometimes referred to as the focus of control.

For Scenario 2, shown in Figure 17-7, insert a comment referring to steps 1 through 4 of Scenario 1, and then add the new message for Scenario 2. The comment simply helps you avoid having to repeat all the steps you've already documented in the previous Sequence diagram. The comment is just a timesaving technique, not a part of the UML or any methodology.

The new message in this case is conditional. The condition "order not found" is placed in square brackets [] before the message description. This indicates that the message will only take place if the order is not found in a previous step.

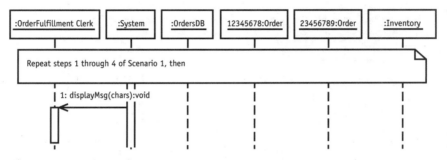

Figure 17-7   *Scenario 2*

For Scenario 3, shown in Figure 17-8, again insert a comment for the repeated steps, 1 through 9 of Scenario 1. The only difference for this scenario is that it loops back to a previous step. There is no additional processing. If I really fleshed this out I might add the exception handling for items not found. For this course I simply indicate that the process loops back to the test to see if the user is "Done" or there are "no unfilled items?"

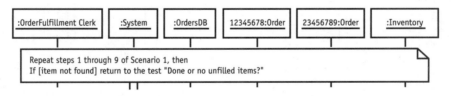

Figure 17-8   *Scenario 3*

**10 Min.
To Go**

For Scenario 4, in Figure 17-9, continue from step 13 of Scenario 1. This time, the process makes it all the way to the end but there are still unfilled items on the Order.

The system tells the Order object to create a backorder in step 1. The Order creates another Order, passing itself as the reference so the backorder can track where it came from (step 2). Note that the minus sign on the operation means that the operation is private (that is, only objects of the same class may invoke it). Step 3 shows that the backorder was successfully created. Step 4 shows the Order telling the System that it finished the task requested in step 1.

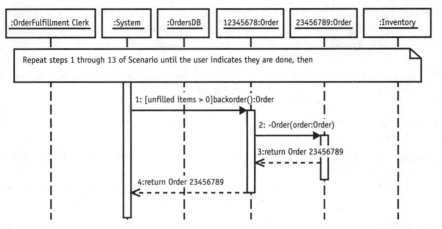

Figure 17-9   *Scenario 4*

The goal of the Sequence diagram is twofold: to discover the interfaces required for each object and to validate that each interface is actually used. I don't know about you, but I've never worked on a project with extra time and money to spend designing, writing, and maintaining unused code. Another major benefit is a much better understanding of the design of the objects and the performance impact on the application as you visualize the volume and complexity of the communication.

Done!

REVIEW

The Sequence diagram models interactions between objects. Because these interactions can be very complex, you typically model a small set of interactions like a single scenario.

To construct the diagram, follow these steps:

1. Identify the participating objects.
2. Line them up across the top of the diagram.
3. Draw a vertical dashed line below each object, representing a timeline.
4. Each message in the sequence becomes at least one horizontal arrow from the sending object's timeline to the receiving object's timeline. The type of arrow depends on the type of message.
5. For a synchronous message or procedure call that requires a reply, draw a solid line with a solid arrowhead. For the reply, place a second horizontal arrow below the first. Use a dashed line-style arrow for replies.
6. Continue to represent each message as a horizontal arrow, placing each new message below the previous one, until all the messages have been translated onto the Sequence diagram.

For subsequent scenarios that incorporate steps already documented on another Sequence diagram, a common convention is to refer to these other messages in a comment, and then add the new scenario's messages.

QUIZ YOURSELF

1. Where do you place the objects on a Sequence diagram? (See "Building a Sequence Diagram from a Scenario.")

2. How do you represent a procedure call (synchronous message)? (See "Building a Sequence Diagram from a Scenario.")

3. What does a line-style arrow mean (versus a solid arrowhead or dashed arrow)? (See "Building a Sequence Diagram from a Scenario.")

4. How do you describe a message? (See "Building a Sequence Diagram from a Scenario.")

5. How do you show that a message may only happen if a condition is satisfied? (See "Building a Sequence Diagram from a Scenario.")

Modeling the Dynamic View:
The Collaboration Diagram

30 Min.
To Go

The Collaboration diagram offers an alternative to the Sequence diagram. Instead of modeling messages over time like the Sequence diagram, the Collaboration diagram models the messages on top of an Object diagram. The Collaboration diagram uses this approach in order to emphasize the effect of the object structures on the interactions.

The Collaboration Diagram

Figure 18-1 shows the same set of interactions modeled in Figure 16-1 using a Sequence diagram. The scenario shows the customer Bill creating an order and adding items to it, checking availability for each item as it is added. Just follow the numbered messages to step through the scenario.

You can accomplish the same thing with both diagrams (that is, you can model the logical steps in a process like a Use Case scenario). In the following sections, I identify the similarities and differences between these two diagrams so that you can know how to choose the diagram that will help you the most with a particular problem in your project.

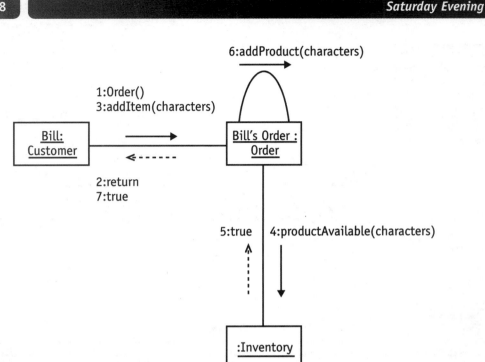

Figure 18-1 *Collaboration diagram of Customer placing an Order*

Diagram similarities

Sequence and Collaboration diagrams model the same two elements: messages and objects. In fact, the two diagrams are so similar that some modeling tools, like System Architect and Rational Rose, provide a toggle feature to switch back and forth between the two views.

Like the Sequence diagram, the Collaboration diagram provides a tool for visually assigning responsibilities to objects for sending and receiving messages. By identifying an object as the receiver of a message, you are in effect assigning an interface to that object. It is kind of like receiving phone calls. You have to own the number the person is calling in order to receive the call. The number is your interface. The message description becomes an operation signature on the receiving object. The sending object invokes the operation.

Diagram differences

The Collaboration diagram places a priority on mapping the object interactions to the object links (that is, drawing the participating objects in an Object diagram format and laying the messages parallel to the object links). This perspective helps validate the Class diagram by providing evidence of the need for each association as the means of passing messages. In contrast, the Sequence diagram does not illustrate the links at all.

This highlights an advantage of the Collaboration diagram. Logically, you cannot place a message where there is no link because there is no physical avenue to send the message across. On a Sequence diagram there is nothing stopping you from drawing an arrow between two objects when there is no corresponding link. But doing so would model a logical interaction that cannot physically take place.

You can take the opposite view that drawing a message where there is no link reveals the *requirement* for a new link. Just make certain that you actually update your Class diagram or, as I said before, you won't be able to implement the message illustrated on the diagram.

An advantage of the Sequence diagram is its ability to show the creation and destruction of objects. Newly created objects can be placed on the timeline at the point where they are created. The large X at the end of a timeline shows that the object is no longer available for use.

Sequence diagrams also have the advantage of showing object activation. Because the Collaboration diagram does not illustrate time, it is impossible to indicate explicitly when an object is active or inactive without interpreting the types of messages being passed.

Collaboration Diagram Notation

**20 Min.
To Go**

The Collaboration diagram uses an Object diagram as its foundation. First, determine which objects will participate in the scenario. Draw the objects with only the name compartment, not the attributes. Then draw the links between them. Because any pair of classes can have more than one association, you need to use the Class diagram as your guide to identify the valid types of links that apply to the current sequence of messages.

Figure 18-2 shows the objects and their links. You may leave the link names off of the links when there is only one type of association between the related classes. Add the names if there is more than one kind of link possible between the two objects and there is a need to clarify which relationship supports the interaction.

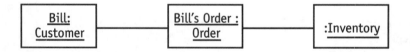

Figure 18-2 *Basic Collaboration diagram notation*

For each step of the scenario, draw the message arrow from the sending object to the receiving object. Place the message arrow parallel to the link between the sending and receiving objects. Having many messages placed on the same link is valid and, in fact, common as long as they really share the same message (arrow) type. Number the messages in the order in which they occur.

The format for specifying a message is the same as on the Sequence diagram:

Sequence-number Iteration : [condition] operation or return

Figure 18-3 models the entire scenario for creating an order. I have added a few twists to the original in Figure 18-1 so that I can demonstrate all the notations.

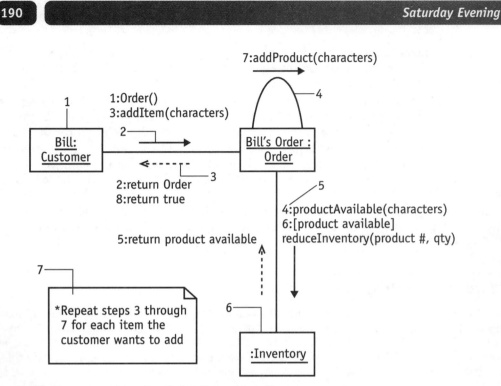

Figure 18-3   *More detailed Collaboration diagram notation*

The following descriptions refer to the numbered items in Figure 18-3 so that you can see the notations used in context:

1. **Object:** This is a fully qualified object name, Bill, of the class Customer. The notation is exactly the same as on the Sequence diagram.

2. **Synchronous event or procedure call:** A synchronous event is a message that requires a reply, so you would expect to see a corresponding return message along the same link sometime later in the sequence. Procedure calls are simply another familiar way to describe this "ask and reply" form of interaction.

3. **Return:** Here is the return message for the message 1. Message 1 told the Order class to create a new Order object, Bill's Order. When the task of creating the object is completed, it passes back a reference to the requestor, Bill.

4. **Self-reference:** A self-reference is simply an object talking to itself saying something like, "It's time for me to get more coffee." In Figure 18-3, the Order is telling itself to use the item information from step 3 to add another product to its list of items.

5. **Sequence number:** Because the Collaboration diagram has no way of showing the passage of time, it uses sequence numbers, like (4:), to reveal the order of execution for the messages. There are no standards for the numbering scheme, so common sense and readability are your guides. The sequence numbers were optional on the Sequence diagram. They are required on the Collaboration diagram.

6. **Anonymous object:** Reference 6 shows another example of valid object notation. You do not have to name the instance if all you need to convey is that any object of this type (Inventory) would behave in this manner.

7. **Comment:** Reference 7 shows *one way* that you can reveal your intention to repeat a set of messages. As with Sequence diagrams, comments can be very helpful for explaining your intentions regarding iteration across a *set of messages* because the iteration notation provided by the UML works only for a single event.

Now I'll change a few items on the diagram so that you can see some new notations. The following descriptions refer to the numbered items in Figure 18-4.

10 Min. To Go

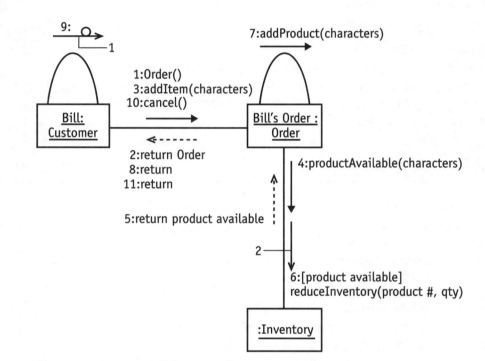

Figure 18-4   More Collaboration diagram notation

Note the following items on the diagram:

1. **Timeout event:** I haven't labeled this message, mostly because a timeout would be a bit unusual for this type of scenario. This way you get to see the notation anyway. Actually, this is a common extension to the UML (that is, it isn't explicitly defined by the UML). The small circle represents a clock and sometimes even shows the clock hands within the circle. A timeout would be used for something like dialing into a network or polling a node on a network. If you don't get a response within a specified amount of time, you abandon the attempt and move on. In this case, if the Order doesn't respond within the specified time limit, the Order is cancelled in step 10.

2. **Asynchronous message:** An asynchronous message does not require a reply. Step 6 has been altered to simply tell the Inventory, "I've taken some of your stock. You might want to update your records. But I'm not going to wait around until you do."

Done!

REVIEW

The Collaboration diagram models pretty much the same information as a Sequence diagram, interactions between objects. It is the perspective that is different. The Collaboration diagram views interactions relative to the structure of the objects and their relationships (links) with one another. The Sequence diagram focuses on timing. Consequently, the advantage of the Collaboration diagram is that it can help you validate the associations between classes or even discover the need for new associations.

The Collaboration diagram is built on top of an Object diagram.

1. Place the participating objects on the diagram.
2. Draw the links between the objects using the Class diagram as your guide.
3. Add each event. Place the message arrow parallel to the link between the two objects. Position the arrow to point from the sender to the receiver.
4. Number the messages in order of execution.
5. Repeat steps 3 and 4 until the entire scenario has been modeled.

QUIZ YOURSELF

1. How are the participating objects represented in a Collaboration diagram? (See "Collaboration Diagram Notation.")
2. How do you know whether a message may be sent from one particular object to another? (See "Diagram differences.")
3. The Sequence diagram uses a timeline to show the order of messages. What do you use on a Collaboration diagram? (See "Collaboration Diagram Notation.")
4. What is a synchronous message? (See "Collaboration Diagram Notation.")
5. What is an asynchronous message? (See "Collaboration Diagram Notation.")

Applying the Collaboration Diagram to the Case Study

Session Checklist

✔ Applying the Collaboration diagram notation to the case study

✔ Explaining the steps in building a Collaboration diagram

✔ Mapping the sequence and Collaboration diagrams to the Class diagram

**30 Min.
To Go**

The Sequence and Collaboration diagrams are both used to model object interactions. In order to emphasize that point, this session takes the same Use Case, Fill Order, used for the Sequence diagram in Session 17 and uses it to build a Collaboration diagram.

Building a Collaboration Diagram from a Scenario

Figure 19-1 provides the flowchart for the Use Case.

You will draw a total of five Collaboration diagrams: one Collaboration diagram for each scenario. When a scenario includes steps already defined in a previous scenario, simply refer to the other diagram and add the events that are unique for the new scenario.

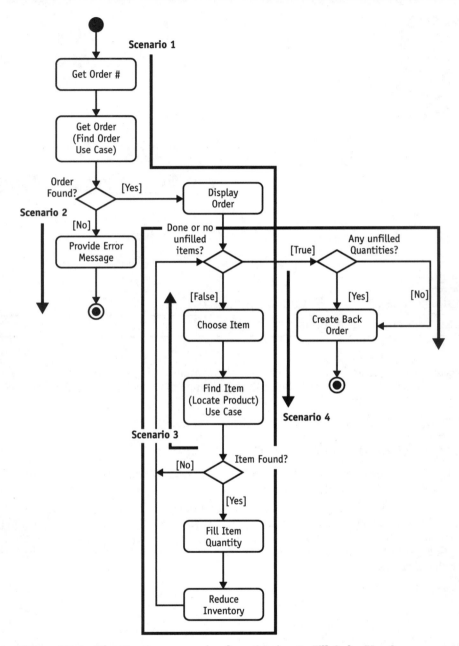

Figure 17-1   *The Use Case scenarios from Session 8: Fill Order Use Case*

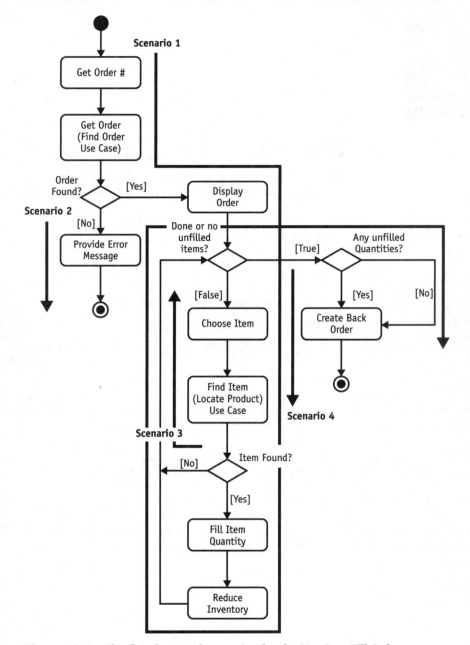

Figure 19-1 *The flowchart and scenarios for the Use Case Fill Order*

The first Collaboration diagram models Scenario 1. The first step in the construction is to identify the objects that participate in the scenario. This scenario has five objects, namely the OrderFulfillmentClerk, the System (the application you will write), the Order, the backorder, and the Orders database. Figure 19-2 shows the object notation. Note that this time you can place the objects anywhere you like. As you add the other information, you will very likely want to rearrange the objects anyway to make the diagram easier to read.

Figure 19-2　*The objects participating in Scenario 1*

Next, add the links between the objects (see Figure 19-3). Be sure to follow the rules established by the Class diagram associations. The links provide the paths over which the interactions take place.

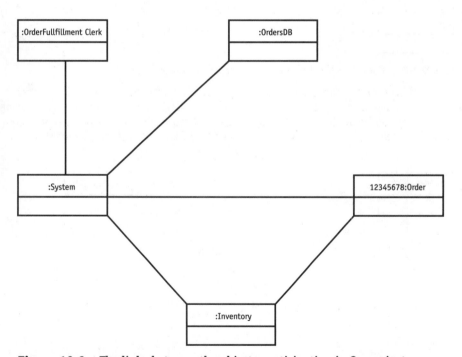

Figure 19-3　*The links between the objects participating in Scenario 1*

Next, each step of the flowchart becomes an event and/or a return on the Collaboration diagram. Start with "Get Order #." The system asks the OrderFulfillmentClerk for the Order #. Imagine this as a screen that is waiting for an entry. The message is from the System object to the OrderFulfillmentClerk object. It is a synchronous type because the System will wait for a reply. Lay the event arrow parallel to the link between the two objects and pointing toward the receiver, in this case the OrderFulfillmentClerk. Label the event arrow with the sequence number and operation. Figure 19-4 shows both the message sent in step 1 and the answer received in step 2. The return arrow uses a dashed line style arrow. Label the return with the sequence number and the data being returned.

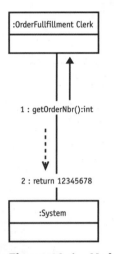

Figure 19-4 *Modeling a synchronous event and the reply*

In the second step of the flowchart, the System tries to find the Order in the Orders database. In Figure 19-5, sequence # 3 from System to OrdersDB is a synchronous message because the System will wait for the answer to the find request. The return in sequence #4 is an Order object, the same Order object that you put on the diagram at the start.

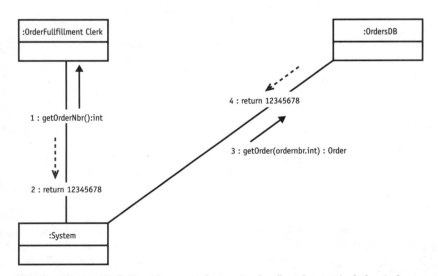

Figure 19-5 *Modeling the second step in the flowchart: Find the Order*

The next step in the flowchart says that the System tells the OrderFulfillmentClerk to display the Order it just found in the database. This sounds a bit odd until you realize that the OrderFulfillmentClerk represents the interface that the Order Fulfillment Clerk will use for this Use Case. So in reality, the System is telling the screen to display the data. Figure 19-6 adds the asynchronous message and line style arrow alongside sequence #1, going in the same direction between the same two objects.

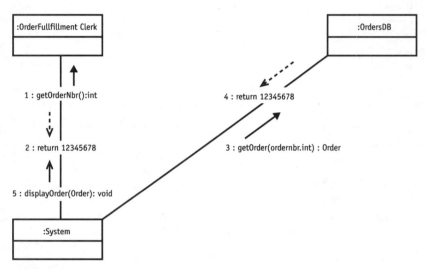

Figure 19-6 *Modeling the next step in the flowchart: Display the Order*

Figure 19-7 shows the completed Collaboration diagram for the first scenario.

 In every synchronous message, I chose to show the return as well. Many people say that you should only show the return if it isn't obvious. Personally, I believe that strategy leaves a lot of room for mistaken assumptions. I also firmly believe that the purpose for modeling is to get the information out where everyone can see it. Using shortcuts hides information.

*20 Min.
To Go*

For the second scenario, insert a comment referring to steps 1 through 4 of Scenario 1, and then add the new event for Scenario 2. This time the message from the System to the OrderFulfillmentClerk is an asynchronous event. The System merely sends the message and goes about its job without waiting for any reply. Figure 19-8 shows the use of the asynchronous solid line style arrow for the displayMsg(char) message.

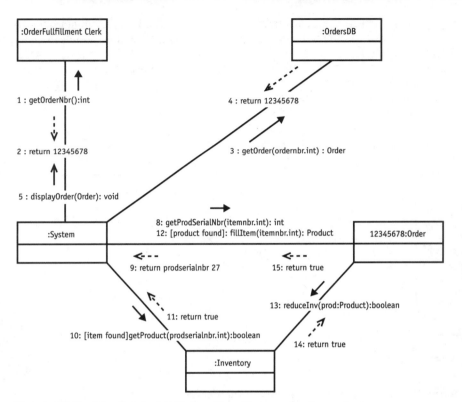

Figure 19-7   *The finished Collaboration diagram for Scenario 1*

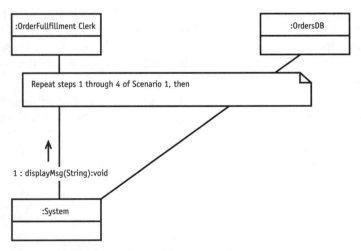

Figure 19-8   *Scenario 2 with an asynchronous event*

The use of comments in this way is not a UML standard. It is merely a useful convention to avoid creating redundant diagrams and increasing the time and cost of maintenance. The goal of the Sequence and Collaboration diagrams is to discover the interfaces required by each object. Once the need for the interface is discovered and justified on one diagram, there is little to gain by repeating it on another diagram.

For Scenario 3, in Figure 19-9, again insert a comment for the repeated steps, 1 through 5 of Scenario 1. Also note that this scenario introduces a new participant, the Inventory object. Add the events for selecting an item and looking up the product availability. These two steps are repeated for every item, so you need a comment to indicate the iteration. Finally, add a comment referring to steps 6 through 10 of Scenario 5.

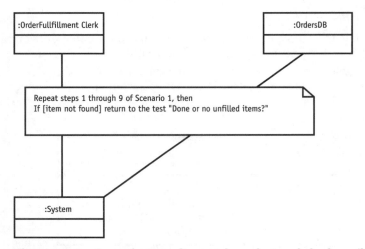

Figure 19-9 *Scenario 3: Look up each product and check availability*

For Scenario 4, in Figure 19-10, continue from step 3 of Scenario 3 and add the new events. Again, complete the scenario with a reference to the steps from Scenario 5.

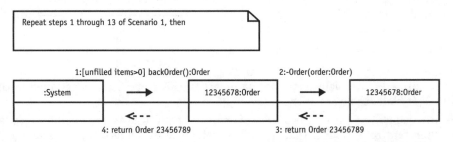

Figure 19-10 *Scenario 4: Mark the order items filled and reduce inventory*

Scenario 5, in Figure 19-11, is the same as steps 1 through 6 of Scenario 1, but the final condition is different. When no unfilled items remain, the Use Case terminates.

See scenario #1, steps 1 through 6

[no unfilled items remain]

Figure 19-11 *Scenario 5: No more items*

10 Min.
To Go

Mapping the Sequence and Collaboration Diagram Elements to the Class Diagram

Because the Class diagram is the source for code generation in object-oriented development, you need to map what you find in the interaction diagrams back to the Class diagram.

Each event becomes an operation on the class of the receiving object. In the classes in Figure 19-12, you can see each of the events declared as an operation on the receiving objects.

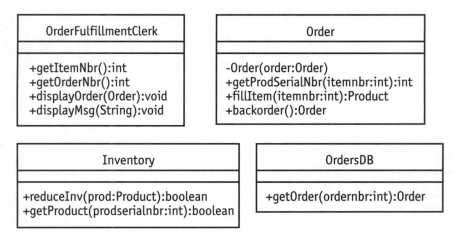

Figure 19-12 *Updated class operations*

The first event modeled in Figure 19-4 was sent from the System to OrderFulfillmentClerk. The event name was getOrderNbr(). The operation is assigned to the OrderFulfillment class, the class of the receiving object.

The return, sequence #2 in Figure 19-4, shows up as the return on the operation signature. It is important to remember that there is no reference to the return on the sending class. Any object may invoke the operation getOrderNbr(). Whichever object invokes the operation at runtime will receive the return. In this scenario, the invoking object in this case happens to be System.

The self-references also become operations. They may be private operations invoked only by the owning object, or they may appear as public, called by other objects in other scenarios. Examine all the scenarios to determine the most appropriate implementation.

Conditions from the Sequence and Collaboration diagrams are placed in the implementation logic of the operation's method.

Done!

REVIEW

The Collaboration diagram models interactions between objects in much the same way that the Sequence diagram does. However, the Collaboration diagram uses the Object diagram as the framework for modeling the events. To construct the Object diagram,

1. Identify the participating objects.
2. Lay them out to provide enough room to arrange the events between them.
3. Draw the links between the objects based on the rules set by the Class diagram associations.
4. Each event in the sequence becomes at least one horizontal arrow from the sending object to the receiving object. The type of arrow depends on the type of event. Regardless of the type, the arrow is placed parallel to the link.
5. For a synchronous event, or procedure call, that requires a reply, place a second arrow parallel to the link running in the opposite direction. Replies use a dashed line style arrow.
6. Continue to represent each event as an arrow running parallel to the links, adding a sequence number to each event to indicate the order of execution, until all the events have been translated onto the Collaboration diagram.

QUIZ YOURSELF

1. What arrangement do you use for the objects in a Collaboration diagram? (See "Building a Collaboration Diagram from a Scenario.")
2. How do you indicate the order of execution in a Collaboration diagram? (See "Building a Collaboration Diagram from a Scenario.")
3. How do you handle the fact that some sets of events need to be repeated? (See "Building a Collaboration Diagram from a Scenario.")
4. Each event becomes an operation. How does the Collaboration diagram help you know what class to add them to? (See "Mapping the Sequence and Collaboration Diagram Elements to the Class Diagram.")
5. How do the return values effect the operations? (See "Mapping the Sequence and Collaboration Diagram Elements to the Class Diagram.")

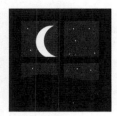

Modeling the Dynamic View:
The Statechart Diagram

Session Checklist

✔ Explaining the purpose of the Statechart diagram

✔ Defining the basic notation for the Statechart diagram

✔ Demonstrating the construction of the Statechart diagram

✔ Defining the Statechart diagram notation for activities, internal events, and deferred events

**30 Min.
To Go**

So far you have seen the dynamic view represented by the Sequence and Collaboration diagrams. Both of these diagrams model the interactions between objects. Now you will see the Statechart diagram that models the effect that these interactions have on the internal makeup of the object. (In fact, in Session 23, I show you how to derive a Statechart from the interactions on a Sequence diagram.)

Describing the Purpose and Function of the Statechart Diagram

The Statechart describes the life of an object in terms of the events that trigger changes in the object's *state*. It identifies both the *external events* and *internal events* that can change the object's state. But what does that mean? The *state* of the object is simply its current condition. That condition is reflected in the values of the attributes that describe that object. There are behaviors in the system that alter those attribute values.

Earlier, I suggested that you notice how parts of speech reflect model elements. A state describes an object, so it typically appears as an adjective in the problem description; for example, an account is open (an *open* account) or an account is overdrawn (an *overdrawn* account).

When the current condition, or state, of the account is overdrawn, the account will respond differently than when the account is in the open condition — checks will be rejected rather than paid or the bank will cover the check and charge you an exorbitant fee for its kindness.

The Statechart has been around a long time. You may know it by the name *state diagram, state machines,* **or** *state transition diagram.*

Next, contrast the scope of the Statechart with that of the Sequence diagram. The scope of the Statechart is the entire life of an object. The scope of the Sequence diagram is a single scenario. Consequently, it is possible to derive a Statechart from the set of Sequence diagrams that use the object.

The Statechart models the events that trigger a *transition* (change) from one state to another state. Each event may have a corresponding *action* that makes the changes in the object (that is, alters the attribute values). While an object is in a state, it may also perform work associated with that state. Such work is called an *activity*.

The Statechart can also be used to model concurrent activities within a state by creating parallel *substates* within a *superstate*. Using the substate and superstate notation, you can explicitly identify split and merge of control for concurrency.

Defining the Fundamental Notation for a Statechart Diagram

The foundation for the Statechart is the relationship between states and events. The following examples illustrate the Statechart notation using the Order object. A state is modeled as a rounded rectangle with the state name inside, as in Figure 20-1, much like the short form of the class icon, where only the name compartment is visible.

Figure 20-1 *State symbol with only name compartment shown (minimum configuration)*

The initial state of an object has its own unique notation, a solid dot with an arrow pointing to the first state. The initial state indicates the state in which an object is created or constructed. You would read Figure 20-2 to say, "An Order begins in the 'Placed' state." In other words, the Order comes into existence when a customer places it.

Figure 20-2 *The initial state notation*

Note that the initial state is the entire image in Figure 20-2. It includes the dot, the arrow, and the state icon. In effect, the dot and arrow point to the first state.

The Statechart event notation is a line style arrow connecting one state to another state. The arrow is actually the transition associated with the event. The direction of the arrow shows the direction of the change from one state to another. Figure 20-3 shows the event "products available" that causes the transition (the arrow) from the state "Placed" to the state "Filled."

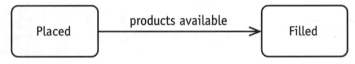

Figure 20-3 *The state transition from "Placed" to "Filled"*

An action is associated with an event. An action is the behavior that is triggered by the event and it is the behavior that actually changes the attributes that define the state of the object. To model the action, place a forward slash after the event name followed by the name of the action or actions you want performed, as in Figure 20-4 where the "products available" event triggers the fillOrder() action. The act of filling the Order alters its contents and redefines its state.

An action is an atomic task, and as such it cannot be broken into component tasks, nor can it be interrupted. There are no break points within it and, furthermore, stopping it midway would leave the object state undefined.

Figure 20-4 *Event/action pair*

An object may reach a *final* state from which it may not return to an active state. In other words, you would never see an arrow going out of this state. A common usage is shown in Figure 20-5. The Order may be archived from either state. But after it is archived, you may never change it. You may still see it and it may still exist, but you can no longer alter its state. The final state may also mean that the object has actually been deleted.

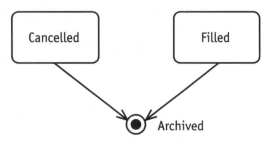

Figure 20-5 *The final state notation*

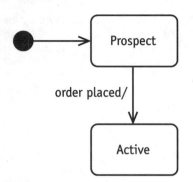

Figure 20-7   *The transition from Prospect to Active*

Now examine the event and determine what, if any, corresponding action needs to occur. Figure 20-8 shows the action addOrder(Order). This operation associates the newly placed order with the customer. According to the client's rules, this makes him an active customer.

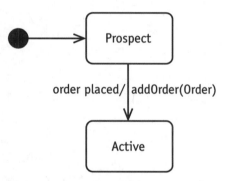

Figure 20-8   *Associating an action with an event*

The second event, payment past due, triggers the transition to On Probation. Figure 20-9 illustrates the new state, the event, the transition from active to on probation, and the action that actually makes the change to the object, setProbation(True).

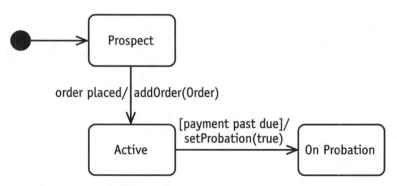

Figure 20-9   *Adding the second transition*

Watching the customer's performance generates the next event. "If he does pay on time and has ordered more than $10,000 in the previous six months, he warrants preferred status." The event is actually a condition that is met. The resulting action is to set the preferred status to true, setPreferred(True). Figure 20-10 adds the new state, the event, the transition, and the action.

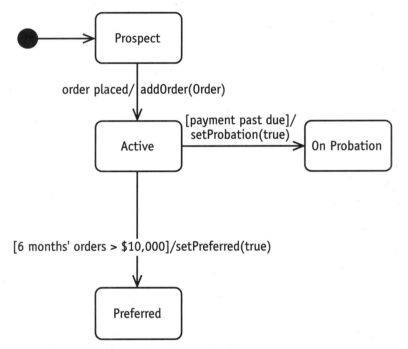

Figure 20-10 *Adding the third transition*

Here is a good place to show how there may be more than one transition between the same two states. Although the example doesn't show it, you could add a second transition from *active* to *preferred* with the event, "The boss says give him preferred status so he will let the boss win at golf." You would have to draw a second transition and label it with the new event and the same action.

10 Min. To Go

The last event addresses how a customer can fall out of preferred status. "Preferred status may be changed only if the customer is late on two or more payments." Again, the event is a condition and the response is an action that alters the state back to active. Figure 20-11 shows the transition back from Preferred to Active.

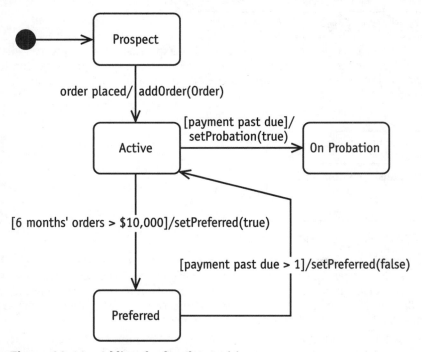

Figure 20-11　*Adding the fourth transition*

This Statechart did not have a final state because within the scope of the problem statement there is no time when a customer object can no longer change. "On Probation" might be a final state because there are no arrows coming out of it, but this happened only because of the limited size of the example.

There is one more very important observation about events on a Statechart diagram. The absence of an event is almost as informative as the presence of an event. In Figure 20-11, the only events that cause a Customer to change from the active state are the conditions *6 months' orders > $10,000,* and *payment past due.* Even though you modeled the event *order placed* in another location, it has no effect when it happens to the Customer while he is in the active state. It simply is not recognized by the active state. You know this because there is no arrow leaving the active state in response to the *order placed* event. So the diagram reveals both the events that an object will respond to while in a state and the events it will not respond to.

Defining Internal Events and Activities

The state icon can also be expanded. The purpose of the expanded form is to reveal what the object can do while it is in a given state. The notation simply splits the state icon into two compartments: the *name compartment* and the *internal transitions compartment,* as illustrated in Figure 20-12.

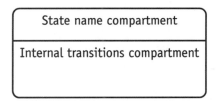

> State name compartment
>
> Internal transitions compartment

Figure 20-12   *The expanded state icon*

The internal transitions compartment contains information about actions and activities specific to that state. You've seen actions associated with events. Here I'm talking about the same actions, only documented as entry and exit actions within a state. But I'm going to hold off until Session 21 to explain entry and exit actions so that I have room to explain them with some illustrations. For now I want to focus on activities.

Activities are processes performed within a state. An activity tends not to be atomic, that is, an activity may be a group of tasks. Activities may be interrupted because they do not affect the state of the object. Contrast this with the earlier definition of an action, which said that you must not interrupt actions because they alter the state. Stopping an action midway could leave the object in an undefined state. Activities just do work. They do not change the state of the object.

For example, Figure 20-13 models the active state of the Customer object. While in that state, the customer object generates a monthly invoice for the customer's purchasing activity and generates monthly promotions tailored to the Customer. To model activities within a state, use the keyword *Do:* followed by one or more activities.

> **Active**
>
> Do : generate monthly invoice
> Do : generate monthly customer promotion

Figure 20-13   *The expanded state icon with activities*

These activities will be performed from the time the object enters the state until the object leaves the state or the activity finishes.

Done!

REVIEW

The Statechart diagram models the life of a single object. The fundamental elements of a Statechart are states and events. A state represents the condition of the object. The state is recorded in the values of one or more of the attributes of the object. An event triggers a change in state, a transition. An action is a behavior triggered by an event, the behavior that actually makes the changes to the attribute values that redefine the state of the object.

The process for building a Statechart is as follows:

1. Identify the state that the object is in when it is first created. Model the initial state.

2. Identify the event(s) that change the object from the initial state to some other state.

3. Name the new state.

4. Draw the transition from the first state to the second. Label the transition arrow with the event that triggers the transition.

5. Identify the action(s) associated with the event and that actually change the object attributes. Add the action after the event name and preceded by a forward slash.

6. Continue the process with each new event until all events have been accounted for.

7. If there is a state from which the object can never leave, convert this state to the final state notation.

QUIZ YOURSELF

1. What does a Statechart illustrate? (See "Describing the Purpose and Function of the Statechart Diagram.")

2. How do you model a transition from one state to another state? (See "Defining the Fundamental Notation for a Statechart Diagram.")

3. How do you model the state an object is in when it is first created? (See "Defining the Fundamental Notation for a Statechart Diagram.")

4. How do you model the behavior initiated by an event and that actually makes the changes in the object's state? (See "Building a Statechart Diagram.")

5. How do you model work that an object performs while it is a state? (See "Defining Internal Events and Activities.")

PART

IV

Saturday Evening Part Review

1. What do you typically use for the basis of a Sequence diagram?
2. How would you show the data returned by an operation?
3. If a scenario covers interactions that are already modeled in another scenario, do you have to repeat them?
4. How do you know where to place an activation bar?
5. What information describes a synchronous event?
6. The Collaboration diagram uses the Object diagram as the basis for modeling events. Why is this advantageous?
7. How does the Collaboration diagram model the order of events?
8. What cannot be seen on the Collaboration diagram that can be seen on the Sequence diagram?
9. On a Collaboration diagram, how do you show that an object refers to one of its own operations?
10. How do you model iteration on a Collaboration diagram?
11. What is the first step in constructing a Collaboration diagram?
12. What is the second step in the construction of the Collaboration diagram?
13. What is the third step in the construction of the Collaboration diagram?
14. What is the fourth step in the construction of the Collaboration diagram?
15. When you encounter a synchronous event, what else can appear on the diagram?
16. How do you start the construction of a Statechart diagram?
17. How is the state of the object actually recorded?
18. What are the elements that make up a state transition?
19. What is a final state? Does every Statechart have to have one?
20. Can there be more than one transition between the same two states?

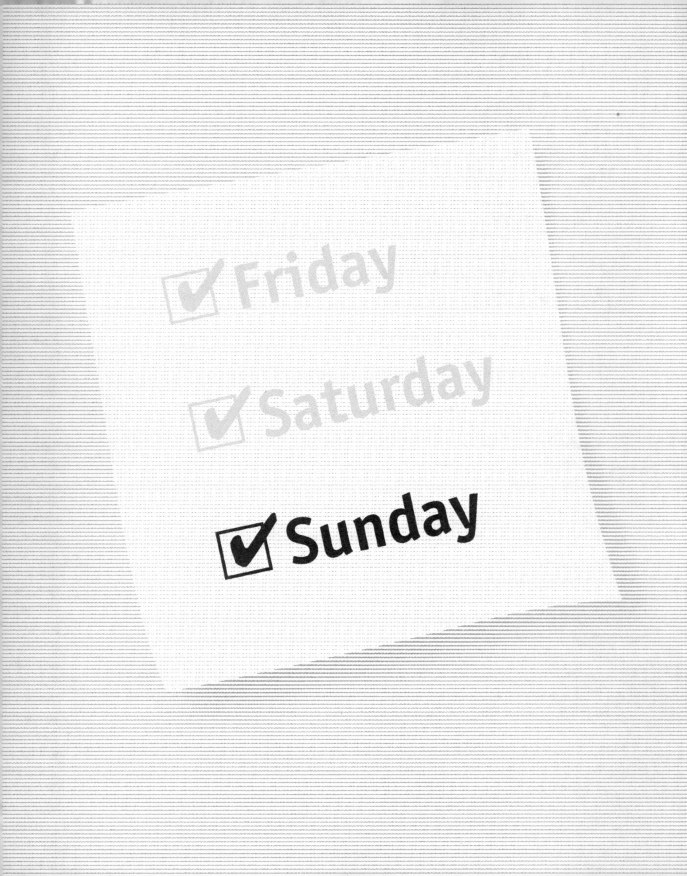

PART

V

Sunday Morning

Applying the Basic
Statechart to the Case Study

Session Checklist

✔ Explaining entry and exit actions

✔ Explaining send events

✔ Explaining the order of event execution

✔ Applying the basic Statechart notation to the case study

**30 Min.
To Go**

The Statechart diagram can become very busy. The UML offers two simplifications called entry and exit actions, along with the ability to send work to other objects. In this session I show you how to take advantage of these features to simplify your diagram for the Order object. I also show you how to construct the complete Statechart diagram for the Order object using the problem statement.

Defining Entry and Exit Actions

Modeling state transitions often results in more than one event that changes the object to the same state. Each of those events may have a corresponding action. For example, in Figure 21-1 the Statechart for the Order object says that you can transition the Order from Tentative to Placed by either receiving the payment for the order or getting an override authorization. But both events require the same action: issue an order confirmation (issueConf()).

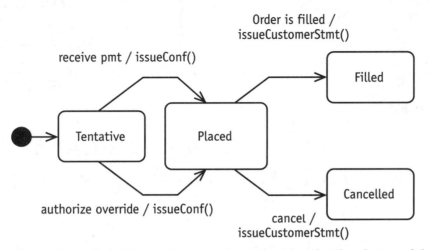

Figure 21-1 *Redundant actions entering and exiting the Placed state of the Order*

In Session 20, you discovered that the state icon could be expanded to reveal the internal transitions compartment. In that compartment you can model something called *entry actions*. Entry actions provide a means to eliminate the redundancy in Figure 21-1.

Whenever you discover an action that must take place with *every* event that transitions to the same state, you can write the action(s) once as an entry action. Figure 21-2 shows the entry action notation, entry/action(s). When the redundant action is replaced by the entry action, you can remove it from the individual event arrows. This simplifies the diagram while preserving the same meaning. You would read the diagram to say, "Every time you enter this state issue an order confirmation."

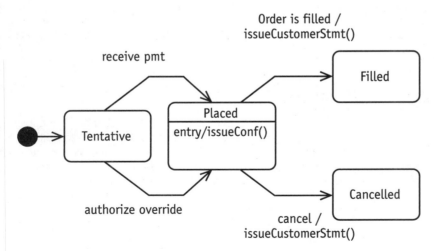

Figure 21-2 *Consolidating the entry actions*

Because we tend to be cautious with our data, it is fairly rare that we literally delete data, so it is equally rare to see the final state. Often, even if an object is flagged for deletion or archive, you leave open the option to undo the deletion or archive to recover from an error or simply change your mind. In this situation, the deleted or archived state would be a normal state (the rounded rectangle).

Building a Statechart Diagram

**20 Min.
To Go**

Now that you know the basic notation, you can step through the construction of a Statechart diagram. In Session 23, I'll show you a way to derive the Statechart from Sequence diagrams. For now, you'll just build a Statechart with the notation you know so far and a simple problem description. The problem statement describes your customers and how you view them for business purposes.

Problem Statement

We track current customer status to help avoid uncollectable receivables and identify customers worthy of preferred treatment. All customers are initially set up as prospects, but when they place their first order, they are considered to be active.

If a customer doesn't pay an invoice on time, he is placed on probation. If he does pay on time and has ordered more than $10,000 in the previous six months, he warrants preferred status. Preferred status may be changed only if the customer is late on two or more payments. Then he returns to active status rather than probation, giving him the benefit of the doubt based on his preferred history.

The first step is to identify the initial state of the customer. The problem statement told you "All customers are initially set up as prospects." To draw the initial state, you need three elements: the starting dot, the transition arrow, and the first state (Prospect). Figure 20-6 illustrates all three elements together.

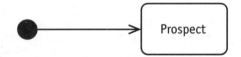

Figure 20-6 *The initial state of the Customer: Prospect*

The next step is to identify an event that could change the prospect state to another state. The problem statement tells you, " . . . when they place their first order, they are considered to be active." To model the change you need at least the event that triggers the change, the transition arrow to show the direction of the change, and the new state that the object transitions to. Figure 20-7 shows all three elements added to the initial diagram.

The same simplification may be used for actions associated with events that leave a state. These are called *exit actions* and are modeled in the same manner as entry actions. If you refer back to Figure 21-1, you will see two events leaving the Placed state. Both events have the same associated action, issueCustomerStmt(). Figure 21-3 shows the *exit/action(s)* notation added to the internal transitions compartment of the Placed state and the actions removed from the event arrows. Compare Figure 21-1 with 21-3 to appreciate the simplification.

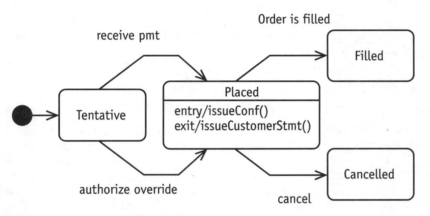

Figure 21-3   *Consolidating the exit actions*

Entry and exit action notations provide a nice simplification for the Statechart diagram. Just remember that they may only be used when the action takes place *every* time you enter (for entry actions) or *every* time you exit (for exit actions) the state. If there is even one exception, the notation may not be used for that action.

Defining Send Events

Figure 21-4 introduces the *send event*. A send event is used when the object in the Statechart diagram needs to communicate with another object. On a Statechart diagram, the source of the incoming events is not shown because the same event may come from any number of other objects and the response must be the same. But an outgoing event must define the receiving object whether it is only one object or a broadcast to many objects. It works in the same way you use your phone. You can receive calls without knowing who is calling. But you cannot place a call without the number you want to call.

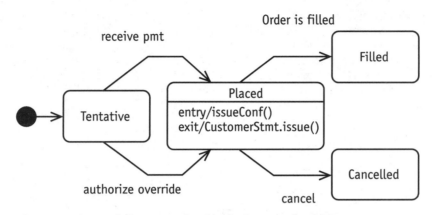

Figure 21-4   *Modeling an action invoked on another object*

In the example in Figure 21-3, when the Order is cancelled, the Order is supposed to issue a customer statement. But the customer statement is another object that takes care of issuing itself. The Order just needs to tell it that it's time to do so. All the actions modeled so far were actions on the same object. To show that the action is invoked on a different object, simply provide the object name followed by a period before the action expression. This is often referred to as the *dot notation*. See the exit action notation in Figure 21-4 where the issue() action is now being sent to the CustomerStmt object.

Order of Events

**20 Min.
To Go**

With all these events, you could end up with a tangled mess of event actions, entry actions, exit actions, and activities. So how do you process all this behavior in a sane fashion? When an event occurs, the order of execution runs like this:

1. If an activity is in progress in the current state, interrupt it (gracefully if possible).
2. Execute the exit: action(s).
3. Execute the actions associated with the event that started it all.
4. Execute the entry: action(s) of the new state.
5. Execute the activity or activities of the new state.

Applying the Basic Statechart Diagram Notation to the Case Study

Now it's time to bring all these concepts together to construct the Statechart for one of the case study objects. This time I use the Product. The problem statement below adds a little more information so that you can exercise the Statechart notation you've learned so far.

Inventory control: Problem statement

Products are first entered into our system when they are ordered using a purchase order (P.O.). Each product keeps a record of the originating P.O. When the product is received, it is placed into inventory by recording the location where it is placed. When the product is received, you have to update the P.O. to indicate that you have received the product.

When a product is sold, the product tracks the order to which it belongs. When a product is sold, it is also packed for shipping and the associated shipment is recorded. When the product is shipped, you need to record the shipper and the date it was picked up. Occasionally, a product is returned. In that case, you put the product back into inventory and record the location.

Constructing the Statechart diagram for the product object

"Products are first entered into our system when they are ordered using a purchase order (P.O.). Each product keeps a record of the originating P.O." The initial state is On Order. The action is to record the purchase order. Notice in Figure 21-5 that an action may be associated with the creation of the object.

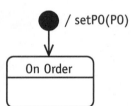

Figure 21-5   *Model the initial state of the product.*

"When the product is received, it is placed into inventory by recording the location where it is placed. When the product is received, you have to update the P.O. to indicate that you have received the product." Figure 21-6 shows that the transition from On Order to Inventoried is triggered by the *receive* event. The associated actions are to update the purchase order object with the product and quantity received and update the product with the inventory location.

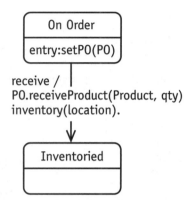

Figure 21-6   *Inventory the product and update the P.O.*

"When a product is sold, the product tracks the order to which it belongs." Figure 21-7 shows the *sell* event triggering the transition to the sold state and the action to record the Order that now holds the product.

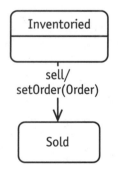

Figure 21-7   *Sell the product and record the order.*

"When a product is sold, it is also packed for shipping and the associated shipment is recorded." Figure 21-8 shows the event *pack for shipping* triggering the transition from sold to packaged. The *pack for shipping* event also triggers the action to record the shipment.

**10 Min.
To Go**

Figure 21-8   *Pack the product for shipping.*

"When the product is shipped, you need to record the shipper and the date it was picked up." Figure 21-9 models the transition from packaged to shipped. The *ship* event is the trigger. The action is *setShipped* with the date and the carrier.

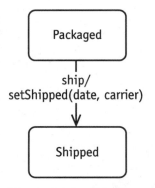

Figure 21-9   *Ship the product.*

"Occasionally, a product is returned. In that case, you put the product back into inventory and record the location." The completed Statechart diagram for the Product object is shown in Figure 21-10. I have added the transition from shipped back to the previous state inventoried. The *return* event requires us to record the inventory location. If you look back to Figure 21-6 you see that the other incoming event also logs the inventory location. Because all incoming events require the same action, you can simplify the diagram using an entry action.

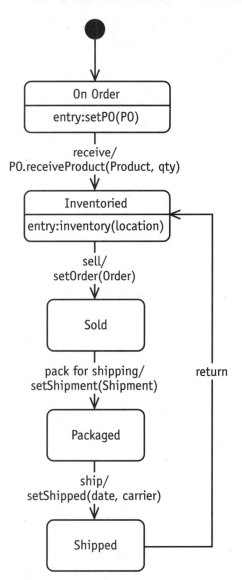

Figure 21-10   *The completed Statechart diagram for the Product object*

Done!

REVIEW

The Statechart allows many events to transition to the same state. Each event may trigger an action. When all the actions associated with the transitions into a state are the same, you can model them as a single *entry action*. Place the entry action description in the internal transitions compartment of the state.

Likewise, the Statechart allows many events to transition out of the same state. Each event may trigger an action. When all the actions associated with the transitions out of a state are the same, you can model them as a single *exit action*. Place the exit action description in the internal transition compartment of the state.

- When an action is directed at an object other than one modeled by the Statechart diagram, use the *dot notation* to qualify the action. Place the object name and a period in front of the action expression.
- When an event takes place it sets off a series of responses in the form of actions and activities. The order of execution for the actions and activities is:
  1. If an activity is in progress in the current state, interrupt it.
  2. Execute the exit: action(s).
  3. Execute the actions associated with the event that started it all.
  4. Execute the entry: action(s) of the new state.
  5. Execute the activity or activities.

QUIZ YOURSELF

1. What is an entry action? (See "Defining Entry and Exit Actions.")
2. What is an exit action? (See "Defining Entry and Exit Actions.")
3. How do you indicate that an action should be performed on another object? (See "Defining Send Events.")
4. What is the first thing that happens when an event takes place? (See "Order of Events.")
5. When an event takes place, which happens first, the exit actions or the actions associated with the triggering event? (See "Order of Events.")

Modeling the Extended Features of the Statechart

**30 Min.
To Go**

S o far you've learned that events trigger transitions between states. Events come in a variety of forms, however. Clarifying at least five different event types, so that you know what to look for when you evaluate the problem statement, will be worth the time. In this section, I cover *call events, time events, change events, send events,* and *guard conditions.* I also explain how you can make these events conditional.

Modeling Transition Events

Figure 22-1 illustrates the Statechart diagram for an Order object. The Order is created in the *initial state* of Tentative. Two events could cause it to change to the Placed state. From Placed it may either be cancelled, or packed and made ready for shipping. After it is packed, it may be shipped. Then, whether it was cancelled or shipped, the Order is archived after 90 days.

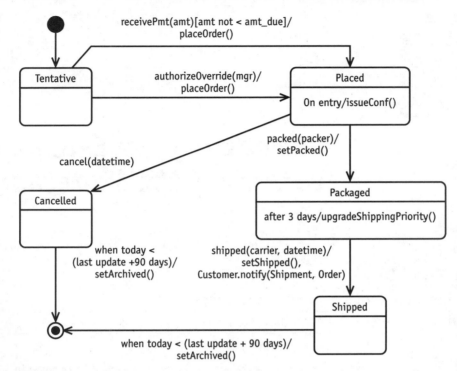

Figure 22-1   *The Statechart for a typical Order object*

Call event

A call event is the most common event type. It is basically the invocation of an operation on the receiving object. This type of event is the merge of an event and an event action. The event itself is an instruction to perform an operation. However, this doesn't prevent you from adding other actions. Figure 22-2 shows the transition from Placed to Cancelled. The transition is triggered by the cancel(datetime) event. "cancel(datetime)" is actually the operation signature on the Order.

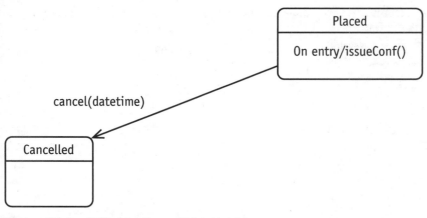

Figure 22-2   *Call event "cancel(datetime)"*

Time event

A time event evaluates the passage of time as a trigger. It implies that the object supports some mechanism to monitor the passage of time. This might be implemented in a number of ways. The mechanism could be a batch program that runs at intervals to update a time attribute. The event could use a polling type of implementation where the object constantly checks to see what time it is.

Use the keyword *after* to specify the time increment to be evaluated. For example, while the Order is in the packaged state, it is waiting to be shipped. But if it has not been shipped within three days, the priority needs to be increased to ensure that it leaves in a timely manner. Figure 22-3 models an internal event within the packaged state called "after 3 days." This implies that there will be code within the object that watches the passage of time to know when to initiate the action "upgrade ShippingPriority()."

Figure 22-3   *Time event "after 3 days"*

Change event

A change event tests for a change in the object or a point in time. Use the keyword *when* with the required test. For example, you might need to know when to run a reporting job or cut invoices so you might say "when 12:00 AM the last day of the month." Or you might watch for a specific condition such as a change in temperature. Then you might say, "when temp > 75 degrees."

Figure 22-4 represents the change events that cause the Order to be archived. In both cases, the Order is waiting until there has been no activity on the Order for 90 days.

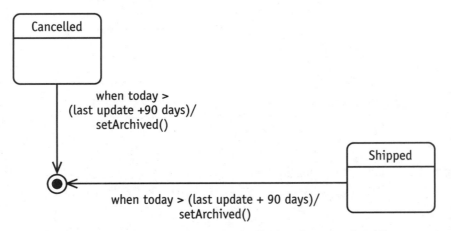

Figure 22-4   *Change event "when today > (last update +90 days)"*

As a reminder, note that this event is only evaluated while the Order is either Cancelled or Shipped. The fact that the event is not drawn from the other states to archived means that the object will not test for that condition while in those states. Remember that what does not show on a Statechart tells you almost as much as what is shown on the diagram.

Making events conditional

A guard condition controls the response to an event. When an event occurs, the condition is tested. If the condition tests true, the corresponding transition takes place along with any and all associated actions; otherwise, the event is ignored.

Figure 22-5 models one of the transitions from the Tentative state to the Placed state. The triggering event is "receivePmt(amt)." But receiving the payment will not upgrade the Order to Placed unless it was actually enough to pay for the Order. The net effect of the event is that the object acknowledges the event, evaluates the effectiveness of the event, and either accepts or rejects it based on the guard condition. If the event is rejected, the object remains unchanged.

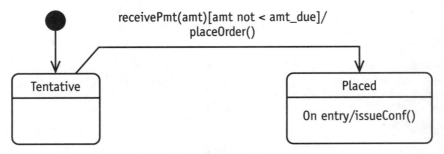

Figure 22-5   *Guard condition [amt not <amt_due]*

Send event

You learned the send event in Session 21. But send events are common enough that it is worth presenting them again briefly in this context. Objects interact to get work done. In the Statechart diagram, you're modeling why and when an object would perform such interactions. A send event models the fact that an object tells another object what to do. A send event may be a response to a transition event or an internal event.

Figure 22-6 models a send event as part of the action required by a transition event. When the shipped(carrier, datetime) event occurs, two actions are triggered with the transition: setShipped() to change the state; and a message to the Customer object to generate a notification to the real customer that her Order has been shipped.

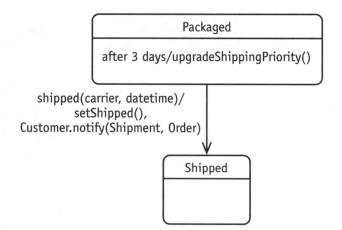

Figure 22-6   *Send event Customer.notify(Shipment, Order)*

Guard conditions as events

A guard condition may actually be used by itself as a triggering event. It simply implies that the object is watching for a condition to be satisfied. For example, your bank account monitors its balance as the deposits and withdrawals are computed. If, at any time, the balance drops below zero, the account jumps at the opportunity to fire off an overdraft charge.

Modeling Superstates and Substates

Modeling often requires different views of a problem. High-level views simplify the model. Low-level views focus on details of a problem. The UML Statechart diagram supports the concept of nested states, allowing both high- and low-level views of object behavior and states.

A *superstate* is simply a state that is expanded to show more detail. The state rounded rectangle icon is expanded and the details are represented as one or more Statecharts within the superstate. The name of the state is placed at the top. Superstates represent a high-level view of a complex situation. They allow you to focus on the bigger, more general problem without getting lost in the details. The substates are placed within the expanded superstate.

A *substate* is a state within a state, a lower level of detail within a state. For example, a car can be in the state of moving forward. Within the *moving forward superstate* are substates of *moving forward in first gear, moving forward in second gear,* and so on. The substates provide a low-level view of a model element so that you can address specific issues individually and in terms of their interactions and interdependencies. This detailed view also allows you to highlight concurrent states and focus on how to control the splitting and merging of concurrent states.

To illustrate these concepts, I'm going to use what I hope is a familiar example, a thermostat. I'm going to simplify it even further and only look at the cooling side of its responsibilities. The thermostat is a typical control-type object. Its job is to direct the work of other objects, much like an application directs the behavior of the screen and the access to the database.

Figure 22-7 models the superstate Cooling with two concurrent substates. In this example, the two substates are both initial states. The diagram says that when the Thermostat enters the Cooling state, it splits into two concurrent substates, that is, it is now doing two things at the same time: It is monitoring the progress of the cooling process, and it is monitoring the cooling device for any problems. The two substates start immediately upon entering the Cooling state.

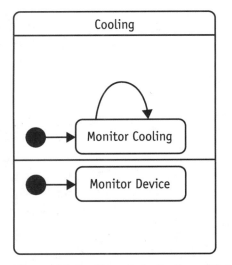

Figure 22-7   *Superstate Cooling with two substates, Monitor Cooling and Monitor Device*

It is also possible to trigger the substates by transition events like a call or time event. In this case, the transition event would extend all the way into the superstate and point directly to the substate. This often involves split of control, which I cover next.

Split of control

Split of control means that, based on a single transition, you want to proceed with multiple tasks. This is exactly the same concept you learned in the Activity diagram session. Split of control is shown by a single transition divided into multiple arrows pointing to multiple states or substates. The divide is accomplished with the fork bar you used in the Activity diagram and is illustrated in Figure 22-8.

Merge of control can be modeled as multiple transition arrows pointing to a synchronization bar, as you saw earlier in learning about the Activity diagram. Synchronization is not shown in Figure 22-8.

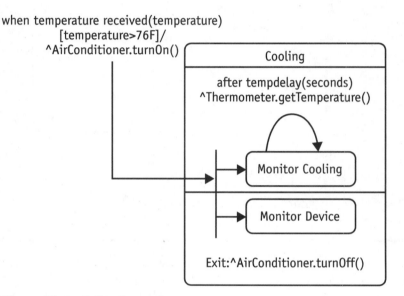

Figure 22-8 *Split of control*

Concurrency

By allowing multiple Statecharts within a state, the UML supports concurrency within a state. To model concurrency, simply split the superstate internal transition compartment into as many separate compartments as needed, one for each sub-Statechart. In the thermostat example, the Thermostat is doing two jobs at the same time: monitoring the cooling device and watching for problems with the device. So the Cooling state internal transition compartment is split in two by a line.

Note that in this particular example each substate provides a different transition out of the superstate. The Monitor Cooling substate is watching for the event "when temperature received(temperature) [temperature < 70]." If it receives this event, it takes the Thermostat out of the Cooling state and back to monitoring the temperature. So what happens to the other substate? Well, this hits on the definition of substate. A substate is a state within a state — in this case, Monitor Device within Cooling. If the Thermostat leaves the Cooling state, by definition it also leaves the Monitor Device state. This is illustrated in Figure 22-9.

The same is true if the Monitor Device state receives the event it is waiting for.

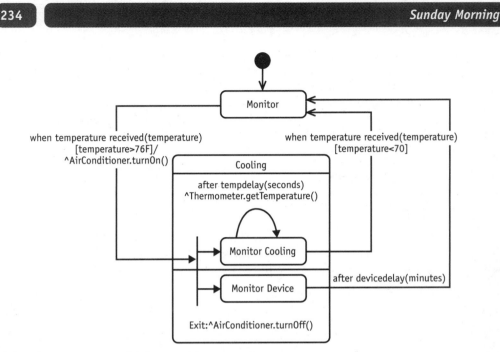

Figure 22-9   *Multiple transitions out of a superstate*

Done!

REVIEW

Different types of events can trigger a transformation in an object:

- Call events are basically messages from other objects telling the modeled object what to do. They are explicit calls to an operation on the object.

- The time event indicates that the object needs to support code that will monitor the passage of time to know when to trigger a change in the object.

- Change events monitor the object and/or its environment for some change.

- Send events describe a message sent by the modeled object to another object. In some respects, this should be called a send action because it happens in response to an event.

- Guard conditions may also act as events. The object watches for the condition to be satisfied. As soon as the condition is met, the object transitions to the next state.

- The UML supports the ability to open up a state and break it into smaller pieces. The smaller pieces are *substates,* states within a state. The larger containing state is referred to as the *superstate.*

- The substates are modeled as a Statechart within a state. All the normal notation of a Statechart is available within a state. When there is more than one concurrent substate, simply split the superstate icon with a line to allow for each independent Statechart.

- Split and merge of control use the fork and synchronization bars, the same bars used in the Activity diagram.

Quiz Yourself

1. What is a call event? (See "Call event.")
2. What is a time event? (See "Time event.")
3. What is a change event? (See "Change event.")
4. What is a superstate? (See "Modeling Superstates and Substates.")
5. What is a substate? (See "Concurrency.")

Applying the Extended Statechart Features to the Case Study

**30 Min.
To Go**

Those who use the UML diagrams often miss the benefit of building and comparing the different diagrams. Each diagram provides a unique view of the same problem. Comparing and contrasting these views can function much like reconciling your checkbook. Given multiple sources of the same information, it is much easier to find and correct errors.

Deriving a Statechart from Sequence Diagrams

The dynamic model provides two diagrams that model changes over time: the Statechart diagram and the Sequence diagram. The key to understanding the relationship between these diagrams is in understanding states and events. Events trigger transitions between states. States capture the condition of an object during the period of time between transitions.

Using this understanding, look at the Sequence diagram shown in Figure 23-1.

In Figure 23-1, each vertical column represents the lifeline for one object. Each event directed at a lifeline represents an event that may trigger a change in that object. The space between events on the lifeline represents a period of time when the object remains in the same condition or state. Because not every event causes a state transition, these periods are referred to as *candidate states* until it's proven that a change, in fact, occurs.

The events pointing outward from the object lifeline represent either return values sent to other objects or send events.

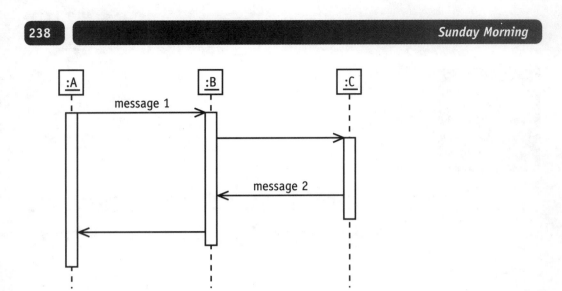

Figure 23-1 *A basic Sequence diagram with events and transitions*

The challenging part of mapping the Sequence diagram to the Statechart diagram is to determine the condition of the object between the events and name it as accurately as possible. The same state may appear in many Sequence diagrams. Accurate naming can prevent confusion when you merge the states from the many Sequence diagrams. To choose an accurate name, remember that the state of an object is defined by its attribute values. Describe the object in terms of its attributes (for example, open, closed, open and overdrawn, or filled and not shipped). Adjectives make very good state names, but you might need more than one adjective to fully describe the current condition of the object.

Figure 23-2 shows how to map the events and corresponding gaps on the lifeline of the Sequence diagram to candidate states and events on the Statechart diagram.

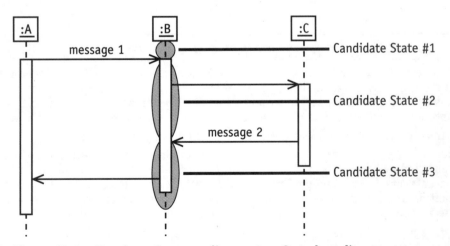

Figure 23-2 *Mapping a Sequence diagram to a Statechart diagram*

Understanding these concepts is a lot easier when you can see an example, so I'm going to derive a Statechart diagram for the Product object and do it a step at a time so you can see the progression. I'll work through the same series of steps for each scenario:

1. Identify the events directed at the lifeline of the Product object.
2. Identify candidate states by isolating the gaps of the lifeline between the incoming events.
3. Name the candidate states using adjectives that describe the condition of the object during the period of time represented by the gap.
4. Add the new states and events to the Product Statechart.

The first scenario is modeled in Figure 23-3. There is one incoming event called Product(PO). This is the constructor operation that creates the object. Before this event, this particular Product object didn't exist, so you have discovered the initial state. I'll name it "On Order" to show that a record of the Product object is created when the Product is first ordered.

The self-transition event setPO(PO) does not change the state of the Product. It only updates a reference that it's tracking, so I didn't identify a state change.

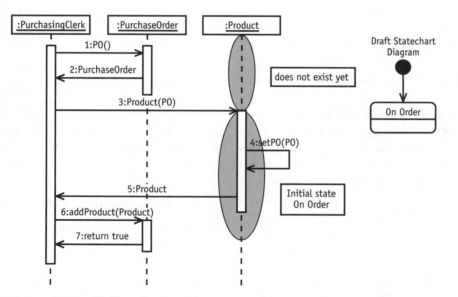

Figure 23-3 *Finding the transition events and candidate states for Scenario 1*

The second scenario, modeled in Figure 23-4, shows the receiving event. There is only one event hitting the Product lifeline, so I identify two candidate states: the one before the event and the one after. The event receive(location) becomes the reason for the transition from On Order to Inventoried.

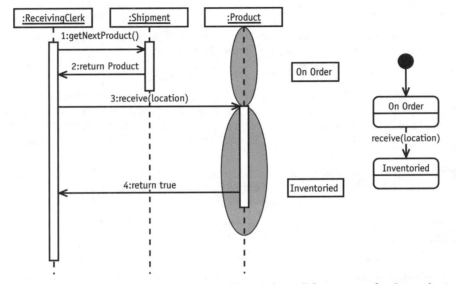

Figure 23-4 *Finding the transition events and candidate states for Scenario 2*

If you're struggling with a name for the state, try to identify the attributes that change in the transition and use them and their values as the descriptors. For example, if the *cancelled date* is set, then call it *Cancelled;* if the product was placed into inventory by entering a location value in the location attribute, call it *Inventoried*.

The third scenario, in Figure 23-5, shows the Product being sold. Before the *sell* event, the Product was sitting in inventory. In fact, if it were not in inventory, I could not sell it. So again, I identify two states and use the incoming event *sell* as the transition event between the two states.

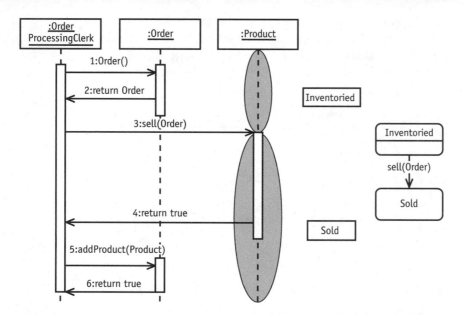

Figure 23-5   *Finding the transition events and candidate states for Scenario 3*

In the fourth scenario, shown in Figure 23-6, the product is packed for shipment. But before the product may be packed for shipping it must have been sold. The *pack* event requires the shipment to update the product with the Shipment information so that we can track it. To show the change, I model a transition from the sold state to a new state labeled Packaged.

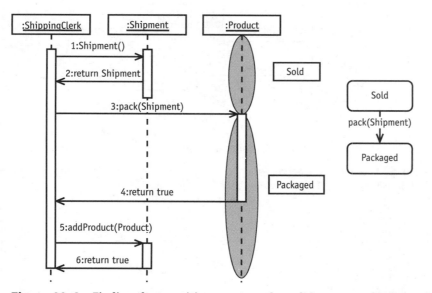

Figure 23-6   *Finding the transition events and candidate states for Scenario 4*

In Figure 23-7, the fifth scenario tells me to ship the product. But before the product may be shipped it must have been packaged for shipment. The *ship* event requires me to update the product with the carrier and ship date. Based on this information, I modeled a transition from the Packaged state to a new state labeled Shipped.

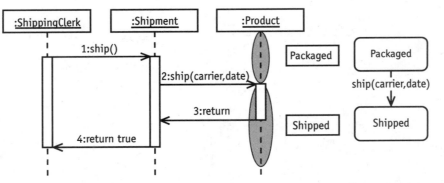

Figure 23-7   *Finding the transition events and candidate states for Scenario 5*

**10 Min.
To Go**

The sixth scenario, in Figure 23-8, illustrates bringing a return back into inventory. But before the product may be returned, it must have been shipped. The *return* event requires the location in inventory where the Product will be placed. When the product is returned to a stock location, it is returned to the previous state called Inventoried.

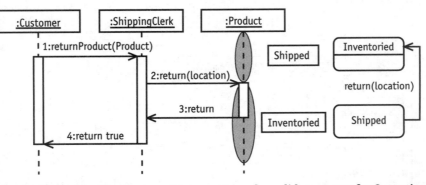

Figure 23-8   *Finding the transition events and candidate states for Scenario 6*

When you put all the little Statechart diagrams together, you get a Statechart diagram that looks like Figure 23-9.

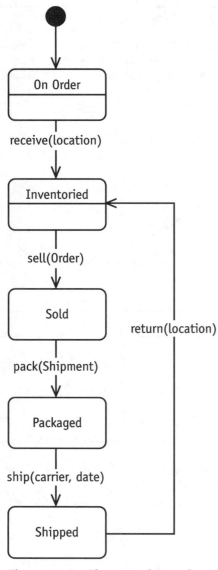

Figure 23-9   *The merged Statechart diagram*

This is just one simple technique for taking advantage of the Sequence diagram to help you build a Statechart. You will very likely encounter a few others. In fact, there are more-formal methods for mapping the two diagrams in a manner that is supported by software. Some modeling tools allow you to work on a Statechart and then automatically generate or update your Sequence diagrams. Likewise, you can create Sequence diagrams and generate the Statechart.

The Statechart and Sequence diagrams can help you a great deal when you're trying to design the behavior of your objects, especially those few objects that are at the heart of your application.

Done!

REVIEW

The Sequence diagram provides the events that can affect an object's condition. It also helps to identify the periods of time between the changes caused by the events. These periods of time when the object remains unchanged may represent states on the Statechart diagram.

To derive the Statechart from the Sequence diagrams, use the following steps:

1. Identify the events directed at the lifeline of the object you're modeling.
2. Identify candidate states by isolating the portions of the lifeline between the incoming events.
3. Name the candidate states using adjectives that describe the condition of the object during the period of time represented by the gap.
4. Add the new states and events to the Statechart diagram.

Remember that the scope of the Sequence diagram is only one scenario. The scope of the Statechart diagram is the entire life of the object, so it may take many Sequence diagrams to build one Statechart.

QUIZ YOURSELF

1. On a Sequence diagram, which events may change an object? (See "Deriving a Statechart from Sequence Diagrams.")
2. How do you identify a candidate state on a Sequence diagram? (See "Deriving a Statechart from Sequence Diagrams.")
3. If an event on the Sequence diagram causes a change to the object, how do you model it on the Statechart diagram? (See "Deriving a Statechart from Sequence Diagrams.")
4. What do you do if an event does not cause a change in the object it is directed at? (See "Deriving a Statechart from Sequence Diagrams.")
5. What kind of word is good for naming a state? (See "Deriving a Statechart from Sequence Diagrams.")

Modeling the Development Environment

Session Checklist

✔ Explaining the purpose and function of packages

✔ Defining the package notation

✔ Creating a Package diagram for the case study

30 Min.
To Go

Throughout the development process, you create a wide variety of diagrams to gather requirements, research those requirements, and ultimately describe the software you want to generate. Without a tool to organize all those work products, the job can quickly become confusing and overwhelming. *Packages* are the UML tool for organizing the diagrams and other work products of the project.

Describing the Purpose and Function of Packages

A package is modeled with a folder icon like the three packages in Figure 24-1. Also illustrated in Figure 24-1 is the fact that packages may be used for three distinct purposes. In one role, they may be used to organize any and all of the diagrams that you create during the project. You can place the diagrams into various packages just like you would place files into various directories on your computer. You name the directories and packages to indicate the purpose of the contained files. Figure 24-1 illustrates this role with the package on the left, a package of deliverables for Project A7, Phase 1.

Packages may contain any of the logical model elements you've learned so far, such as Use Case diagrams, Sequence diagrams, Class diagrams, and even other packages. In fact, most modeling tools provide a navigation mechanism based on packages that look and function exactly like a directory structure. Because this use of packages is so general, you may use virtually any stereotype with it to explain how you are using the particular package.

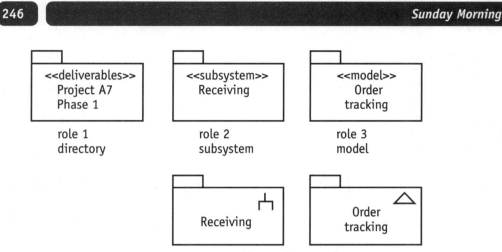

Figure 24-1   *Three uses for packages: directories, subsystems, and models*

In the second role, the package can represent a *subsystem*, like the Receiving subsystem in Figure 24-1. A subsystem is a UML-defined stereotype that identifies a cohesive subset of the total system. For example, the Inventory Control System might be organized into a Receiving subsystem and a Shipping subsystem, among others.

Elements placed in a subsystem type of package are, by default, visible only within the package. However, the visibility of individual model elements within the package may be defined as public, private, or protected. Every subsystem package must have at least one public interface (that is, at least one class with a public interface).

The third use of packages is called a *model*. A model is also a UML-defined stereotype, similar to a subsystem in that it contains a cohesive set of elements of the system. The difference is that the model focuses on a topic or type of behavior within the system. For example, information about the Order Tracking topic of the third package in Figure 24-1 will very likely appear in most of the Inventory Control subsystems. Also, because the model is focused on one topic, it will not contain any system elements that do not help explain the topic.

Packages Provide a Namespace

All these package types provide a separate namespace for the model elements contained within them, including other packages. Naming elements within a package requires two pieces of information: the element name and the element type. For example, a package may contain something called Product of type Class and something called Product of type Statechart diagram. Names must be unique across elements of the same type within a package but do not have to be unique across different types. A package could not contain two items called Product that are both of type Class.

Model elements in different packages may have the same name. But whenever the two elements are used together, they must be qualified with the owning package name. A fully qualified element name uses the notation *package :: element,* for example *Receiving :: Product* and *Shipping :: Product*.

Defining the Notation for Packages and Package Diagrams

The package icon looks like a tabbed folder. Packages reference one another using the dependency notation, a dashed arrow. Read the example in Figure 24-2 as "the Receiving subsystem depends on, or needs help from, the Purchasing subsystem package."

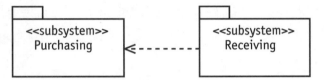

Figure 24-2　*Package icon and dependency notation*

Package stereotypes

In Figures 24-1 and 24-2, each package icon contains a stereotype like <<subsystem>> or <<deliverables>>. You can put almost anything you want in a package, so the package description often requires a bit of clarification. The stereotype allows you to characterize the contents of the package and still provide specific naming of its contents. For example, the Receiving package is characterized as a subsystem. This prevents us from interpreting it as the directory containing the receiving documents, or some other resources besides the subsystem classes.

Be careful though. Stereotypes are not part of the package name, so they do not help make it unique. Two packages at the same level called <<documentation>> Receiving and <<subsystem>> Receiving would be in conflict and probably would not be allowed by most modeling tools. On the other hand, if the packages themselves are contained within other packages, then they are qualified by their containers, making them unique. However, you need to check how your modeling tool implements these rules.

Package dependency

Figure 24-2 also shows a dashed dependency arrow from Receiving to Purchasing. The dependency relationship means that at least one class in a package has to communicate with at least one class in the other package. The dependency in Figure 24-2 could mean that the Receipt class in the Receiving package (Receiving :: Receipt) needs to be able to get the details of the PurchaseOrder class in the Purchasing package (Purchasing :: PurchaseOrder) in order to validate incoming products.

It is entirely valid for a dependency to run both directions, indicated by an arrowhead on both ends of the dashed line. Figure 24-3 shows an example where Shipping might need to update an Order in the Order Processing subsystem. But Order Processing might also need to check the status of a Shipment containing the Products on an Order.

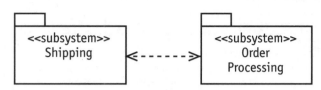

Figure 24-3 *A bi-directional dependency*

For simplicity's sake, all the other dependencies illustrated in this session go only one direction.

Dependency stereotypes

The package dependency may be labeled with a stereotype to describe the nature of the dependency. The UML defines two dependency stereotypes, <<import>> and <<access>>. The <<import>> stereotype in Figure 24-4 means that the Receiving package adds a Purchasing class (in this case the PurchaseOrder class) to itself at run time, allowing *internal references* (references within the package) to the class without specifying the source package name.

Figure 24-4 *The* <<import>> *stereotype on a dependency*

 For Java programmers, the <<import>> **stereotype has the same effect as the** *import* **statement in Java.**

 The <<access>> stereotype in Figure 24-5 says that the Shipping subsystem will want to communicate with the Receiving subsystem but will not actually pull the classes from Receiving into Shipping at run time. At run time, you would then expect to see some object from the Shipping subsystem making calls in the interface of the Receiving subsystem.

20 Min. To Go

Figure 24-5 *The* <<access>> *stereotype on a dependency*

There are a number of other stereotypes described in the UML specification in the file 01-09-78 UML 1.4 Appendix A UML Standard Elements.pdf.

Model elements in a package

One of the most common uses for the package is to hold your diagrams. In most modeling tools, packages provide a nesting mechanism (that is, a package may contain other packages, which in turn contain diagrams). The packages in this scheme refer to systems, subsystems, and diagrams, respectively. The scheme can contain as many levels as the problem requires. Figure 24-6 shows an example of the package Shipping that holds the Class diagram that supports the functions of the Shipping subsystem.

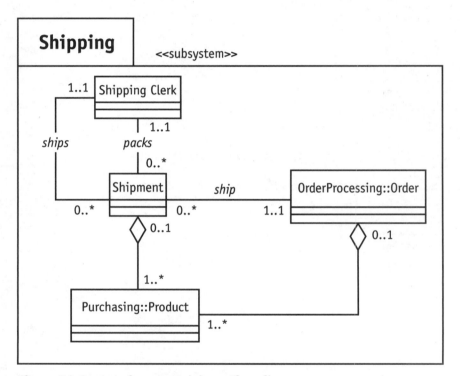

Figure 24-6   *A package containing a Class diagram*

Actually, the more common way to represent this in a modeling tool is to open a package and get a diagram in a new window or canvas. Conceptually, the diagram resides in the package as I have represented in Figure 24-6. But the tool does not represent it that way.

Figure 24-6 also shows two examples of the import relationship. The Order and Product classes use the qualifying notation *package :: element*. This notation tells you that the two classes came from the named package (that is, Order is imported from the OrderProcessing package and Product is imported from Purchasing). This clearly identifies the fact that the class is defined in another package but is referenced in this package.

Constructing a Package Diagram for the Case Study

Next I'll step through the creation of a Package diagram using the subsystem stereotype to organize the Inventory Control System elements that we have discovered so far. Note the use of the package icon, the package stereotype, dependencies, and dependency stereotypes.

1. Add a package to represent the Purchasing subsystem. Draw the package icon (a folder). Add the name "Purchasing." Add the stereotype <<subsystem>> to clarify what you want to represent in the package. Figure 24-7 illustrates this first package.

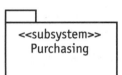

Figure 24-7   *Step 1: A package containing a Class diagram*

2. Add the Shipping and Receiving subsystems. Figure 24-8 shows the new additions.

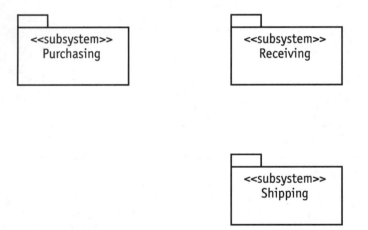

Figure 24-8   *Step 2: Adding the new subsystems*

3. Create a dependency between Receiving and Purchasing to show that Receiving needs help from classes in the Purchasing package. Figure 24-9 shows a dashed arrow from Receiving to Purchasing. Receiving needs the help. Purchasing is the place that Receiving looks to get the help.

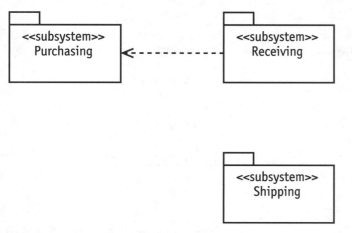

Figure 24-9   *Step 3: Adding a dependency*

4. Stereotype the dependency between Receiving and Purchasing as <<import>> to show that Receiving makes references to classes within Purchasing by adding them into its own set of classes at run time. Figure 24-10 shows the addition of the <<import>> stereotype.

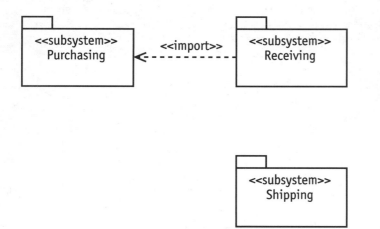

Figure 24-10   *Step 4: Adding the <<import>> dependency stereotype*

**10 Min.
To Go**

5. Add the <<access>> stereotype to the dependency between Shipping and Receiving to show that Shipping needs to communicate with classes within Receiving without actually making them part of the Shipping subsystem at run time. Instead, the classes in the Shipping subsystem will make calls to one or more classes in Receiving. Figure 24-11 places the <<access>> stereotype on the dashed dependency arrow between Shipping and Receiving.

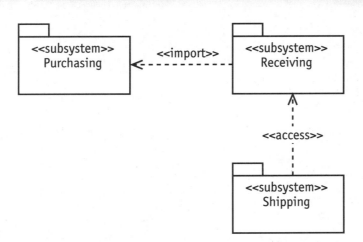

Figure 24-11   *Step 5: Adding the* <<access>> *dependency stereotype*

6. Add a package to handle the order processing requirements of the system. The new package, Order Processing, is modeled as a folder icon just like the other packages. The name is placed inside the icon. The package should be recognizable as a subsystem, so the stereotype <<subsystem>> is placed above the name. The Order Processing package needs to use the Inventory class in the Receiving package, so it pulls the class into itself to work with it. This requirement is implemented in Figure 24-12 with a dashed dependency arrow from Order Processing to Receiving using the <<import>> dependency stereotype.

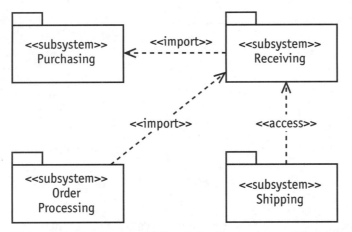

Figure 24-12   *Step 6: Adding Order Processing and the* <<import>> *dependency stereotype*

7. The Shipping package needs to use the Order class in the Order Processing package but will simply communicate with it rather than add it to itself. Figure 24-13 models this change with a dashed dependency arrow from Shipping to Order Processing using the <<access>> dependency stereotype. Figure 24-13 models the addition of the dependency.

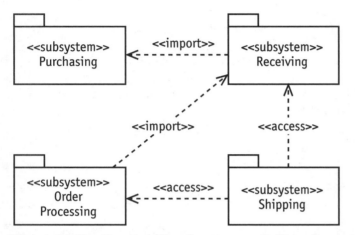

Figure 24-13   *Step 7: Adding the <<access>> dependency stereotype*

Done!

REVIEW

The package notation provides a versatile tool for storing work products of the software development process. The package notation may be used just like a directory structure to store artifacts, documentation, and just about anything you can put in a file.

- The package notation may also be used to represent a breakdown of the system into subsystems and finally to diagrams that represent the subsystems. This is by far the most common use of the packages in modeling tools.

- Packages provide separate namespaces for the elements contained in them. This results in the UML naming standard package :: name to fully qualify each element.

- The package is modeled with a folder icon, a name, and often a stereotype to distinguish how the package is being used. The UML defined stereotypes include <<subsystem>> and <<model>>.

- Packages contain elements that may need to interact. This need is expressed as a *dependency,* a dashed arrow between the two packages. The type of dependency is described using a stereotype like <<import>> or << access>> placed on the dependency arrow. The dependency may be uni-directional or bi-directional.

QUIZ YOURSELF

1. How do you model a package in the UML? (See "Describing the Purpose and Function of Packages.")

2. What is a package stereotype? (See "Defining the Notation for Packages and Package Diagrams.")

3. What is a dependency? (See "Defining the Notation for Packages and Package Diagrams.")

4. What is a dependency stereotype? (See "Defining the Notation for Packages and Package Diagrams.")

5. What does the <<import>> stereotype mean? (See "Defining the Notation for Packages and Package Diagrams.")

Modeling the Static View: The Component Diagram

Session Checklist

✔ Describing the purpose and function of the Component diagram

✔ Defining the notation for Component diagrams

✔ Creating a Component diagram for the case study

**30 Min.
To Go**

O nce the logical design is completed, the next step is to define the physical implementation of your design. The physical implementation must address three different problems: the software, the hardware, and the integration of the two.

Explaining the Component Diagram

The Component diagram models the physical implementation of the software. The Deployment diagram models the physical architecture of the hardware (the Deployment diagram is covered in Session 26). Combined, they model the integration and distribution of your application software across the hardware implementation.

Just as Class diagrams describe the organization and intent of your software design, components represent the physical implementations of your software design. The purpose of the Component diagram is to define software modules and their relationships to one another. Each component is a chunk of code that resides in memory on a piece of hardware. Each component must define an interface, which allows other components to communicate with that component. The interface and the internal implementation of the component are encapsulated in the classes that make up the component.

The UML groups components into three broad categories:

- Deployment components, which are required to run the system
- Work product components including models, source code, and data files used to create deployment components
- Execution components, which are components created while running the application

Components may depend on one another. For example, an executable (.exe) may require access to a dynamic link library (.dll), or a client application may depend on a server side application, which in turn depends on a database interface.

Components may be dependent on classes. For example, to compile an executable file, you may need to supply the source classes.

Given the key elements, component, component interface, and dependencies, you can describe the physical implementation of your system in terms of the software modules and the relationships among them.

Defining the Notation for Components and Component Dependencies

A *component icon* is modeled as a rectangle with two small rectangles centered on the left edge. The name is placed inside the icon, as in Figure 25-1.

OrderEntry.exe

Figure 25-1 *Component icon and name*

The two small rectangles are left over from an old notation that used to put the component interfaces in the rectangles.

Component stereotypes

Component stereotypes provide visual clues to the role that the component plays in the implementation. Some common component stereotypes include:

- <<executable>>: A component that runs on a processor
- <<library>>: A set of resources referenced by an executable during runtime
- <<table>>: A database component accessed by an executable
- <<file>>: Typically represents data or source code
- <<document>>: A document such as a page inserted into a Web page

These stereotypes refer to classifiers (implementations of the classes defined earlier in the process) and artifacts of the implementation of the classifiers, such as the source code, binary files, and databases.

Component interfaces

A component *interface* may be modeled in either of two ways. One way is to use a class with the stereotype <<interface>> attached to the component with a realization arrow, as shown in Figure 25-2. The realization arrow looks like the generalization symbol with a dashed line. To *realize* the interface means to apply it to something real like the executable.

Figure 25-2 *Interface notation using a class and stereotype*

A second, more common, technique is to use a "lollipop" attached to the component with a solid line, as shown in Figure 25-3. If you look into the UML specification examples, the circle on the end of the lollipop is very small. This is a bit distorted from the typical notation employed by modeling tools.

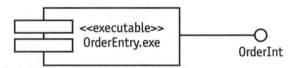

Figure 25-3 *Interface notation using the lollipop*

The interface implemented by a component is actually implemented by the classes within the component, so the interface should already have been defined in your Class diagrams. Also, a component may implement as many interfaces as it requires. The number and exact type of interfaces are dictated by the classes implemented by the component.

**20 Min.
To Go**

Component dependencies

Dependencies between components are drawn with the dashed arrow from the dependent component to the component it needs help from. In Session 24, you learned that package dependencies could be stereotyped to clarify the nature of the dependency. The same is true for component dependencies. In Figure 25-4, the OrderEntry depends on the OrderEntry.exe component. The UML stereotype <<becomes>> means that the OrderEntry file literally becomes the OrderEntry executable at runtime. OrderEntry would be the code sitting on a storage device. At runtime it is loaded into memory and possibly even compiled. Then during execution the OrderEntry.exe component would depend on the three other components: orders.dll, inventory.dll, and orders.tbl.

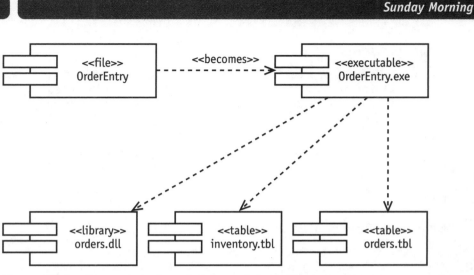

Figure 25-4   *Components dependencies and dependency stereotypes*

Building a Component Diagram for the Case Study

To review the notation for the Component diagram, I'll show you how to build one using each of the new model elements you just learned.

The diagram will model the Receiving application. The application consists of two executable components, a shared interface, and three library components. The Receiving application consists of the classes that implement the Use Case ReceiveProduct, the server side application, and the client application (the UI). The other components represent the implementations of the classes used by receiving, Product, PurchaseOrder, and Inventory.

1. In Figure 25-5, create the Receiving.exe component. Name it and add the <<executable>> stereotype.

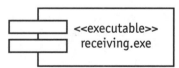

Figure 25-5   *Step 1: Creating the Receiving.exe component*

2. Figure 25-6 adds the purchaseorder.dll library component so that the Receiving component can validate incoming products against the purchase orders. The purchaseorder.dll component is the implementation of the PurchaseOrder class. It then draws a dependency from Receiving.exe to the purchaseorder.dll to show that the Receiving.exe needs help from the purchaseorder.dll to check the received products against the purchase order.

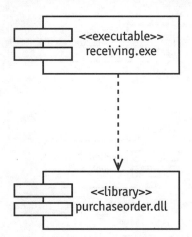

Figure 25-6 *Step 2: Adding a library component and drawing the dependency*

3. Figure 25-7 adds two more resource components. The product.dll component allows the Receiving application to update the product status to received. The inventory.dll component supports checks on the availability of locations where they can put the new product. It then adds the dependency from the Receiving.exe to the product.dll to show that the Receiving.exe needs access to the product.dll, and the dependency from the Receiving.exe to the inventory.dll to show that the Receiving.exe needs access to the inventory.dll in order to update inventory.

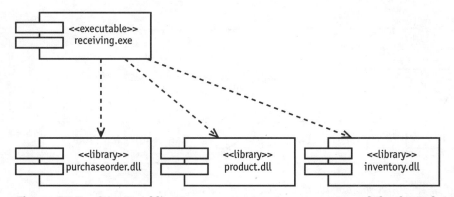
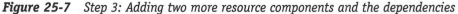

Figure 25-7 *Step 3: Adding two more resource components and the dependencies*

4. Figure 25-8 adds the client application that manages the user interface. The Receiving application provides the PO (or Purchase Order) interface. Figure 25-8 models the interface using the lollipop notation. The user interface application (ui.exe) accesses the Receiving application using the PO interface. This access is modeled as a dependency from ui.exe to the PO lollipop style interface to illustrate that the ui.exe will not work properly unless it can access the receiving application through the PO interface.

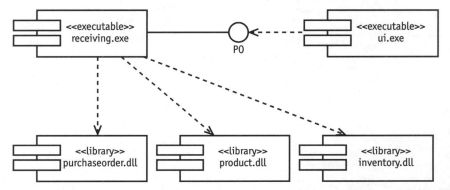

Figure 25-8   *Step 4: Adding the user interface application and the shared interface*

Mapping the Logical Design to the Physical Implementation

Making components from classes involves choices about how to assemble these classes into cohesive units. The interfaces of the classes in the component make up the interface to the component. Figure 25-9 shows a database table component, orders.tbl, which implements the classes that define an order, namely Order, LineItem, and Product, and their association.

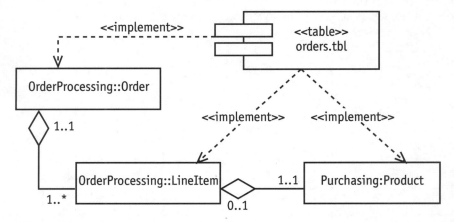

Figure 25-9   *A component is created from classes.*

In like manner, the main program in an application may implement some or all of the key classes in the logical model. To create the executable in Figure 25-10, you compile the classes together into a single executable.

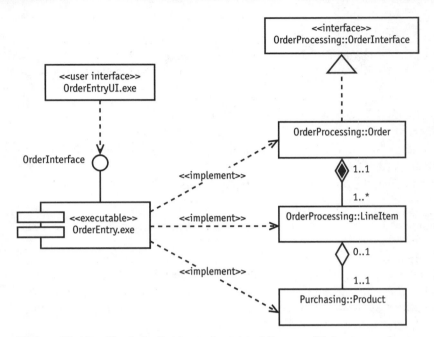

Figure 25-10   *The OrderEntry.exe is created from multiple source classes.*

Quite often, however, a component consists of a single class implemented as an executable, file, library, table, or document. In Figure 25-11, the order entry executable references a set of library components for the individual classes rather than compiling the classes into one component. The user interface application is broken into two html components. The result is a more modular design.

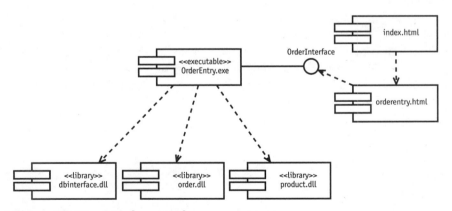

Figure 25-11   *One class equals one component.*

Finally, components can be organized into packages just like other diagrams and model elements. This can be very helpful when managing application distribution. The result is a directory containing all the software elements needed to implement the system or subsystem represented by the package.

Done!

REVIEW

The purpose of the Component diagram is to define software modules and their relationships to one another. Each component is a chunk of code that resides in memory on a piece of hardware.

- The UML groups components into three broad categories:
  - Deployment components, which are required to run the system
  - Work product components including models, source code, and data files used to create deployment components
  - Execution components, which are components created while running the application

- The component icon is a rectangle with two small rectangles on the left edge. The interface to the component may be modeled two different ways:
  - The lollipop notation represents the interface as a small circle connected to the component by a solid line and with the name of the interface near the circle.
  - The second method uses a class with the stereotype <<interface>> with a realizes relationship drawn from the component to the interface class. A component may realize (implement) as many interfaces as it requires.

QUIZ YOURSELF

1. What is a UML component? (See "Explaining the Component Diagram.")
2. What is the icon for a UML component? (See "Defining the Notation for Components and Component Dependencies.")
3. What notation shows that one component needs access to another component? (See "Defining the Notation for Components and Component Dependencies.")
4. What notation is used to show that a component implements an interface? (See "Defining the Notation for Components and Component Dependencies.")
5. True or False: Each component implements a class. (See "Mapping the Logical Design to the Physical Implementation.")

Modeling the Static View: The Deployment Diagram

Session Checklist

✔ Describing the purpose and function of the Deployment diagram

✔ Defining the notation for Deployment diagrams

✔ Mapping software components to an architecture

✔ Applying the combined diagrams to the case study

30 Min. To Go

When the logical design is completed, the next step is to define the physical implementation of your design. The physical implementation must address three different problems: the software, the hardware, and the integration of the two. The Component diagram, from Session 25, is used to model the physical implementation of the software. The Deployment diagram is used to model the physical architecture of the hardware. Combined, they model the distribution of your application software across the hardware implementation.

Describing the Purpose and Function of the Deployment Diagram

The Deployment diagram describes the physical resources in much the way a Class diagram describes logical resources. The focus of the Deployment diagram is the nodes on which your software will run.

Each *node* is a physical object that represents a processing resource. Most often this means a computer of some type, but it may mean a human resource for manual processes. Each node contains, or is responsible for, one or more software components or objects. The software components on different nodes can communicate across the physical *associations* between the nodes.

The purpose of a Deployment diagram is to present a static view, or snapshot, of the implementation environment. A complete description of the system will likely contain a number of different Deployment diagrams, each focused on a different aspect of the system management. For example:

- One diagram might focus on how software components are distributed, such as where the source code resides and where it is shipped for implementation.
- Another diagram might model how the executable is loaded from one node to another node where it actually runs.
- For a multi-tiered application, the Deployment diagram would model the distribution of the application layers, their physical connections, and their logical paths of communication.

 Remember that the Component and Deployment diagrams are relatively new for most people and there are a lot of different ideas out there about how to use them. These tools can be very helpful, but they will not make or break an implementation. Use good judgment. Practice. Find out where the benefits lie for your project. Exploit the tool for your success instead of just following a standard.

Defining the Notation for the Deployment Diagram

By now, the pattern for these physical diagrams should be getting pretty familiar (that is, resources and connections). Just like the Package and Component diagrams, the Deployment diagram has two types of elements: nodes (resources) and associations (connections).

The *node icon* is drawn as a 3D box (the shading is not necessary). Figure 26-1 models four types of nodes: Server, Client, Database Server, and Printer. The lines between the nodes are physical *associations* that are represented as a solid line from one node to another. Use multiplicity notation to define the number of nodes on each end of the association. For example, Figure 26-1 says that each Server is connected to one or more Client nodes, and each Client node is connected to exactly one Server node.

Naming the node associations poses an interesting problem. Because all the associations are physical connections, they could all end up with the same name, "connects to." Instead, you may want to use stereotypes to describe types of connections. Figure 26-1 says that the Server node and Client nodes are connected by an Ethernet connection using the <<Ethernet>> stereotype.

The node is a classifier (like classes, Use Cases, and components), so it can have attributes and specify behaviors in terms of the executables it deploys. Figure 26-2 shows an object-level view of a Deployment diagram. The object-level diagram models instances of each node just as an Object diagram models real entities. The name compartment on top identifies the node name and type, as well as the optional stereotype. The attribute compartment in the middle defines the properties of the node. The operations compartment at the bottom defines the components that run on the node.

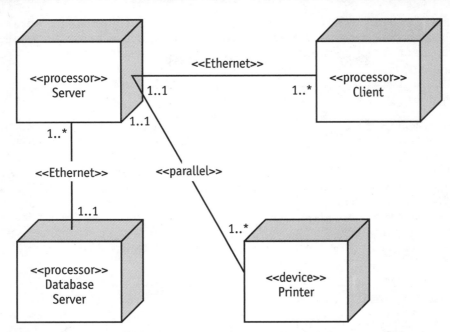

Figure 26-1   *Component diagram with four nodes and three associations*

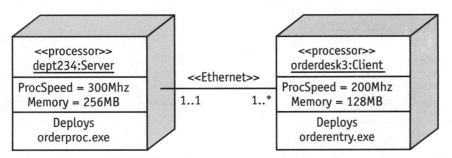

Figure 26-2   *An object-level Deployment diagram*

The object-level view is not supported by many modeling tools even though it is supported by the UML Metamodel.

Draw the Deployment diagram as though each node on your physical architecture is a class on a Class diagram. Each node fulfills a specific purpose. Each node has communication associations with other nodes that represent the physical connections that support communication.

Deployment diagrams can also function like network diagrams to illustrate the make-up of your network. The object-level Deployment diagram can function as a requirements specification for each node, defining the memory, processor, and storage requirements.

**20 Min.
To Go**

Mapping Software Components to an Architecture

The more common technique for modeling the components on a node is to combine the two physical diagram notations for components and nodes. Model the component icons inside the expanded node to show containment. To show the logical communication between the components, draw a dashed dependency arrow just like you did on the Component diagram.

In Figure 26-3, the orderentry.exe resides on the server but is loaded onto the client at runtime. The stereotype <<becomes>> specifies this runtime migration. After the executable is loaded, it depends on the orderproc.exe for help. Note that I could have drawn this at the class level just as easily. But here I am modeling the fact that the logical design represented by the classes has, in fact, been implemented in this physical architecture.

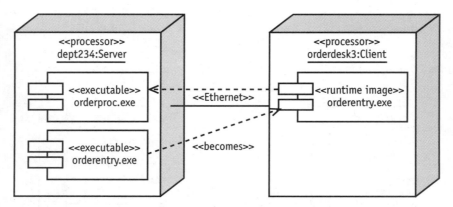

Figure 26-3   *Combined Component and Deployment diagrams*

Applying the Combined Diagrams to the Case Study

In this section, you'll build the combined Deployment and Component diagram for the case study step by step.

1. The hardware architecture consists of three kinds of devices: the client PC, a middle-tier server, and a database server. Draw three nodes, one for each kind of hardware resource (see Figure 26-4).

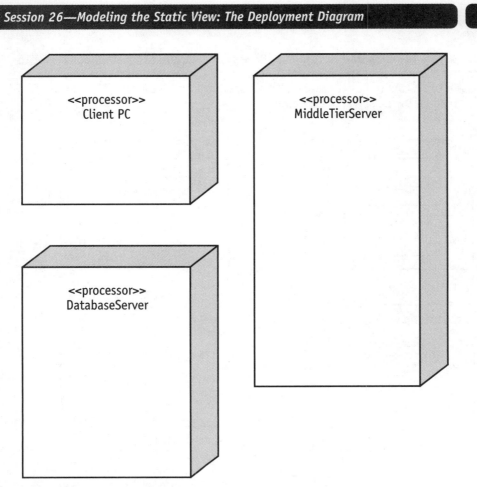

Figure 26-4   *Modeling the three nodes on the Deployment diagram*

2. Each client PC runs a client UI for receiving. Each client PC contains the receiving components (see Figure 26-5).

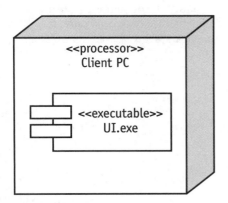

Figure 26-5   *Adding the executable component to the Client node*

3. As shown in Figure 26-6, the client and server nodes are associated, one server to many clients, using an Ethernet connection. The server and database servers are associated, one to one, using an Ethernet connection. The client PC nodes are connected to the server via Ethernet.

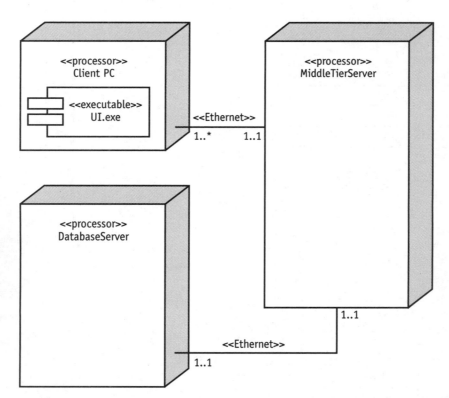

Figure 26-6 *Supplying the node associations to represent the physical connections*

4. The server application uses two resources: the purchase order library and the product library. The server also uses the database access library to communicate with the database server. The server contains three components: the purchase order library component, the product library component, and the database access library component (Figure 26-7).

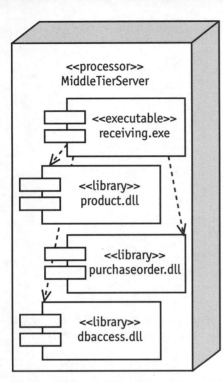

Figure 26-7 *Adding the components (and their dependencies) that reside on the MiddleTierServer node*

5. The database server runs the database management system (DBMS) and the database. The database server node, shown in Figure 26-8, contains the DBMS component and the database component.

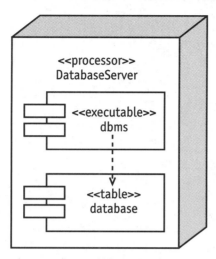

Figure 26-8 *Adding the database management system and the database components to the DatabaseServer node*

6. Show the fact that the UI component needs help from the server-side application. Draw a dashed dependency arrow from the client UI application to the server application component, as in Figure 26-9.

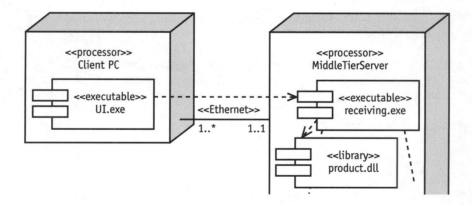

Figure 26-9 *Modeling the logical communication between the components as a dependency from the UI.exe component to the receiving.exe component*

7. Show the fact that the server dbaccess component needs help from the dbms on the database server. There is a dashed dependency arrow from the server dbaccess component to the database server dbms component (Figure 26-10).

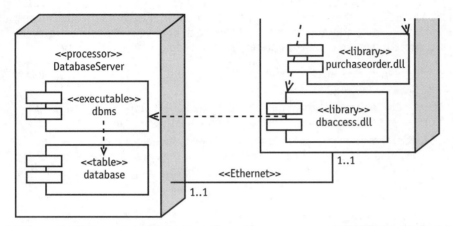

Figure 26-10   *Adding the dependency from the dbaccess.dll component to the database management system component*

The completed Deployment diagram is presented in Figure 26-11.

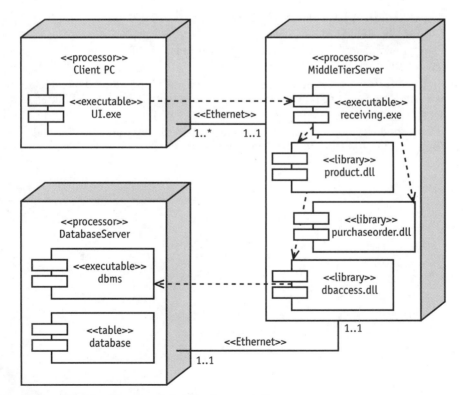

Figure 26-11   *The completed Deployment diagram*

Done!

REVIEW

The Deployment diagram models the hardware architecture by identifying the processors. Processors are typically computers but may also be people who perform manual processing. Nodes, or processors, may contain and run software components. Node connections are modeled as associations, complete with stereotypes for names and multiplicity.

- A node may be modeled like a class with attributes and behaviors. However, many modeling tools do not support this view.
- Component and Deployment diagrams may be combined. Components reside on a node. Component icons are placed inside the expanded node icon.
- Communication between components on the nodes is modeled as dependencies. The dependencies model the logical communication requirements. The nodes model the communication associations that represent the physical communication paths like TCP or Ethernet.

QUIZ YOURSELF

1. What is a node? (See "Describing the Purpose and Function of the Deployment Diagram.")

2. How do you represent the connections between nodes? (See "Defining the Notation for the Deployment Diagram.")

3. What can a node contain? (See "Describing the Purpose and Function of the Deployment Diagram.")

4. What is the difference between an association between nodes and a dependency between components? (See "Defining the Notation for the Deployment Diagram" and "Mapping Software Components to an Architecture.")

5. What elements do you use to define a communication association between nodes? (See "Defining the Notation for the Deployment Diagram.")

PART

V

Sunday Morning Part Review

1. When are you allowed to use an entry action?
2. When are you allowed to use an exit action?
3. What change would cause you to remove an exit action?
4. How do you indicate that an action is to be performed on another object?
5. When an event impacts an object, what type of behavior is interrupted and why doesn't this damage the object?
6. What is a call event?
7. What is a time event?
8. What is a guard condition?
9. What is a change event?
10. How do you model a substate?
11. What is the state of an object? How is it expressed in the UML diagrams?
12. Where would you look to find candidate states on a Sequence diagram?
13. What events illustrated on a Sequence diagram can affect the state of an object?
14. What is the best way to name a state?
15. How many Sequence diagrams are required in order to create a Statechart diagram?
16. Describe two common uses for the Package diagram.
17. What is the purpose of a package stereotype? Give two examples.
18. What is the purpose of a dependency arrow? Give an example.
19. What is the purpose of a dependency stereotype? Give an example.
20. If a package is stereotyped as <<subsystem>>, what can it contain?
21. What is a component?
22. What types of components are defined by the UML?
23. How is an interface specified for a component?

24. How is the relationship modeled between components when one component needs access to another component?

25. What is the relationship between classes and components?

26. What is a node?

27. How do you represent the connections between nodes?

28. What can a node contain?

29. What is the difference between an association between nodes and a dependency between components?

30. How do you name a node?

Introduction to Web Development with Java

Session Checklist

✔ Explaining the challenges that Web development poses to traditional UML modeling

✔ Explaining and illustrating the basic architectural model for Web development

✔ Explaining the Java technologies that can be applied to Web development

✔ Explaining and illustrating Web architectures that lead to high cohesion and maintainability

✔ Explaining how UML can be utilized to model Web systems

**30 Min.
To Go**

Web application development has become one of the most prevalent forms of software development. A whole new industry of Web-based e-commerce businesses (such as Amazon.com) has emerged to utilize the ease and simplicity of the Web to sell merchandise. Many companies that previously used heavy client GUIs for remote access to their databases and other enterprise resources are now using lightweight Web clients to access these resources.

The Value of UML in Web Development

Throughout the second half of the '90s, the initial shortage of Web developers, coupled with the high demand and visions of future wealth, fueled a gold-rush mentality of Web development. In 2000 and 2001, that gold-rush mentality hit its first major crash as slews of dot-com businesses struggled to survive and many traditional businesses reevaluated their unsuccessful Web ventures. One key reason for the crash was the lack of appropriate analysis, design, and modeling of the software. Without proper analysis, many of the Web projects did not meet the business requirements they were designed to support. Without proper design, many of the systems were difficult to adapt and rescale as the business requirements or number of users changed. Without a model of the system, such as a UML model, many of the Web systems were difficult to trace and maintain.

The dot-com crash did not demonstrate that the Web was less useful than people thought; instead it demonstrated that successful Web development necessitates better business planning and better software analysis and design. As a result, the importance of utilizing the UML in Web development is clearer than ever. This session and the two sessions following explore how the UML can be applied to Web development. This session presents an introduction to Web development concepts for those readers who are new to Web development. Session 28 explores design and architectural issues of Web application development. Both of these sessions will use UML diagrams to demonstrate the Web concepts. Session 29 will bring the concepts together by modeling a Web application case study using the UML.

Issues in Using the UML in Web Development

The UML was developed primarily for traditional object-oriented application development. Web applications have several differences from traditional object-oriented applications that require adapting the UML to work with the Web architecture model.

Some of the key aspects of Web development that affect the use of the UML models include

- Web applications almost always involve markup languages such as HTML and XML that are not inherently object-oriented. Session 28 considers some mechanisms that can be used to show an object representation of markup language documents using a Class diagram.

- Web applications are inherently very network-dependent architectures. Consequently, Deployment diagrams are very helpful for modeling Web applications.

- Web applications frequently involve a wide variety of different technologies integrated together. Component diagrams can be very helpful for showing the relationships between these architectures.

- Many Web technologies are not object-oriented, which may lead the reader to think that Sequence diagrams, Collaboration diagrams, Object diagrams, and Class diagrams would be of little use. Nonetheless, these modeling techniques can support the development of highly modular designs that are more easily developed and maintained.

 This session is designed to give readers with no Web development experience a brief introduction to these technologies. If you already have done a lot of Web development, you'll probably want to skim over parts of this session. Take note of how the UML is used in this chapter to show the Web architecture.

Basic Web Architecture and Static Web Content

For simplicity, first consider the static Web content, which is the Web content that never or infrequently changes. Suppose that your company wants to have a Web site that has some fixed text, images, and hyperlinks to other pages. In this case, you would write an HTML page with this content and place it on your Web server. A shell of the HTML page is shown in Listing 27-1. (HTML is a markup language that is composed of plain text accompanied by markup *tags* to specify how to format the text. HTML can be stored in a plain text file and does not need to be compiled or processed in any way before it is placed on the Web server.)

Listing 27-1   *HTML sample*

```
<html>
  <head>
    <title>Next Step Education</title>
  </head>
  <body>
    <h1>Next Step Education</h1>
    (...more content...)
  </body>
</html>
```

 HTML is the most common form of Web content and is the form I focus on in this session. However, this session's discussion of generating and sending HTML can also be applied to other forms of Web content, such as XML for data interchange.

Usually, HTML files are stored on a Web server and loaded over a network such as the Internet. This architecture is shown in the UML Deployment diagram in Figure 27-1. When the user types a URL into a Web browser, the browser needs to communicate with a Web server to get that document, in this case "index.html." The HyperText Transfer Protocol (HTTP) defines the communication protocol for that communication between the Web browser and the Web server.

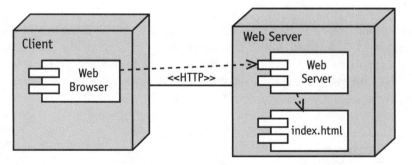

Figure 27-1   *UML Deployment diagram, HTML on a Web server*

The full sequence of events for retrieving a Web document is shown in the UML Sequence diagram in Figure 27-2. When the user enters a URL, the Web browser creates an *HTTP request,* which is a packet of information including the name of the Web server, the name of the document, and other information about the request being made. The Web browser then sends that HTTP request over the network to the Web server that was specified in the URL. The Web Server then looks up the Web page "index.html" and returns it as part of the response.

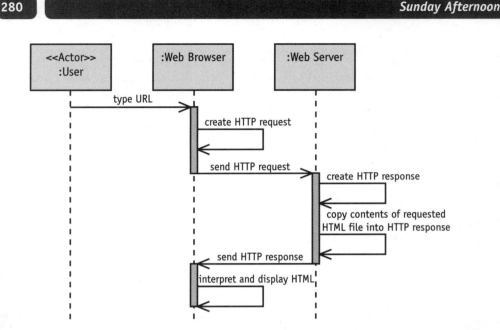

Figure 27-2 *UML Sequence diagram, HTTP protocol*

For example, if the URL entered is `www.nextstepeducation.com/index.html`, the Web request will be sent to the Web server on the machine with a domain name of `www.nextstepeducation.com`. When the Web server receives the request, it will create an HTTP response, which is a packet of information that includes the requested document or error message and other metadata about the response. The Web server will look for the file that was specified in the URL. In the example in Figure 27-2, the Web server will load the index.html file and place the contents of that file into the HTTP response. The Web server will then send the HTTP response back across the network to the Web browser that made the request. The Web browser will take the HTML out of the HTTP response, interpret it, and display the content with the specified formatting.

Some people may question the choice of "objects" in the Sequence diagram in Figure 27-2. In truth, a Web browser is simply a larger, more complex object than a customer or an order. This approach is common practice when modeling interaction between systems (that is, when modeling the systems as objects).

Dynamic Web Content

20 Min.
To Go

The previous section showed how HTTP is used to send static HTML content to Web browsers. Most Web applications require dynamically generated content. For example, when you go to a weather forecast Web site, you don't want it to give you the contents of an HTML file that was saved a month ago; you want it to generate an up-to-date weather forecast for you on the spot and return it to you. Furthermore, you want to be able to access weather information for a certain city. Thus, there must be some programming logic that can take your user input and adapt the result to your request. So a weather Web site would need to have some programming logic that generated the HTML for the HTTP response. The same is true of any e-commerce site where you want to be able to do activities such as search for items, place items in a shopping cart, or make purchases. All those activities require some code on the Web server that reacts to the HTTP request by completing some processing and then returning Web content such as HTML or XML. In reality, almost all modern Web sites include at least a few pages of dynamically generated content.

Consider further how a weather Web site might be implemented. For a moment, if you ignore the Web aspect of this system, imagine how you could write code in almost any programming language to query a database or other information source to gather data on the weather, calculate statistics, generate weather map images, and produce HTML of the results. The only problems that need to be solved are to find a way to trigger that code with an HTTP request arriving at the Web server, and then to have the HTML results placed in an HTTP response and have the HTTP response sent to the Web browser. CGI scripts and Java servlets are two technologies that solve this problem by hooking your code into the HTTP Web protocol.

This general solution is shown in the UML Deployment diagram in Figure 27-3. The diagram refers to your weather reporting code as the Web application code. This code that you have written is just normal code that can do almost any of the normal things you can do in that language, usually including talking to resources such as databases, making calculations, sending e-mails, and outputting HTML, which is included in the HTTP response. You place this code on the Web server and map it to a particular URL. The HTTP protocol will be used in the same way that it was for static content: The Web browser generates an HTTP request object corresponding to the URL entered by the user, and sends that HTTP request to the Web server. The Web server recognizes that this URL was mapped to your Web application code and calls your code to go gather the data and output the Web content into the HTTP response, which is sent back to the Web browser.

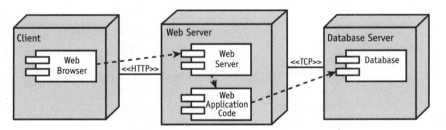

Figure 27-3 *UML Deployment diagram for dynamic Web content*

CGI Scripts were the original solution to the problem of generating dynamic Web content. They allow you to write scripts in a wide variety of languages, including Perl and C. They then provide the mechanism for hooking your script into the HTTP request/response mechanism. CGI Scripts were very commonly used and are still used frequently, although they are gradually being used less in favor of a variety of newer solutions I discuss in the next section.

Java servlets

Java servlets provide the same basic functionality as CGI scripts. They allow you to write a class in Java that will generate the dynamic Web content. Listing 27-2 shows how a Web page that displays the current date could be created as a Java servlet. If you haven't studied Java programming, this example may seem a bit confusing. But the important thing to notice is not the syntax, but how the HTML is generated and placed into the HTTP response (the HTML is the bold text in Listing 27-2). Notice that the servlet is a class and, in this case, it only has one method, which is called doGet. The servlet container will call this method to service the request whenever a Web browser sends an HTTP request for this servlet. The doGet method always takes two parameters that represent the HTTP request coming in and the HTTP response going out. The variable named out is a reference that allows you to write content to the body of the HTTP response. Thus, all the HTML and other content in the out.println method calls is placed into the HTTP response and sent by the Web server back to the Web browser, which displays the HTML. In this case, the Web content is almost all static content, except that it places "new java.util.Date()" into the output. This puts the current date and time onto the Web page. Notice that all the handling of the HTTP response and HTTP request is done behind the scenes. All you have to write is how you want to service the request. Servicing the request could include querying or updating databases, sending e-mails, calling legacy code in other languages using CORBA, or a wealth of other activities that may be accomplished with Java.

Listing 27-2   *Java Servlet*

```
1 import javax.servlet.http.*;
2 import java.io.*;
3 import java.util.*;
4
5 public class DateServlet extends HttpServlet {
6   public void doGet(HttpServletRequest request,
7                     HttpServletResponse response)
8         throws IOException {
9
10    response.setContentType("text/html");
11    PrintWriter out = response.getWriter();
12
13    out.println("<html>");
14    out.println("<head>");
15    out.println("<title>Current Date and Time</title>");
16    out.println("</head>");
17    out.println("<body>");
18    out.println(new Date());
19    out.println("</body>");
20    out.println("</html>");
21
22    out.close();
23  }
24}
```

Java servlets offer a powerful technology for developing dynamic Web content and complete Web applications. Java servlets are simply regular Java classes that follow a few special rules. As a result, servlets have all the traditional benefits of Java. These benefits include cross-platform code that can run on any kind of computer with a Java Virtual Machine (JVM), a fully object-oriented language, and massive libraries of pre-written code to simplify tasks such as database access and remote method invocation.

Despite frequent confusion, Java and JavaScript are very different technologies. JavaScript is a scripting language usually written alongside HTML and executed in the Web browser. JavaScript can be useful for small tasks such as validating form input before it is sent to the server. You could place JavaScript inside of the out.println statements of the Java servlet, just as the HTML was placed in those statements.

Template pages

There is one substantial problem with using servlets in the manner that I just showed. When using servlets for producing Web content such as HTML, you have to place the HTML inside the Java code. Whether you're talking about HTML and Java, SQL and business logic code, or almost any other combination of technologies, mixing different technologies almost always leads to more complicated development and maintenance. It requires that the developer and maintainer of that code be proficient in both technologies. It also means that a change in one of the technologies impacts the other — a symptom of tight coupling, which results in high maintenance costs. Thus, to achieve loose coupling and good maintainability, you should usually try to avoid mixing technologies.

This general principle is particularly true for HTML and Java. There are few people who are both experienced programmers and talented Web content developers. Even if you happen to have both of these skills, developing Web content inside of programming code can be difficult. In addition, maintenance is more difficult because changing the Web page layout requires entering the Java files to change the HTML. CGI scripts have the same drawback of mixing Web content with a programming language. So using servlets or CGI scripts to generate Web content can be costly and awkward, and may lead to low cohesion.

Template pages are a major part of the solution to this development and maintenance problem. Template page technologies such as JSP, ASP.NET, PHP, and Cold Fusion allow you to mix code or special tags inside a markup language page, such as an HTML page.

JavaServer Pages

JavaServer Pages (JSPs) are Java's version of template pages. Listing 27-3 shows a JSP that will produce an identical Web page to the Java servlet in Listing 27-2.

10 Min. To Go

Listing 27-3   *JavaServer Page*

```
<html>
  <head>
    <title>Current Date and Time</title>
  </head>
  <body>
    <%=new java.util.Date()%>
  </body>
</html>
```

If you glance too briefly at this JSP page, you may mistake it for an HTML page. In fact, it is all HTML except for line 6, which is a line of Java code that inserts the current date and time. A JSP page is composed of your Web content, such as HTML, with Java code inter-mixed to insert the dynamic content. Comparing the Java servlet in Listing 27-2 and the JSP page in Listing 27-3, you can probably see why JSP code is usually far easier to write and develop than a servlet for producing Web content. A JSP page generally has less compli-cated Java logic, is usually easier to read, and is much easier to maintain. A JSP page also doesn't need to be compiled by the programmer and may be easier to deploy into the Web server, which makes the development and maintenance process a bit simpler. Other template page technologies like ASP, PHP, and Cold Fusion work in a similar way, although each has its own specific features, advantages, and disadvantages.

It is worth noting that JavaServer Pages turn into servlets. The JSP container class auto-matically writes a Java servlet much like the one in Listing 27-2 (although significantly harder to read) that has the same functionality as the JSP page that you wrote. All requests for your JSP page will actually be handled by the Java servlet that represents it. Thus, JSP is simply an easy way to write a Java servlet without having to write as much Java code. The UML state diagram in Figure 27-4 explains this. The programmer writes a JSP. At or before the first request for that JSP, the JSP container automatically writes the servlet that represents that JSP and compiles it. From this point on, the lifecycle of a JSP is the same as a servlet. When a request comes in, the servlet will be instantiated and the same instance of the servlet will be used for all requests until the JSP container decides that the servlet should be unloaded, usually due to the container shutting down or a long period with no requests for that JSP. If the programmer changes the JSP, that servlet will be permanently unloaded and the lifecycle starts over with the new version of the JSP being translated.

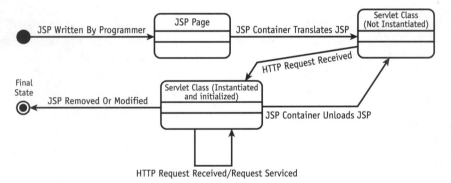

Figure 27-4 *UML state diagram, JSP Lifecycle*

You may think that writing only JSPs, as opposed to writing servlets, would be easier, but that isn't actually the case. If you need to write a servlet or JSP that primarily gener-ates Web content, then it will almost always be easier to write it as a JSP. If you need to write a servlet or JSP that has a lot of logic and generates very little or no content, then it will usually be easier to write it as a servlet.

Done!

REVIEW

The UML is a useful tool for modeling Web systems. The UML was not designed for the purpose of modeling Web systems, so some adaptations must be made.

- Non–object-oriented technologies are often viewed as objects in order to demonstrate their characteristics and behaviors in Class, Sequence, and Collaboration diagrams. Non–object-oriented hierarchies such as XML may be mapped to class hierarchies in a Class diagram to represent their structure.

- Sequence or Collaboration diagrams can model the interactions of architecture elements like Web browsers, Web applications, and HTML pages. Component diagrams are frequently used to show how mixed technologies are integrated.

- Component diagrams can model the relationships between the architecture elements.

- Deployment diagrams are frequently used to show the network aspects of a Web system.

- The basic Web architecture is based on a request/response protocol called HyperText Transfer Protocol (HTTP). Web browsers make HTTP requests to Web servers, which generate or load Web content such as HTML and return it to the Web browser. This communication is often modeled using a Sequence or Collaboration diagram.

- CGI scripts, Java servlets, and JavaServer Pages (JSP) are just a few of the wide variety of technologies that you can use to dynamically generate Web content. Both Java servlets and JSPs provide the power and flexibility of the Java language for dynamic Web development. JSPs are easier to code, debug, and maintain for pages that are exclusively or primarily producing Web content. Java servlets are easier to code, debug, and maintain when they are generating little or no Web content.

QUIZ YOURSELF

1. What makes modeling a Web application in UML different from modeling a non-Web application? (See "Issues in Using the UML in Web Development.")

2. What UML diagram could you use to model the communication between a Web browser and a Web server? (See "Basic Web Architecture and Static Web Content.")

3. What UML diagram would you use to model the lifecycle of a JSP? (See "JavaServer Pages.")

4. What UML diagram could you use to model how components of your system are deployed on the client machine and on the Web server? (See "Dynamic Web Content.")

Analysis and Architectural Design of a Web Application

Session Checklist

✔ Explaining how requirements gathering and analysis are done in a Web system

✔ Explaining the Model View Controller design principle

✔ Illustrating how the View and Controller can be separated in a Java Web application

✔ Explaining and illustrating how UML can be used in the analysis and architectural design of a Web system

**30 Min.
To Go**

Congratulations! You have almost completed your UML crash course. This weekend, you have learned an incredible spectrum of techniques and strategies for using the UML to model and develop applications. Sessions 28 and 29 will demonstrate how to model a Web application from start to finish. You'll see that the process of modeling a Web application is primarily the same process used to model any application, but I will also point out some special tricks and techniques that you can apply to Web modeling with the UML.

The Friendly Reminder Case Study

Sessions 28 and 29 will consider the development of a project that is a typical Web application. In this project, your contracting firm is asked by a software company to develop a Web component for its existing Visual Basic application, which is called Friendly Reminder. The client's initial project specification states that the current Friendly Reminder system allows users to track their appointments and contacts by allowing them to

- Enter contact data such as names, phone numbers, and addresses.
- Enter appointment data such as date, time, and description.
- Associate contacts with appointments.
- Search for specific contacts or appointments.
- Receive notification when an appointment is approaching.

The current system is a standalone application with no network component. Friendly Reminder is a well-established product with a loyal customer base, but the company has received many requests from users who would like to be able to view their appointments on the World Wide Web. The customers complain that they have no way to check appointments when they're away from their own computer. The client's initial project specification requests that you develop a small application that will allow their users to

- Upload all their appointments and contacts to a server where they can be remotely accessed.
- Query those appointments and contacts whenever and from wherever they wish.

Requirements Gathering

Regardless of whether you're developing a Web or standalone application, the requirements-gathering phase is a process of careful communication with the client to discover and document the business requirements and to ensure that the development team knows what it must create in order for the customer to be successful.

In the case study, the clients required that users be able to upload all their appointments and contacts to a server where they can later access them remotely. Because the client is a very conservative company and is a little bit apprehensive about moving onto the Web, it specifies a constraint that the new system must pose the smallest possible risk to the reliability of their current system. Because the current application has no network component, all appointments are stored in a file on the user's machine. Based on this experience, the client adds a constraint that all appointments must still be saved on the local machine while a *copy* of the appointment data can be uploaded to a server for remote access. Also due to its apprehension, the company wants to limit users to entering appointments only in the existing Visual Basic application and not on the Web.

In these discussions, we also find out that the users have been requesting access to their appointments and contacts from traditional wired Web devices such as PCs, as well as from wireless devices like cell phones. After some discussion, this is identified as a key functional requirement that can be fulfilled and will be factored into the cost of the project.

In design, as you craft a solution to these requirements, the technological options are more critical and more extensive in a Web system than a standalone system. Here are some of the factors you should consider when evaluating technology in a Web system:

- **Availability and reliability:** Must the system be available 24/7 with virtually no failures? It is possible to make a Web system that almost never fails or is never unavailable, but that kind of reliability comes at a substantial cost. In the case study, the client protects the reliability of the current system by specifying that the Web system only keep a duplicate of the data and that nothing in the standalone system should be dependent on the new Web system.

- **Performance:** How rapidly must the system reply to user requests? Web systems sometimes have more performance limitations than standalone systems. The client specifies constraints for the responsiveness of the system.

- **Scalability:** How many concurrent users must the system be able to support now and in the future? Many Web systems can be bombarded with hundreds or thousands of concurrent users. To keep the project cost lower, the clients decide that moderate growth potential (scalability) is acceptable for now as long as the system is easily adaptable to a more scalable solution in the future.

- **Security:** How much and what kind of security protection is required? Any kind of networked system can potentially be very vulnerable to malicious attacks. As is true with most requirements, the greater the security, the greater the cost of the software and hardware. The client wants to ensure reasonable security and defines the budget limitations accordingly.

- **Adaptability:** How easy should it be to modify the system to meet new requirements? A more adaptable system will generally be far less expensive to maintain in the long run and may survive longer before it becomes obsolete. However, developing a system with high adaptability takes more time and money. The client has put a very high priority on high adaptability because it expects that this is just the first cautious step onto the Web and the company expects to add a lot more functionality to this system later.

For a detailed description of the requirements gathering process and the problem statement, see Session 4.

Creating the Use Case diagram

During the requirements-gathering phase for this project, you will again develop a Use Case model. This model will not be fundamentally different for a Web system than it is for a non-Web system. The Use Case model helps you to better understand who will use your system and what features they will use. Figure 28-1 shows the Use Case diagram for the case study. There is a Use Case for the user to *create an account* that will allow him to *log in* so that he can store and query his appointments and contacts. The *Upload Appointments and Contacts* Use Case will upload a copy of his appointment and contact data onto the Web server for querying. The user has a general Use Case for *querying his appointments* and another for *querying his contacts.*

Customers using wireless devices such as cell phones will require a different kind of markup language and will require very different interfaces for the querying to make it usable on these very limited devices. The requirements-gathering team decided that the functional differences between traditional wired Web clients (like desktop and laptop computers) and wireless Web clients (like cell phones) justified separate Use Cases. However, because they are similar, you show a Use Case generalization to indicate that the four specific querying Use Cases inherit from the two general querying Use Cases. All the querying and uploading Use Cases are extended by the Log In Use Case, because the user must be logged in to run any of these Use Cases.

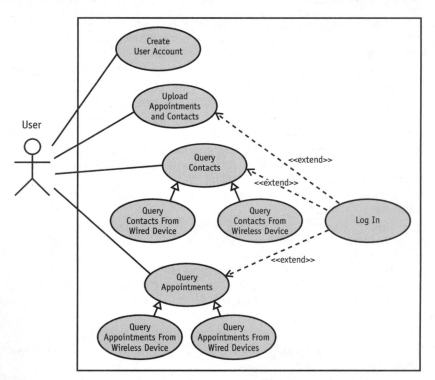

Figure 28-1 UML Use Case diagram, Friendly Reminder system

The requirements-gathering team then develops the details behind each of these Use Cases by developing Use Case narratives and possibly Activity diagrams. They also find all the Use Case scenarios for each Use Case to provide the basis for the test plan.

 The steps for developing Use Case narratives and finding Use Case scenarios for a test plan are outlined in Sessions 7 and 8.

Analysis

20 Min. To Go

In the requirements-gathering phase, you considered what the system must do to meet the needs of the client. In the analysis phase, you expand your understanding of the business problem and create a Class diagram that represents the business problem. Because the analysis phase is more about the business problem than the technical solution to that problem, this phase, like the previous one, will be essentially the same for Web and non-Web applications.

In this case study, one of the areas you need to analyze is how appointments are represented in the system. Through an analysis of the existing system and the business problem, the analysts create a conceptual Class diagram of The Friendly Reminder appointments and contacts. This diagram is shown in Figure 28-2. A User makes zero to many Appointments and tracks zero to many Contacts. Each Appointment has a date, time, description, priority, notes, and Contacts related to that Appointment. A Contact is anybody about whom the customer wants to store information such as name, home phone, work phone, e-mail, notes, and addresses. A Contact has two associations to the Address class, one for a home address and one for a work address.

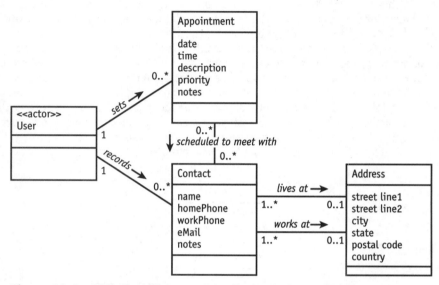

Figure 28-2   *UML Class diagram, Friendly Reminder appointments*

Architectural Design

The design phase is the point at which the design team will see how to utilize the Web and non-Web technologies to meet the customer's requirements. The UML will help them to visualize and specify their decisions.

During the initial design phase, some major architectural decisions need to be made. The project architect decides to use Java servlets and JavaServer Pages for the Web implementation because of their flexibility and robustness, and because of the development team's extensive Java experience. In return for these advantages, the team pays a small performance hit compared to some of the other Web technologies, but they believe they can easily compensate for that with an efficient design and good hardware.

Model View Controller

In the last session, I explained that for high cohesion and ease of maintainability, it is always advisable to keep the different technological aspects and functional aspects of your system in different classes or segments of code. You can take this recommendation a step further by considering the Model View Controller (MVC) design pattern. MVC recommends that you keep three aspects of your code separate:

- **Model:** The code for dealing with the data model, database logic, and direct manipulation of the data
- **View:** The user interface or presentation of the data viewed by the user

- **Controller:** The code that reacts to user requests, modifies the data, and controls the flow of the application

This basic structure is shown in Figure 28-3. MVC may be applied to almost any application you develop, whether it is Web based or not. For a non-Web application, your application may have a set of classes for your data model that coordinate database access and data manipulation, another set of classes for your GUI views, and a third set of classes for your controlling event-handling code. One of the most important advantages of MVC is that it allows you to more easily change one aspect of the system without affecting the other aspects, exemplifying loose coupling. For example, you may want to offer different interfaces for the traditional wired Web devices and the wireless devices without changing or duplicating the data model. If you have intermixed your database access with your GUI code, then changing the GUI without changing the data model will be much more difficult. Because the programmer who is good at writing data model code is likely not the same programmer who is good at writing GUI view code, another advantage of MVC is that it simplifies the independent development of these components.

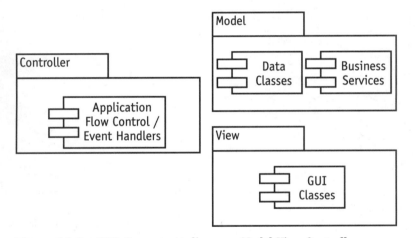

Figure 28-3   *UML Component diagram, Model View Controller*

In Web development, the view is the Web content such as HTML. The model is the business logic for data manipulation and database access and is usually written in a programming language like Java. The controller is the code for verifying the data coming in from the HTTP request, interacting with the data model, and selecting the next view (Web page) to be sent to the user. Just as in non-Web application development, separating these three aspects will greatly simplify your maintenance and improve both cohesion and coupling. In the remaining portion of this session, you separate the model from the view. In Session 29, you separate out the controller.

JavaBeans

The JSP in Session 27 contained an unusually small amount of Java code because it had extremely little dynamic content, but most JSPs will have to use a lot more Java code for querying and updating databases, calculating data, and other operations. The result is that you have a lot of Java code inside your Web content. With this usage, a JSP is really just a servlet turned inside out; instead of having HTML in your Java, you have Java in your HTML. So simply switching from servlets to JSPs isn't enough to successfully separate your HTML view from your Java model and controller. Thus, there must be another way to get the Java code out of the JSP pages.

A simple solution to this problem would be to move any large chunks of Java code from your JSP page into regular Java classes and have your JSP page contain method calls to the methods in those classes. This would remove a very large quantity of Java code from the JSP, but the JSP page would still have Java syntax method calls in it. JavaBeans represent a refinement of this solution. For this purpose, a JavaBean is just a regular Java class with private attributes and public get/set methods for accessing the attributes. Figure 28-4 shows a UML Class diagram of a simple JavaBean for tracking a customer order. Creating a JavaBean is as simple as it sounds; with proper encapsulation, you will probably meet the requirements of JavaBeans without even trying.

OrderBean
- item: String - quantity: int - costPerItem: double
+ setItem (i: String): void + getItem (): String + setQuantity (q : int): void + getQuantity () : int + setCostPerItem (c : double) : void + getCostPerItem () : double + getTotalCost () : double + submitOrder () : boolean

Figure 28-4   *UML Class diagram, JavaBean*

JSP has special markup tags that can be used to call the get and set methods of the JavaBean. Thus, the Java syntax method calls can be replaced with markup tags. For example, the Java syntax and the JSP tag syntax shown here are equivalent method calls, but it may be easier for a content developer to use the JSP tag syntax.

- Java Syntax: `<% order.setItem("UML Weekend Crash Course"); %>`
- JSP Tag Syntax: `<jsp:setProperty name="order" property="item" value="UML Weekend Crash Course"/>`

Typically, the code that you move from the JSP pages into JavaBeans will include your application data, database access code, and business services. What is left in your JSP is largely the Web content, which is the view of that data. Thus, by using JavaBeans, you can separate your view from your model and take the first step towards an MVC Web architecture.

This section addresses JavaBeans, not Enterprise JavaBeans (EJB). EJB is a far-more-involved technology and is beyond the scope of this book.

MVC pattern in the case study

**10 Min.
To Go**

The case study requirements specify that users must be able to query their appointments and contacts from both traditional wired Web clients and wireless Web clients such as cell phones. For the wired Web clients, customers will access the system via Web browsers such as Internet Explorer or Netscape Navigator and the system will generate HTML for those Web browsers to display.

Wireless devices such as cell phones usually have extremely limited display capabilities, very limited input devices such as keypads, limited network bandwidth, and unreliable network availability. As a result of these limitations, they have their own browsers, protocol, and markup languages for their special requirements. In North America, most wireless Web clients have a micro Web browser that communicates via the WAP protocol and interprets Wireless Markup Language (WML). WML looks very similar to HTML, but it is more compact and more limited to meet the needs of the restricted wireless devices. Because most of the case study wireless users have devices that use WML, the architects decide to use that for the wireless interface.

The system requires two views for interfaces to the querying parts of the application: an HTML view for traditional wired Web clients and a WML view for wireless Web clients. In addition, the layout and flow of those views are different because wireless Web clients must be carefully designed to be easily usable on limited devices. On the other hand, the fundamental business logic and data business services are the same for both interfaces. The Model View Controller design pattern principles make this a very simple problem to resolve. Because your JSPs are the view of the system, there are two sets of JSPs: one with HTML content, and one with WML content. Both sets of JSPs talk to the same JavaBeans for the business logic and data manipulation. This is shown in the UML Component diagram in Figure 28-5.

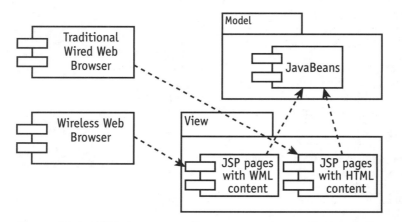

Figure 28-5　*UML Component diagram, two views with MVC design*

The next thing to consider is whether the system requires any special software or hardware configuration to communicate with the wireless Web clients. Wireless Web clients communicate using the WAP protocol instead of the HTTP protocol. Because traditional Web servers are designed to communicate using the HTTP protocol, you might reasonably think that the system would need another Web server that uses a WAP protocol. In fact, it can still use a regular HTTP Web server. The wireless network providers have systems called WAP

Gateways that translate between WAP and HTTP. All you have to do is write JSP pages containing WML, specify the MIME content type for WML, and place them on your normal Web server. The WAP Gateway, which is usually provided by the wireless network provider, not by you, automatically takes care of the rest. Figure 28-6 shows a Deployment diagram with the hardware (traditional wired device, wireless device, WAP Gateway, and the Web Server). The components from Figure 28-5 are placed onto the nodes of the Deployment diagram to show where they will reside.

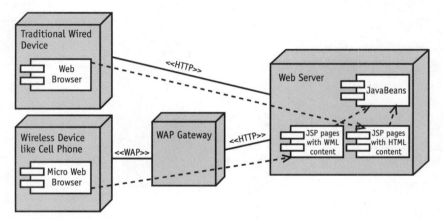

Figure 28-6 *UML Deployment diagram, WAP Gateway*

Done!

REVIEW

- Because requirements gathering and analysis are more about the business problem than the technical solution to it, the process for these phases should not be any different for a Web system than for a non-Web system. One exception to this general rule is that the customer should consider additional technological factors such as scalability, reliability, availability, performance, and security — considerations that may not be as important when designing a standalone system.

- The Model View Controller (MVC) design pattern simplifies development and enhances maintainability by separating the data model, user interface views, and controller logic aspects of your system. MVC can be adapted to Java Web applications by separating the model into JavaBeans and the view into JSP pages. Session 29 will show you how to separate out the controller. MVC also makes it easier to have two views, such as a WML view and an HTML view.

QUIZ YOURSELF

1. What additional kinds of technological factors should a customer consider with a Web system? (See "Requirements Gathering.")
2. Which UML diagram would you use to model a resource like a JavaBean? (See "JavaBeans.")

3. How would you use the Component diagram in the development of a Web system? (See "MVC pattern in the case study.")

4. What is the purpose of the Model View Controller (MVC) pattern? (See "Model View Controller.")

Design of a Web Application

30 Min. To Go

I n the last session, you partially implemented a Web Model View Controller (MVC) design by separating out the model into JavaBeans and the view into JSPs. This partial implementation of the MVC pattern provides significant advantages: independent development, better cohesion, and easier maintainability. For a full MVC architecture, though, you need to know how to separate out the controller elements as well.

Model 2 Architecture

The Model 2 Architecture was presented by Sun Microsystems in the early versions of the servlet specification. It is now a popularly used and discussed Model View Controller architecture for Java Web applications. The Model 2 Architecture is an MVC architecture that will separate out the controller elements. This architecture is shown in the UML Component diagram in Figure 29-1 and the UML Sequence diagram in Figure 29-2. The Model 2 Architecture separates the model (JavaBeans) and the view (JSPs) just as you did in the last session. In addition, it has a single servlet used as the controller. All HTTP requests for any part of the Web application will be directed to this controller servlet. The servlet will verify the input data from the HTTP request and call methods on the JavaBeans to update the data model. The servlet controller will then forward the request on to a JSP that will render the view. The JSP will access the JavaBeans to get the data that should appear on the Web page.

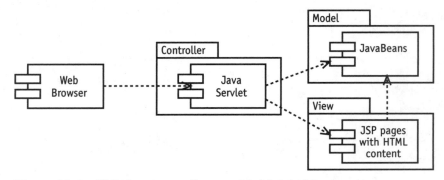

Figure 29-1   *UML Component diagram, Model 2 Architecture*

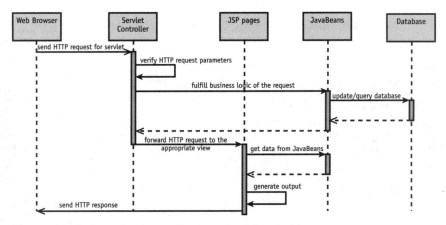

Figure 29-2   *UML Sequence diagram, Model 2 Architecture*

The controller servlet of the Model 2 Architecture offers some additional benefits beyond the high cohesion and good maintainability of MVC. Because all requests for the Web application come through one servlet, the developer can place generic security checks and audit logging code in the servlet and that code will be run for any request for any part of the Web application.

In the discussion of the case study in Session 28, the two JSP views were separated from the model. For a full Model 2 Architecture, the development team now adds a single servlet that will receive all requests that are sent by the Web browser for any part of the Web application. In this case, the development team decides that having separate controllers for the wired Web clients and wireless Web clients could enhance maintainability. Thus, they use two servlet controllers instead of the usual one. Their new architecture is shown in Figure 29-3.

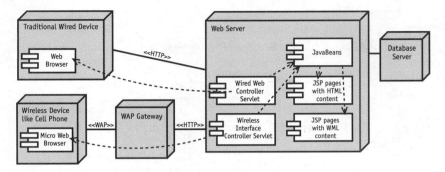

Figure 29-3   *UML Deployment diagram, Model 2 Architecture*

Uploading Appointments and Contacts

The case study architectural team has now completed the architecture for querying appointments and contacts. They now consider the architecture needed to allow the customers to upload their appointments and contacts from the existing Visual Basic application to the database on the server. Having the existing Visual Basic application communicate directly to the database could decrease the security of the system. It could also decrease adaptability, because changing the database logic would then require distributing a new version of the client application to the users. Instead, the project designers decide to have the Visual Basic application trigger a Java servlet that will insert the data in the database. You may wonder how Microsoft Visual Basic can talk to a Java servlet. This is actually no problem; any kind of system that can generate an HTTP request can talk to a servlet. Visual Basic, like most programming environments, is perfectly capable of generating an HTTP request to communicate to a Java servlet.

The designers could have the Visual Basic application communicate with one of the controller servlets in the current architecture, but they decide it would be more cohesive to create a new servlet for this purpose. This servlet will not use any JSP pages because it will not be returning any HTML or other Web content to the Visual Basic client. The Visual Basic client sends all the appointment and contact data to the Java servlet, the servlet saves the data to the database, and it returns back to the Visual Basic application the number of records saved. This is shown in the UML Deployment diagram in Figure 29-4. The design team then considers what format to send the data in. They want a clear, verifiable, adaptable format. Because XML meets all these requirements and is an excellent way to send data between systems, they decide to send the appointment and contact data in an XML format.

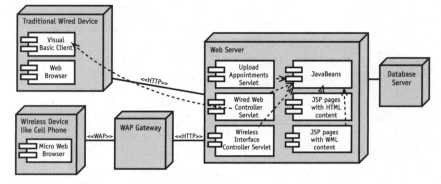

Figure 29-4   *UML Deployment diagram, Visual Basic client*

Detailed Design

**20 Min.
To Go**

The design team has now completed the high-level architectural design of the system. They have chosen the technologies that they will be using and the organization of those technologies required to solve the business problem. In the detailed design, they will specify how each individual part of the system will be implemented. The Component and Deployment diagrams illustrate how the different Web technologies will be organized. In the detailed design, the component and deployment diagrams will be used less and the Class, Object, Sequence, and Collaboration diagrams will tend to be used more.

Querying appointments and contacts

In the detailed design phase, the designers want to create a roadmap for the programmers, specifying how the browsers, servlets, JSP pages, JavaBeans, and databases will work together to allow customers to query for appointments and contacts. Because there isn't space or time to explore the entire detailed design, we will focus on the design of appointment querying by customers using traditional wired Web clients.

The development team first makes the Collaboration diagram in Figure 29-5 to show how the user will move from one Web page to another. This particular diagram is not meant to show the inner workings of the system. Because it only shows what the user will see, this diagram will only contain JSP pages. The diagram shows that the user must use the Login JSP page to log in prior to accessing the AppointmentQueryForm JSP page. This form will allow the user to enter criteria for the appointments he wants to search for. When he submits the query form, if there are matching results, he will be sent to the AppointmentQueryResults JSP page, which will display those results. If there are no matching results, he will be sent to the No Appointments JSP page, which will inform him that there were no matches to his query.

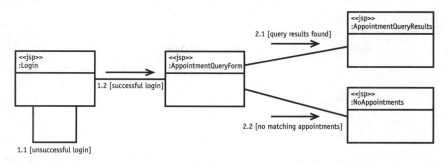

Figure 29-5   *UML Collaboration diagram, querying appointments page flow*

The design team now wants to model how the appointment querying shown in the last diagram will be implemented in the system. For this purpose, they develop the Sequence diagram in Figure 29-6 that shows all the components involved. For simplicity, they chose not to show the Login process, but instead to begin this Sequence diagram with the request for the query form. All requests from the Web browser go to the controller servlet. The initial request to the servlet is forwarded to the AppointmentQueryForm JSP page so the user will be presented with the query form to make his request. When the user fills out and submits that form, the servlet sends the query request to the JavaBeans to run the query and return the results. If the query bean returns some appointments, then the request is forwarded to the AppointmentQueryResults JSP page so that the user will see the matching appointments. If there were no matching results, then the request is forwarded to the NoAppointments JSP page.

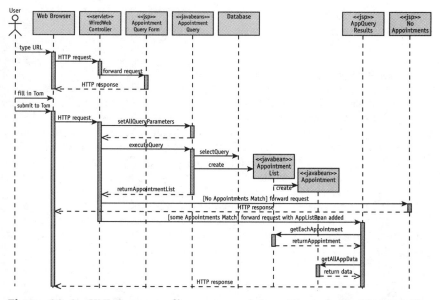

Figure 29-6   *UML Sequence diagram, appointment querying implementation*

Web technologies on an implementation Class diagram

Sometimes you may wish to show JSP pages, servlets, HTML content, JavaScript, and other Web technologies on a Class diagram. Figure 29-7 shows some ways you can include these technologies on a Class diagram. Servlets are regular classes in Java, so they can be shown normally on the Class diagram. JSP pages are represented by servlets, so you could simply represent the servlet class that is generated from the JSP page. In the Class diagram, I chose to show the JSP page without detailing any attributes or methods. The servlets don't have an association with the JSP pages, but they have a dependency based on the fact that they redirect the HTTP request to the JSP page. The diagram also shows that the JSP page builds the HTML page and that the HTML page contains an HTML form and some JavaScript. Each of the classes has a stereotype to show what kind of technology it is.

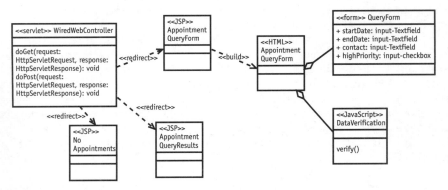

Figure 29-7   *UML Class diagram with Web technologies*

XML

**10 Min.
To Go**

Although only a few years old, XML has become extremely popular and is being used for data transfer in more and more systems. XML is an excellent way to transfer data between systems. An XML document holds data that is being stored or transferred. XML documents can be validated with an XML schema or DTD. (For simplicity, I won't go into the distinction between the two; instead, I will just use schema.) The schema defines the rules for all documents of a certain type. Thus, the relationship of schemas and documents is like the relationship of a UML Class diagram and an Object diagram. An Object diagram shows a set of objects that follow the rules and relationships defined on a Class diagram. Likewise, an XML document has a set of data that follows the rules and relationships defined by the XML schema. An XML schema can specify what data will be stored in the documents, the structural associations between the data, the multiplicities of how many of one type of data entities are associated to another type, and the types of the data.

The advantages of using XML include:

- XML is a simple and effective way to store data.
- Validation tools can automatically validate an XML document against a schema.
- Parsing tools can automatically parse the data out of an XML document.
- Schemas allow you to standardize the structure of the data so that a whole industry can agree to share data in one standard format.

- XML documents can be shared easily by virtually any combination of programming environments.

UML modeling of XML

XML has a hierarchical structure that can be modeled as an object hierarchy in the UML using generalization in a Class diagram. XML schemas can be generated from UML Class diagrams, and XML documents can be generated from UML Object diagrams. The Object Management Group (OMG), which maintains the UML Specification, also maintains the XML MetaData Interchange (XMI) specification. This specification describes a standard for mapping UML models into XML. The primary purpose of this specification is to create an industry standard for UML modeling tools to share UML models.

Many UML tools now have an option to save your UML model as an XML file in accordance with XMI. That means that you can start developing your UML model in one UML modeling tool, save it in this standard format, and then load it in any other UML modeling tool that supports the XMI specification. XMI functionality is also useful for the purpose of generating XML schemas and documents for an application based on the application UML model.

Appointment XML in the case study

The architecture team decided to use XML to transfer the appointment and contact data from the existing Visual Basic application to the Java servlet that will save the data to the database. Now the designers have to come up with the XML document structure and schema that represents the format for how the data will be sent. The first thing they do is refine their analysis Class diagram from Figure 28-2, which showed how appointments and contacts were related. Figure 29-8 shows a simplified portion of that Class diagram. To prepare to generate the XML, the designers ensure that no attributes or associations are missing, that all attributes have data types, that the direction of traversal arrows is shown, and that role names have been specified. The team also adds an enumeration called PriorityLevel, which specifies the legal values for the priority attribute of the Appointment class.

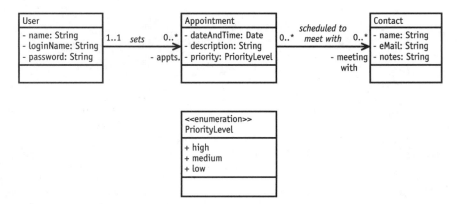

Figure 29-8   *UML Class diagram for XML modeling*

As mentioned earlier, UML Class diagrams are comparable to XML schemas. Both define the rules for how data is organized. The development team can use their modeling tool's XMI functionality to automatically generate an XML schema from the Class diagram, or they can generate it by hand. I don't show the XML schema here because reading XML schemas is a large topic in and of itself. Instead, I show a sample XML document. The UML Object diagram in Figure 29-9 is a valid instantiation of the Class diagram in Figure 29-8 and has the same data and structure as this XML document.

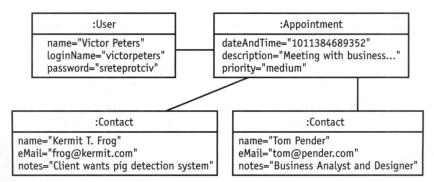

Figure 29-9   *UML Object diagram*

The Object diagram in Figure 29-9 maps to the XML document in Listing 29-1. The User object becomes the <user> element. That element contains one sub-element for each attribute of the user class. Each attribute, like <User.name>, has the value of the attribute followed by an end tag </User.name>. The link from User to Appointment is shown as a sub-element of the <user> element and contains all the attributes in the Appointment class. Notice that the dateAndTime (stored in Java milliseconds format) and priority are attributes instead of being separate elements because they are simple values.

Listing 29-1   *XML for the Appointments Object diagram*

```
<User>
 <User.name>Victor Peters</User.name>
 <User.loginName>victorpeters</User.loginName>
 <User.password>sreteprotciv</User.password>
 <User.appt>
  <Appointment dateAndTime="1011384689352" priority="medium">
<Appointment.description>Meeting with business analyst and client
</Appointment.description>
   <Appointment.meetingWith>
    <Contact>
     <Contact.name>Kermit T. Frog</Contact.name>
     <Contact.eMail>frog@kermit.com</Contact.eMail>
     <Contact.notes>Client wants pig detection system</Contact.notes>
    </Contact>
   </Appointment.meetingWith>
   <Appointment.meetingWith>
    <Contact>
```

```
            <Contact.name>Tom Pender</Contact.name>
            <Contact.eMail>tom@pender.com</Contact.eMail>
            <Contact.notes>Business Analyst and Designer</Contact.notes>
          </Contact>
        </Appointment.meetingWith>
      </Appointment>
    </User.appt>
  </User>
```

Web Application Extension

Jim Conallen of Rational Software created an extension to the Unified Modeling Language to facilitate Web modeling in UML. He devised a set of strategies, stereotypes, and icons for UML Web modeling. This extension is called the Web Application Extension (WAE). These three sessions do not explicitly use the WAE, because you may be using tools that do not support WAE. On the other hand, the strategies recommended in these sessions are completely compatible with the WAE. Reading about the WAE may give you a few extra strategies for enhancing your UML Web models. In addition, WAE recommends a set of icons that can be used in UML diagrams instead of using textual stereotypes. For example, rather than using the standard component with a <<servlet>> stereotype shown on the left in Figure 29-10, you could use the WAE servlet icon shown in Figure 29-10 on the right.

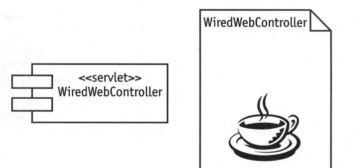

Figure 29-10 *Standard UML component with <<servlet>> stereotype and WAE servlet icon*

Many tools, such as Rational Rose and Popkin's System Architect, support WAE. Check the Help file of your UML modeling tool to see if and how it supports WAE. You can also get more information from Jim Conallen's Web site at `www.conallen.com/technologyCorner/Webextension/welcome.html` or do an Internet search on "WAE UML."

Done!

REVIEW

- The Model 2 Architecture is an MVC architecture for Java Web development. JavaBeans are used for the data model and business data services. JSP pages are used to display the view of the data. A single Java servlet is used for the controller, which verifies HTTP parameters, prompts the JavaBeans to do business processing, and selects a JSP page view to be returned to the user. No matter what technologies you use to develop Web applications, you can apply the goals and concepts of the Model 2 Architecture. In particular, keep your Web content separate from your business logic and controller code whenever possible.

- UML Deployment and Collaboration diagrams are very handy for showing the architecture of your Web application. UML Sequence, Collaboration, Class, and Object diagrams are useful for showing the details of your Web application design. Sometimes, to get the most use out of these diagrams, you'll need to be a bit liberal with the definition of *class* or *object* when deciding what you can place on a diagram. Remember: The goal of UML is to be useful, so although you shouldn't recklessly abuse the rules of UML, you can bend them to meet your individual needs.

- XML hierarchies can be shown in UML. An XML schema can be generated from an XML Class diagram, and an XML document can be generated from a UML Object diagram. XMI is an OMG specification for mapping UML to XML.

QUIZ YOURSELF

1. What does MVC stand for when describing the MVC pattern? (See "Model 2 Architecture.")
2. What two diagrams can be used to show how the Web components talk to each other during execution of the application? (See "Querying appointments and contacts.")
3. How would you model the XML structure used in your Web application? (See "Appointment XML in the case study.")
4. What diagram could represent the instantiation of an XML document? (See "Appointment XML in the case study.")
5. Has anyone come up with a standard way of using the UML to model Web applications? (See "Web Application Extension.")

UML Modeling Tools

Session Checklist

✔ Explaining the purpose and function of modeling tools

✔ Explaining evaluation criteria for modeling tools

✔ Evaluating UML modeling tools

**30 Min.
To Go**

Y ou have undoubtedly found that working with the UML diagrams by hand can be time-consuming and difficult. The problem increases in complexity when you attempt to maintain the integration between the models. You are not alone. Many people in the industry have come to appreciate the value of the modeling tools but have been hindered by the sheer magnitude of the task.

Explaining the Purpose and Function of Modeling Tools

This is where modeling tools come in. The idea behind these modeling tools is simply that you should be able to use the power of the computer to draw the diagrams, store the information about the diagrams, and use the computer to run the cross checks, maintain the integrity, keep track of versions, and ultimately generate the code.

Unfortunately, the early attempts at these tools did not go well. The developers tried to anticipate how you should write your code. In trying to account for every possibility, they delivered tools that generated bloated, unreadable code. The result was that no one trusted the code or the tools.

The good news for modeling tools came in the form of object-oriented programming. The elements of the OO diagrams now map so well to elements of OO code that there is little if any difference between the diagrams and the code.

So what is a modeling tool? Figure 30-1 shows you a screenshot of a typical modeling tool interface. This particular tool is System Architect by Popkin Software, the tool used to generate most of the diagrams in this book.

Take a look at the central elements of the tool:

Main Menu: At the top of Figure 30-1, you see the typical menu. In a modeling tool, you will also find a menu, often called Tools or something similar, that gives you access to the code generation features, database schema creation, export and import of models, and links to related tools like data modeling tools and Integrated Development Environments (IDEs) or coding environments.

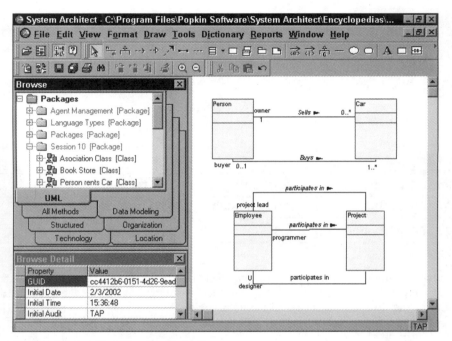

Figure 30-1 *Modeling tool interface*

Model Navigation: Each tool typically provides a navigation window. Figure 30-1 shows the navigation window in the left side panel. The upper portion looks a lot like a directory tree. Notice that it uses packages (folder icons) containing diagrams and definition files.

The lower half of the left side is a detail window that displays the properties of the currently selected item. Often this is a thumbnail view of a diagram or audit details about a package or other selected item.

Canvas: The large white area on the right side of Figure 30-1 is the drawing canvas. This is where you create, view, and maintain all your diagrams. Just above the canvas is a row of buttons, or a toolbar, for each diagram element. This toolbar may also appear to the immediate left of the canvas or float over the canvas depending on the tool. The contents of the toolbar change depending upon which diagram you are drawing.

Explaining Evaluation Criteria for Modeling Tools

The next big question is, "How do I choose the right tool for my project?" As with any decision, you first must decide what your needs are. Modeling tools come in all shapes and sizes. Costs range from free to over $5,000. As with any product, you often get what you pay for. But the fact is that not all of us need the best or the most expensive or the most popular. Frankly, some of the low-end products are really worth taking a close look at. So I've provided some evaluation criteria to assist you in your discussions with vendors and in your own evaluations of the products you want to investigate.

The basics

First I cover the features that should pretty much be provided by every modeling tool. The distinctions come in how they implement them. Modeling tool vendors will usually give you access to an evaluation copy of their software. Often, it is as simple as downloading it from their site. I'll provide you a convenient site to gain access to most of the existing tools at the end of this session.

Type and version of the UML supported

As of this printing, the current UML version is 1.4. UML 1.5 is due to be completed by OMG sometime in 2002, with UML 2.0 to follow after that. Since there are generally schedule delays with updates to the UML spec, UML 2.0 will probably not be official until sometime in 2003.The real question is whether the tool really supports 1.4. A substantial number of changes exist between 1.3 and 1.4. Many tools seem to have a blend of both.

Use the diagram notations in this book to help you verify the support. Get an evaluation copy of the product and create one of each of the diagrams to try out the modeling features and check out the standard. You can even duplicate the diagrams created in this book as a benchmark.

Platform support

You need to run the tool on your operating system(s). Verify that the tool is supported on each platform you require. Beware that the versions for different platforms are not always in sync. Some of the vendors bypass this problem by writing the tool in Java. Even so, differences in virtual machines may surprise you.

Printing

One of the primary reasons you will create the UML diagrams is to share your ideas. Check out the printing capabilities. Some tools require add-ins to get all the features you need. Many of these diagrams can be very large, so the print features should support either plotters or easy-to-use multi-page layouts. A print preview feature can also be a great time saver when preparing presentations.

HTML documentation

Most of the time, there will be a limited number of people actually using the tool, but a much larger number of people who need to see what is being produced. Printed output is good for meetings but impractical for wide and frequent dissemination. Many of the current tools support the generation of reports and diagrams in HTML format so that they may be published on the Web. Again, some tools build this in as a standard feature while others use add-ins.

Repository

A *repository* is simply a place to store all the work you do in the tool. Most often the repository is a database. In a few tools, the repository is a proprietary format. This means that you will be limited to the vendor's own tools to create reports and do queries. The added software can be a hidden cost.

Some tools use a relational database, which allows you to augment their reporting features with standard SQL tools.

Still others use an object database. This can provide some significant productivity advantages with performance and when working with team development. Object-level locking allows multiple users to view the same diagram and edit individual elements of the diagram while others observe the changes.

Code generation

Code generation is one of the big selling features of modeling tools. It is also one of the biggest sources of skepticism. Modeling tools have had a poor history of code generation, but the advent of object-oriented programming and object-oriented modeling changed the problem significantly. Now the diagrams and the code line up so well that there is very little difference between the two.

The list of languages supported in modeling tools is surprisingly long. The most common languages include Java, C++, and Visual Basic. Many tools are now supporting Microsoft's C# programming language. You will also find CORBA IDL, JavaScript, SmallTalk, C, and Ada, among others.

One key feature of code generation to be aware of is code markers. A *code marker* is one line (or sometimes two lines) of code that identifies where the code fits into the model. It is generated along with the code. The result is a listing that is two and sometimes three times longer than you expected. The markers can make the code very difficult to work with. The upside is that the tools that use this method will often provide an editor that hides the markers. But then again, you have to use that vendor's editor.

Most tools have avoided the problem of markers. The result is just the code you wanted and the freedom to use whatever editor you like.

Integrated editor

Speaking of editors, the situation used to be that you worked either with modeling tools doing the modeling or you worked with an Integrated Development Environment (IDE) writing and maintaining code. The line between the two products is becoming blurred. Some modeling tool vendors have literally built the coding features into the modeling product. Others have formed partnerships with IDE vendors so that the user (you or I) can move almost seamlessly between the two. Practically speaking, that's how it really works. There are some things best done in a modeling tool and some things best accomplished in an IDE. One very common situation is the need to define operations. A modeling tool only supports the operation signature. An editor or IDE is required to add the method to the operation.

Version control

Version control is a fact of life on every project and modeling vendors know it. Most vendors either provide the version control features in the modeling tool itself or they provide integration with a tool like Program Version Control Software (PVCS), StarTeam from Starbase, ClearCase/ClearQuest from Rational, Visual SourceSafe from Microsoft, and others. The remaining vendors save their projects as an encyclopedia or directory of some sort that is easily identified and managed by any third-party version control package.

Version control is also especially valuable with object-oriented modeling. The diagrams are used throughout the development process. The same diagram initially created in the early phases is continuously changed through analysis and design and finally through implementation. Without version control, you lose the history of the diagrams that explains how you arrived at the current image.

Extended features

The rest of the features listed don't appear in all tools; however, they are very valuable. These features and how well they are implemented can set a tool apart from the rest. They can also add substantially to the cost.

Round-trip engineering

Round-trip engineering is a hotly debated subject. It sounds great but can be challenging to accomplish. The concept involves four types of translation between models and code. Figure 30-2 provides a visual explanation to reference while you read through the following definitions:

- *Forward engineering:* A Class diagram is used to generate code that never existed before.
- *Reverse engineering:* Code is used to create a Class diagram that never existed before.

Maintenance involves work in both directions:

- *Diagram updates the code:* The diagram changes so you need to regenerate the code. Some tools replace the existing code, while others are smart enough to isolate the changes and even comment out the replaced or deleted code.
- *Code updates the diagram:* The code has changed so you need to update the diagram to keep in sync. This is not as easy as it sounds. Always do it in very small increments. Also, some diagram concepts, like aggregation and composition, are not reflected in code. So you will need to modify the diagram to make certain that it continues to represent your model accurately.

The maintenance phase is one of the reasons that vendors introduced *markers*. The markers can represent modeling concepts that do not have code equivalents. Using this technique, they can preserve the non-code constructs when the code is converted back into a diagram during reverse engineering and code-to-diagrams updates.

Data modeling integration

Nearly every application requires a database. Most databases nowadays are relational. The better tools have taken measures to incorporate data modeling options into their product. Others have partnered with data modeling or database management vendors to provide the linkage between a Class diagram and a data model.

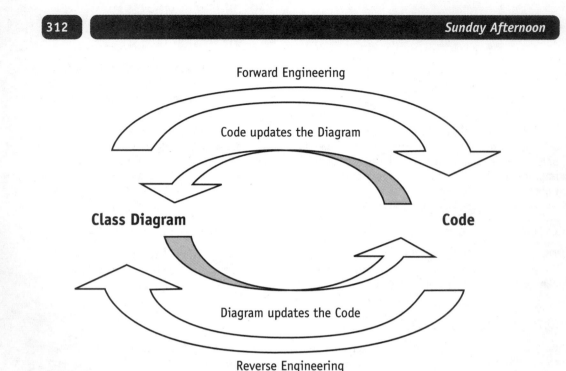

Forward Engineering

Code updates the Diagram

Class Diagram   **Code**

Diagram updates the Code

Reverse Engineering

Figure 30-2   *Round-trip engineering*

One simple way to incorporate data modeling is to support code generation in DDL, the language needed to create tables in a relational database. A problem with this approach is that the Class diagram is rarely designed for the database or according to database performance standards. A better solution is to port the Class diagram to a tool that supports true data modeling. This solution works equally well whether the data modeling capabilities are built into the modeling tool or separate.

Customization

**10 Min.
To Go**

Inevitably you will want to change certain things about the tool. Vendors know they can't keep everyone happy, so they often provide you with the ability to make the changes yourself. The modifications are accomplished with a scripting language, usually something common like Visual Basic. Because much of the code to generate reports and generate code is written in this scripting language, the vendor allows you to modify the code or create your own. Some even build in an editor to help you.

It is worth noting that Visual Basic for Applications (VBA) is the industry standard for Windows-based modeling tools, and as such provides the user with the same language and IDE (within the modeling tool) offered in Microsoft Word, Excel, and so on. (VBA is a stripped down version of VB, invented expressly for such purposes.)

XML Metadata Interchange

Just what you need — another acronym! The XMI (XML Metadata Interchange) details are something that you may never need to know. But XMI is a feature that you should look for if you expect to use a set of tools from different vendors. Earlier in this chapter, I talk about using your Class diagrams to create data models, perhaps in an entirely different tool. XMI is one facility that will support the sharing of models created in one product with many other products. XMI not only supports sharing of Class diagrams, but sharing of all the UML diagrams.

XMI uses standard XML to describe the diagrams. OMG specifies XMI via a UML.DTD, which is updated for every revision of the UML specs. Some modeling tools import/export XML to their own DTD. Because correct XMI support means the tool is supporting the UML metamodel correctly, correct XMI import/export becomes a 'kosher stamp' on whether the tool is supporting UML well or not.

The fact that XMI uses standard XML means that you can export your diagrams to a variety of tools that can exploit the information for other purposes like reporting, software metrics, and project management.

Team development

Many projects require a number of people to contribute to the modeling effort. This implies that they need to share the same diagrams, each working on different aspects but everyone sharing each other's products. Vendors have come up with a variety of techniques to support such team development. Some require a check-out/check-in method where one person has exclusive access to the checked out portion of the model. Others provide diagram or even element-level locking so that many people may have the same diagram or element open, but only one person may modify the diagram or element until they release it.

Evaluating UML Modeling Tools

Since the release of the UML standard, the modeling tool market has exploded. The best single source I've found for a list of the current tools is a Web site at www.cetus-links.org. The Cetus Team is a group of private individuals who support the content of the site. The site has over 18,000 links to everything you ever wanted to know about object-oriented anything.

On the first page, you'll find a section on Architecture and Design. Under that heading, you'll see OOAD Tools, which stands for Object-Oriented Analysis and Design Tools (what I have been calling modeling tools). The list provides everything from university and freeware projects like ArgoUML to high-end products like System Architect, Together Control Center, and Rational Rose. Be wary of the free stuff. Most of it is work in progress. But some of the less expensive products like Poseidon or MagicDraw might be everything you need.

Unfortunately, I've never found a single source that contains reviews of all the currently available products. So you're on your own. I suggest the following plan of attack:

1. Identify your financial limits. These tools cover a range from $100 to $7,000 fully configured. Remember to look into site and concurrent user types of licenses. Be realistic about the number of people you expect to use the tool.
2. Identify the features that are most valuable to you. Look over the list in this session and determine what you can't live without, what would expedite the project, and what you can live without.

3. Get an evaluation copy. Nearly all the tools are available either by download or by contacting the vendor for a CD. Beware that some of the evaluation periods are as short as 15 days.

4. Create each type of UML diagram to make certain that the tool supports UML 1.4 and that it doesn't work in some of its own funny ways of doing things.

5. Generate some code. Review the code. See whether the tool uses markers. Find out why and whether the use of markers will be a benefit or a hindrance. Find out what types of customization the tool supports for code generation (class headers, audit trails, and so on).

6. Reverse engineer some code. This is difficult no matter how you do it. But you may find yourself needing to reverse existing code to gain an understanding of its structure so that you can make changes with more confidence.

7. Generate all the reports. If you created one of every diagram, then you should get some meaningful reports. Find out about customizing reports and adding your own.

8. For those features that don't work the way you like right out of the box, find out if the vendor supports customization through scripting. Try to change the report or code generation using the scripting language to find out how easy or difficult it is to use.

Done!

REVIEW

A modeling tool supports the creation and maintenance of UML diagrams, generating code, reverse engineering code, and interfaces to related tools like data modelers, IDEs, report generators, and others.

- A typical modeling tool provides an interface that supports navigation through the work products created by the tool, a drawing canvas and associated toolbar, and menu options to access the other tools like code generation.

- The most common features of the current modeling tools include, but are not limited to, support for the current version of the UML, support for various platforms, printing, HTML documentation, code generation, an integrated editor, and version control.

- Additional features include data modeling integration, customization using scripting, XMI (XML Metadata Interchange) import export, and support for team development.

QUIZ YOURSELF

1. What is a modeling tool? (See "Explaining the Purpose and Function of Modeling Tools.")

2. What is a repository? (See "Explaining Evaluation Criteria for Modeling Tools.")

3. What is round-trip engineering? (See "Explaining Evaluation Criteria for Modeling Tools.")

4. What is team development? (See "Explaining Evaluation Criteria for Modeling Tools.")

5. How can you make certain that the tool supports UML 1.4? (See "Type and version of the UML supported.")

PART

VI

Sunday Afternoon
Part Review

1. Compared to modeling non-Web applications, Web development requires you to pay more attention to the software and hardware that make up the implementation environment. What UML diagrams do you use to represent the implementation environment?

2. What UML diagram(s) could you use to show the process of how your Web components work together to implement your system?

3. What UML diagram could you use to model the logical business process that you want to implement in the Web application?

4. During the execution of your application, the objects like the Java Server Pages go through a number of transformations that affect their behavior. What UML diagram shows why these changes happen and how the object changes?

5. Is it redundant to use Class, Sequence, Component, and Deployment diagrams to model your Web application? How does each diagram make a unique contribution to your model?

6. How would you use the Sequence and Collaboration diagrams in a Web system?

7. How would you use the Deployment diagram in a Web system?

8. How would you use the Statechart diagram in a Web system?

9. How would you use the Activity diagram in a Web system?

10. Session 29 showed how to model an XML data hierarchy as an object hierarchy on a Class diagram. Could you apply the same strategy to the tag structure of an HTML document?

11. The Model 2 Architecture is based on a pattern that divides the application design into three loosely coupled segments. What is the pattern?

12. What tools could you use to model the implementation environment that contains the Web browser and the Wired Web Controller on a Web-based solution?

13. How would you model the structure of each Web resource and the relationships between them?

14. Does the UML allow for any customization, or do you have to use it exactly as defined in the standard?

15. What are the main features of a modeling tool interface?

16. Why is HTML documentation valuable for a project?

17. Why is version control especially important in an object-oriented project?

18. What are the four types of translation between models and code?

19. What is team development and how does a modeling tool support it?

Answers to Part Reviews

Friday Evening Review Answers

1. The UML is a diagramming notation standard. The UML does not include anything about how to build software. The UML does not include anything about how to perform analysis and design. It only specifies the diagramming models used to capture the results of these tasks. Finally, the UML is not proprietary.

2. The UML was the merger of most of the current object-oriented methods. Elements from nearly all the leading methods have been included in the UML. Although Booch, Rumbaugh, and Jacobson took an aggressive stance to push the development of the UML and even now play the part of stewards of the documentation, many others joined them. The OMG is the coordinating standards representative only.

3. The Object-Oriented Analysis and Design Task Force RFP asked for a metamodel for specifying software solutions. The RFP specifically avoided methodologies. The visual notation is actually left up to the vendors, whereas the underlying element definitions (the metamodel) are required to be consistent among vendors.

4. The UML may be extended by using stereotypes to qualify element descriptions. Stereotypes are defined in the UML and have a suggested notation for their use. You are not allowed to alter the standard; otherwise, it would not be a standard. The set of diagrams is part of the specification. To create a new one would be outside of the UML standard. Although you're allowed to choose your own icons for existing elements, you may not arbitrarily add your own.

5. The metamodel includes definitions of the modeling elements. The UML does not specify usage at all. The specification defines function and relationships among elements only. The UML only suggests a visual icon for each element, leaving the final choice to the vendor. The UML is explicitly independent of any programming language used to implement the models.

6. The three elements are the process, the notation, and the guidelines and rules. The process describes how to go about the development effort. The notation defines the appearance and meaning of the work products. The guidelines and rules define how you will assess the quality of the work products and the process.

7. The UML standard is a common notation that may be applied to many different types of software projects using very different methodologies. The variations appear in the use of the UML extensions, like stereotypes, and the emphasis placed on different diagrams for different types of projects.

8. The hallmarks of RUP are the two terms *incremental* and *iterative*. The goal of the methodology is to deliver an executable release of a product, an increment of the product, for every pass, or iteration, through the process. The motivation for this approach is to keep delivery times short and deliveries frequent. This prevents the historical problem of projects that run for months, or even years, before they actually produce anything. It also supports early review and early problem detection.

9. The Shlaer-Mellor Method is based on an integrated set of models that can be *executed for verification,* and an innovative approach to design that produces a system design through a *translation of the analysis models.* The method is built on a set of well-defined rules for the construction of the models and the translation of those models from analysis to design and finally to implementation.

10. The CRC card captures the information about one class. The class name is written on top of the card. The next two lines are reserved for the listing of superclasses and subclasses. The body of the card is divided in half. The left column or half lists the responsibilities of the class and the right column or half lists the other objects that it works with, the collaborators, to fulfill each responsibility.

11. The Use Case view consists of Use Case and Activity diagrams, narratives, and scenarios. It is tempting to include policies and procedures, but policies and procedures are captured within a number of the models. Depending on the specific nature of the procedures or policies, they may be captured in one or more of the static or dynamic view diagrams or even the physical models (Component and Deployment).

12. The static view includes the Class and Object diagrams. The Class diagram models the rules that govern the objects that make up the system. The Object diagram models facts about the objects that make up the system. The Class diagram is the source for generating code. The Object diagram is used to model tests and examples.

13. The Activity diagram models processes, conditional logic, and concurrency, much like the old flowcharts, but with some enhancements suited to object modeling.

14. The Collaboration diagram models the way objects communicate. The Sequence and Collaboration diagrams are subtly different views of the same concepts, object communication.

15. The component view defines the bundling of classes and components into a functional unit. The Component diagram is often combined with the Deployment diagram to represent the implementation environment.

16. Focus on results rather than process.

17. Three categories of requirements are user requirements, resource requirements, and functionality requirements.

18. Resources can be anything that the users or the system may need to accumulate, manipulate, create, store, destroy, and retrieve.

19. Assumptions, replicating the existing system, and confusing user preferences with requirements.

20. I assume that the screen design offered by the user has been approved by all the users who will need to use it. The client assumes that I already know the laws that govern insurance terms for international shipping.

21. If you replicate the system, you have not fixed the problem that was the justification for the project.

Saturday Morning Review Answers

1. A person may function in many roles. A person may perform many different functions and use the system in many different capacities when using a system. There really is no limitation other than the nature of the problem domain to restrict the possible number of roles that a person may play. The same person may even use the same Use Case from different roles.

2. Associations identify interactions between actors and Use Cases. Associations simply indicate that there is some sort of communication, no matter what that communication is. To get the details, you need to look at the Use Case narrative or one of the other models such as the Sequence or Collaboration diagrams. An association has no way of showing the data flowing between the two elements.

3. The dependency stereotype <<include>> indicates delegation of part of a task to another Use Case. "Used" Use Cases are typically autonomous Use Cases that may also be referenced much like you would seek help from a friend.

4. The dependency stereotype <<extends>> indicates a conditional reference to a Use Case. During the execution of one Use Case, a condition may be encountered that requires access to a feature handled by another Use Case. When that condition is encountered, the extension is invoked. When the condition is not met, the extending Use Case is not invoked.

5. Generalization may be used to identify an existing actor or Use Case whose definition forms the basis for a more specialized actor or Use Case.

6. Few, if any, systems function in a void. Other systems, the business itself, and the people who use the system all influence how we interpret the role of the system and its value.

7. Identify the actors that interact with the Use Cases. In order to interact, they have to be aware of one another. An association defines who knows whom.

8. When the first Use Case must always (unconditionally) call on the second Use Case for help, model the relationship as a dependency with the <<include>> stereotype. Draw the dependency arrow from the first Use Case to the second Use Case.

9. When the first Use Case only calls on the second Use Case for help because it encounters a pre-defined condition, model the relationship as a dependency with the <<extend>> stereotype. Draw the dependency arrow from the second Use Case to the first Use Case.

10. When two or more Use Cases share common properties, the common properties can be defined in a single Use Case. Then the two specialized Use Cases only have to define what they add to or override from the generalized Use Case. The same concept may be applied to common properties of actors.

11. We need to know how to start the Use Case. Do we simply say "start" as in select-ing a menu option, or do we trigger an event? Does the Use Case start because of time or because of a state within the system? Sometimes the starting mechanism can tell us whether a Use Case should actually be more than one Use Case.

12. Both define conditions that must be true in order for the Use Case to work prop-erly. But the Use Case takes on the responsibility for testing the condition defined in the preconditions, where it does not test the conditions defined in the assump-tions. The Use Case literally assumes that another Use Case has satisfied the assumption prior to the execution of this Use Case.

13. The dialog is the conversation between the actor/Use Case and the system in the execution of the Use Case. It describes how they communicate with one another in order to complete the goal established for the Use Case.

14. They are defined separately mostly for visibility, to make certain that the dialog has addressed all the possible outcomes. We also define them separately because some termination options are difficult to describe in textual form (for example, concurrency options like canceling in the middle of an operation).

15. Typically, you only include what the user would be able to see during his interac-tion with the system. So you wouldn't normally see things like saving items to the database, closing connections, and so on. But there are always exceptions.

16. A Use Case is a single goal that the system is expected to accomplish. A scenario is one possible way that the Use Case might execute when it attempts to accomplish the goal.

17. Scenarios help you define all the functional requirements for the execution of the Use Case. By doing so, they also provide the basis for a test plan to ensure that the Use Case can and does work exactly as expected.

18. The Use Case narrative and the Activity diagram illustrating the Use Case narrative can both be used.

19. Avoid redundancy. Isolate the unique segments of the logic into separate paths rather than repeat the same series of steps in multiple scenarios. Then to describe a complete scenario, simply combine and/or repeat the execution of individual test segments.

20. Use the scenarios as a guide to develop test cases. Taken together, the set of scenar-ios for all Use Cases in the system form the basis for your acceptance-level testing.

21. The Class diagram establishes the rules that govern the creation and use of objects. The Object diagram represents the facts about actual objects. Consequently, the Object diagram is a valuable tool for testing the accuracy and correctness of the Class diagram.

22. A constraint is a rule or set of rules that dictate the values that may be assigned to the attribute.

23. Constraints on an operation typically specify the logic or rules for the proper execution of the operation.

24. The name compartment includes the name of the class, optionally a stereotype, and optionally a set of properties (or constraints).

25. No. The UML allows you to show or hide as much or as little of the class notation as you need for the current problem you are working on, though typically you would always show at least the name compartment.

26. It should express the purpose of the relationship (that is, why the objects are working together).

27. Use role names when a verb or verb phrase does not clearly express the relationship. Place the roles at each end of the association next to the type of object that plays the role.

28. A constraint is a rule that defines the conditions under which an object may participate in the relationship.

29. You most often spot the need for them in a many-to-many association.

30. Use a qualified association to simplify and to speed up the navigation across associations with a many-to-many multiplicity.

Saturday Afternoon Review Answers

1. *Single point of control:* One of the objects in the relationship is the designated point of control for all communication with the set of objects. *Function like a single object:* The behavior of the set of objects associated by aggregation is coordinated through the aggregate (the single point of control) so the set of objects is managed and behaves like one big object.

2. Composition is a type of aggregation so it has all the properties of an aggregation association. It differs from aggregation in that the assembly object controls the creation and destruction of the member objects. So a member object cannot exist outside of the assembly. In aggregation, a part may be created outside the assembly and later added to the assembly or even removed and placed into storage or into another aggregate object. In composition, the part is created and dies within the assembly.

3. When the multiplicity on the aggregate end of the association is 1..1, it is safe to assume that the association is a composition type. In fact, some people don't show the multiplicity on composition for this very reason. The 1..1 multiplicity means that the part must be associated with exactly one aggregate. The part object cannot exist without an associated assembly object. An aggregation relationship where the aggregate is required by the part defines a composition relationship.

4. Specialization examines the objects in a class to identify what makes them different from one another (using the five objective criteria). Generalization looks at objects in a number of subclasses to see what the objects have in common. The common properties are then isolated within a superclass.

5. A multiplicity of 0..1 says that the referenced type of object is optional, so the object on the other end of the association can exist without it. For example, an order can be placed even if there is no shipment for it. The shipment end of the association would be set to 0..1. A multiplicity of 1..1 says that the relationship is required. The object on the other end of the association cannot exist without the relationship. If the shipment end of the association was set to 1..1, then you could not place an order until you had a shipment ready.

6. Qualifiers provide the mechanism for reducing the number of objects that have to be accessed to find the specific desired object. They work much like keys in a database.

7. The pattern defines the materials needed to solve the problem and how to make them work together. But the implementation may be tailored to the specific type of application and the technology used for the implementation, not to mention the preferences of the developer for the peculiar needs of the application.

8. The pattern notation would indicate to everyone using the model that you have chosen to apply a standardized solution rather than a homegrown solution that would take more time to evaluate and approve because it has not been tested to the degree that a pattern has been tested.

9. The roles define the behavior of the participating objects much like job description or task assignments help clarify how members of a team will coordinate their efforts to finish the project.

10. The Class diagram models rules, but the Object diagram models facts. The facts may prove or disprove the accuracy of the rules, so the Object diagram is valuable for determining what the rules should be and whether the existing rules are accurate.

11. The object name may be similar to the name of an object of another type. Including the class name prevents misinterpretation of the diagram.

12. The Class diagram declares the rules that constrain the values that you can use in the attribute. The Object diagram records the actual value. The Class diagram defines all the rules about the information, whereas the Object diagram is used to model real examples or test cases.

13. An association defines the rules about how objects may be related to one another. Links identify how objects are related to one another. A link is to an association as an object is to a class.

14. Operations are only the declared part of behavior. The declaration would be the same for all objects of the same class, so including them in the Object diagram would be redundant.

15. Logical processes include workflows, Use Cases, and operations. The workflow describes when and how people will use the features of the system. The Use Case logic explains how the actors will interact with the system to accomplish one specific goal. Each operation describes the logic required to implement the behavior that the operation offers.

16. The diamond is used for decisions and as a merge point. The bar is used for initiating multiple threads or processes and for synchronizing multiple threads or processes.

17. Place a guard condition on the transition using text enclosed in square brackets [ ].

18. No. You can have multiple transitions out of an activity, each labeled with a guard condition to show the direction to take based on the outcome of the activity.

19. False. An Activity diagram has one start but may have many end points.

20. There should be one end point for every termination option. But you can use a single end point for many transitions (that is, you can have many transition arrows point to the same end point).

21. If the completion of the activity results in criteria needed to make the decision, then use the activity itself. If the criteria are an explicit decision by the actor, or the accumulation of information from many previous activities, then use a decision diamond.

22.　Draw the logic in sequential fashion using all the activity features needed to represent the flow properly. When you encounter the need to loop back to a previous point, insert a diamond merge point symbol at the return point in the logic.

23.　The fork bar allows you to show the point in the flow where a number of processes begin at the same time. Each logical process is modeled independent of the other until they meet at a synchronization bar. Meeting at the synchronization bar indicates that each process has ended and the original initiating process continues on its own.

24.　Place a guard condition on the transition. The guard is an expression enclosed in square brackets [ ] that must test true in order to follow the transition.

25.　The objects that participate in the work. The object lifelines that allow you to represent the order of the events. The events that express what the objects say to one another.

26.　The event is expressed as an operation that is being invoked on the other object, using the name of the operation, the arguments, and the return type.

27.　It uses a self-reference, an event that leaves the object lifelines and loops back to the same lifeline.

28.　The object usually becomes active in response to a message or signal (an event) that tells it to start performing an operation.

29.　The first represents a synchronous message, the invocation of an operation on the object it is pointing to. The second represents a reply or the return value from the operation that was invoked.

Saturday Evening Review Answers

1.　It's usually best to use a Use Case scenario because it is a single discrete piece of logic. But a Sequence diagram can also be used for a single operation or just about any other discrete piece of logic in the design.

2.　Returns are drawn with a dashed line style arrow and the description of the data being returned.

3.　No. You can refer to them in a comment. The goal of the diagram is to identify the interactions. Once identified, your goal has been achieved. Showing them more than once is just more work with no value.

4.　The activation bar is placed on the object lifeline. The activation bar begins when an event is sent to the object and ends when the object sends back a response or finishes the requested operation.

5.　The operation signature includes the name, arguments, and return type (optional). You may also show the sequence number and the operation visibility.

6.　The Object diagram represents the structure of the objects and their relationships. The structure is what makes the interactions possible. Using the structure, the Collaboration diagram can validate that the messaging is taking place across existing connections. The Collaboration diagram can also reveal the need for new connections when an interaction is needed but not currently supported by the structure.

7. The Collaboration diagram numbers the events. The numbering scheme is not standardized, so care should be taken to decide ahead of time on a consistent technique for your team.

8. The Sequence diagram can illustrate when an object is created and destroyed. On a Collaboration diagram, you have to depend on the event names to know that these things have happened. Also, the Sequence diagram can show activation where a Collaboration diagram cannot.

9. Use a self-reference. Draw a link that loops out of and back to the object. Place the event along that loop.

10. There are two types of iteration. Iteration of a single event is modeled with the iteration qualifier in front of the event name. Iteration through a set of events can be modeled with a comment, referring to the sequence numbers of the events involved.

11. Identify the objects that participate in the scenario or operation.

12. Arrange the objects on the diagram with enough space between them to write the events. They do not have to be lined up across the top as in a Sequence diagram.

13. Use the Class diagram to determine the links that connect the participating objects. Draw the links between the objects. The link names are not necessary unless there is more than one valid type of link between the same pair of objects. Then the name should be shown to distinguish the link that makes the interaction possible.

14. Each event in the sequence becomes at least one horizontal arrow from the sending object to the receiving object. The type of arrow depends on the type of event. Regardless of the type, the arrow is placed parallel to the link.

15. For a synchronous event, or procedure call, that requires a reply, place a second arrow parallel to the link running in the opposite direction. Replies use a dashed line style arrow. The return is technically optional but strongly recommended.

16. Identify the condition of the object when it is first created. Draw the state. Then draw a dot and an arrow from the dot to the state. This configuration identifies the initial state of the object.

17. The state of the object reflects its condition as recorded in the values of one or more of the attributes. A change to one or more of these values can redefine the state of the object.

18. The transition itself is modeled as an arrow between two states. The event that triggers the transition is written along the arrow. Any actions that are triggered by the event are written after the event with a forward slash between the event and the action.

19. A final state is a condition from which an object cannot change. You can spot a final state as a state that has no outgoing arrows. No, a final state is not required on every Statechart. In fact, they are rather rare.

20. Yes. There may be as many transitions as the problem statement dictates.

Sunday Morning Review Answers

1. When all the actions associated with the transitions into a state are the same, you can model them as a single *entry action*. Place the description of the action you want the object to perform whenever it enters the state in the internal transition compartment of the state.

2. When all the actions associated with the transitions out of a state are the same, you can model them as a single *exit action*. Place the description of the action you want the object to perform whenever it leaves the state in the internal transition compartment of the state.

3. If an outgoing transition is added that does not require the action, you cannot use the exit action. An exit action means that the action will *always* be performed when the object exits that state.

4. In front of the action expression put the object name; separate the name from the action with a period. This is often called dot notation.

5. Activities. Activities may be interrupted because they do not alter the state of the object.

6. A call event is the most common event type. It is basically the invocation of an operation on the receiving object.

7. A time event evaluates the passage of time as a trigger. It implies that the object supports some mechanism to monitor the passage of time. Use the keyword *after* to specify the time increment to be evaluated.

8. A guard condition controls the response to an event. When an event occurs, the condition is tested. If the condition tests true, the corresponding transition takes place along with any and all associated actions; otherwise the event is abandoned.

9. A change event tests for a change in the object or a point in time. Use the keyword *when* with the required test.

10. A *substate* is a state within a state, a lower level of detail within a state. The substates are placed within the expanded superstate.

11. The state of an object expresses its current condition. The condition is reflected in the values of the attributes of the object. A change in the attribute values that define the state redefines the state of the object.

12. A Sequence diagram models a timeline for each object. It also models events that affect the object. The spaces on the timeline between those events represent periods of time when the condition of the object does not change. These periods of time, the gaps on the timeline, represent candidate states.

13. Typically, only the events pointing at the object's timeline affect a change in the object. The outgoing arrows represent messages to other objects. (Sending a message usually does not change a state unless it causes a wait state until the reply arrives.)

14. A state describes an object. An object is usually named with some form of noun. Words that describe nouns are called adjectives. So the object Order may be described as a Placed Order, a Filled Order, or a Cancelled Order.

15. A Sequence diagram only models one scenario. An object may participate in many scenarios. So you need to use all the Sequence diagrams in which the object participates to build one complete Statechart diagram for the object.

16. The Package diagram may be used just like any directory structure, to hold files of any type including UML diagrams, documentation, and sample documents. The most common usage is to organize the parts of the system into subsystems and finally down to the Class diagrams that model the resources of the system.

17. The package stereotype helps to characterize the usage of the package. For example, the <<subsystem>> stereotype describes a package that will only contain classes and other packages that describe the makeup of the system. The <<deliverables>> stereotype characterizes the package as a repository for project work products.

18. The dependency arrow shows that one or more classes in one package needs to interact with a class or classes in another package. The direction of the arrow indicates who has the need (the base of the arrow) and who supplies the help (the head of the arrow).

19. The dependency stereotype describes the nature of the dependency. The <<import>> stereotype indicates that at run time the dependent package will bring the class from the other package into itself to use along with its own classes. The <<access>> stereotype indicates that the dependent package will want to call on the class or classes at run time without bringing them into itself.

20. A <<subsystem>> package typically only contains other packages, a Class diagram. But it may contain any of the UML diagrams.

21. Components represent the physical implementations of your software design.

22. Deployment components, which are required to run the system. Work product components including models, source code, and data files used to create deployment components. Execution components, components created while running the application.

23. One way to draw a component interface is to use a class with the stereotype <<interface>> attached to the component with a realization relationship. A second, more common technique, is to use a "lollipop" attached to the component by a realization relationship, which is shown simply as a solid line when the lollipop notation is used.

24. Dependencies between components are drawn with the dashed arrow from the dependent component to the component it needs help from.

25. A component may be built from one or more classes. The interfaces of the classes in the component make up the interface to the component.

26. A node is a physical object that represents a processing resource. Most often, this means a computer of some type, but it may also mean a human resource.

27. The connections are modeled as associations. The association is labeled with a stereotype that describes the type of connection.

28. A node may contain components and objects (that is, only run time resources).

29. An association between nodes represents a physical communication path like a cable. The dependency between components is a logical communication requirement. This is why the mapping of the components onto the nodes is so valuable.

It maps the logical need to the physical capability to ensure that the application can in fact work properly.

30. The node is labeled with a name and a type in the format "name : type." But actually both elements are optional, although exercising that option doesn't make your diagram very descriptive.

Sunday Afternoon Review Answers

1. The Deployment diagrams illustrate the hardware and the connections that make communication possible between the devices (nodes). Use Component diagrams more frequently to show how mixed technologies work together in the Web application.

2. The Sequence or Collaboration diagrams are ideal for showing how Web components work together to complete a process.

3. The Activity diagram is used to model any logic process, whether it is business work-flow, business transactions, computations, or communication. When the objects that will take responsibility for the process have been identified, the Activity diagram can be translated to a set of Sequence and/or Collaboration diagrams.

4. The Statechart diagram models the condition of the object at different points in time and the events or stimuli that cause the changes that redefine the condition of the object (its state).

5. No, it is not redundant. Component diagrams show a big-picture view of the architectural solution, whereas Class diagrams show a more detailed view of that solution. Deployment diagrams contribute a network view of the solution. Sequence diagrams show the process for how all the classes and components work together to complete the process. Thus, it is often useful to use all four diagrams together.

6. Use the Sequence and Collaboration diagrams to show how objects in the system interact to complete a process. Many non-OO technologies may be viewed as objects for the sake of these diagrams.

7. The Deployment diagram is particularly useful in Web systems, because Web applications are usually distributed over multiple machines. The Deployment diagram models how the software is distributed across the various pieces of hardware.

8. You may use Statechart diagrams to show how objects change over time and why. This would work well for modeling how the user's session state changes and how the behavior of the application changes along with it.

9. A Web application is a business process much like any other. Any place in the development process where you need to model a logic sequence of behaviors and decisions, the Activity diagram may be applied to help bring greater precision and visibility to the effort.

10. Sure. Although the rules are less formally enforced in HTML, HTML documents have a hierarchical structure of tags just like XML. You could make a Class diagram that represents each tag as a class.

11. The pattern is the Model/View/Controller pattern. The model represents the information resources. The view represents the presentation portion. The controller

represents the application logic that manipulates the model and feeds information to the view.

12. The Component diagram shows the dependency between the Web components. Superimposing the Component diagram on the Deployment diagram provides a complete picture of where the software resides on the network.

13. The Class diagram supports the description of the structure of each resource as well as their relationships and dependencies.

14. The UML allows customization through the use of stereotypes and alternative icons. As a point of further study, you might check out the UML discussion on *profiles,* complete schemas for applying the UML modeling standards to more-diverse domains like business process modeling (see UML 1.4 chapter 4 UML Example Profiles).

15. The main features of a modeling tool interface are the main menu, which includes the tools and diagrams selections, the browser navigation area, and the drawing canvas.

16. Usually there are a limited number of licenses but a large number of project participants who need to see the work products created in the tool. The HTML documentation can be created and distributed to a larger audience. The documentation can also be maintained to keep everyone up to date, again without tying up the tool.

17. Class diagrams are used throughout the development process. The same diagram initially created in the early phases is continuously changed through analysis and design and finally through implementation. Without version control, you will lose the history of the diagrams that explains how you arrived at the current image.

18. The four types of translation between models and code are

   1. *Forward Engineering:* A Class diagram is used to generate code that never existed before.

   2. *Reverse Engineering:* Code may be used to create a Class diagram that never existed before.

   Maintenance involves work in both directions:

   3. *Diagram updates the Code:* The diagram changes so you need to regenerate the code. Some tools replace the existing code while others are smart enough to isolate the changes and even comment out the replaced or deleted code.

   4. *Code updates the Diagram:* The code has changed, so you need to update the diagram to keep in sync. This is not as easy as it sounds. Always do it in very small increments. Also, some diagram concepts, like aggregation and composition, are not reflected in code, so you will need to modify the diagram to make certain that it continues to represent your model accurately.

19. Many projects require a number of people to contribute to the modeling effort. This implies that they need to share the same models, each working on different aspects but sharing each other's products. Vendors have come up with a variety of techniques to support such team development. Some require a check-out/check-in method where one person has exclusive access to the checked out portion of the model. Others provide diagram or even element-level locking so that many people may have the same diagram or element open but only one person may modify the diagram or element until they release it.

What's on the CD-ROM?

This appendix provides you with information on the contents of the CD that accompanies this book. For the latest and greatest information, please refer to the ReadMe file located at the root of the CD. Here is what you will find:

- System Requirements
- Using the CD with Windows and Macintosh
- What's on the CD
- Troubleshooting

System Requirements

Make sure that your computer meets the minimum system requirements listed in this section. If your computer doesn't match up to most of these requirements, you may have a problem using the contents of the CD.

For Windows 2000, Windows NT4 (with SP 4 or later), or Windows XP:

- PC with a Pentium processor running at 200 Mhz or faster
- At least 64 MB of total RAM installed on your computer; for best performance, we recommend at least 128 MB
- Ethernet network interface card (NIC) or modem with a speed of at least 28,800 bps
- A CD-ROM drive

Using the CD with Windows

To install the items from the CD to your hard drive, follow these steps:

1. Insert the CD into your computer's CD-ROM drive.
2. A window will appear with the following options: Install, Browse, eBook, and Exit.

Install: Gives you the option to install the supplied software and/or the author-created samples on the CD-ROM.

Browse: Allows you to view the contents of the CD-ROM in its directory structure.

eBook: Allows you to view an electronic version of the book.

Exit: Closes the autorun window.

If you do not have autorun enabled or if the autorun window does not appear, follow the steps below to access the CD.

1. Click Start ⇨ Run.
2. In the dialog box that appears, type **d:\setup.exe**, where *d* is the letter of your CD-ROM drive. This will bring up the autorun window described above.
3. Choose the Install, Browse, eBook, or Exit option from the menu. (See Step 2 in the preceding list for a description of these options.)

What's on the CD

This book's CD-ROM includes some helpful additional information and a copy of the UML standard PDF files. The CD is divided into the following sections.

Supplements

During the course of my lecturing I have developed some visual aids to illustrate many of the key concepts explained in the course. Among the illustrations are discussions of abstraction, cohesion, and coupling; roadmaps for the phases of the development process and how to apply the diagrams; and cheat sheets on association, aggregation, and composition.

I've also added a small piece on swimlanes in the Activity diagram. This topic is not covered in the book, but I thought that some people might appreciate a brief introduction to this part of the UML notation.

UML 1.4 Documentation

The CD contains the full text of the UML 1.4 documentation in PDF format. You will want to focus on the Notation chapter and possibly the Glossary. But if you want to get the background, you will also find the Preface, Summary, and Semantics chapters interesting. Chapter 4 covers profiles for the software development process and business modeling. Chapter 5 covers the XMI, the XML Model Interchange format.

Version 1.5 is due out any time now, but it has only minor changes. The tools currently on the market typically support the UML 1.4 standard, so you should be able to get a lot of mileage out of this version. But any time you want to check on the latest developments, just hop onto the OMG Web site at www.omg.org.

Trial Software

The CD includes trial versions of two modeling packages, *System Architect* by Popkin Software, Inc. (the tool used to generate most of the diagrams in the course, thanks to Lou Varveris), and *Describe Enterprise by* Embarcadero Technologies, Inc. I suggest you try them out to draw the diagrams in the course. But I do caution you that if trying to understand the mechanics of the tools distracts you from the course, step back and use pencil and paper. After you understand the topic in the course, go back to the tools and step through the chapters again using them. Every tool has its idiosyncrasies, but they will get the job done. Overall, I believe you will be pleasantly surprised with the power of these tools.

Shareware programs are fully functional, trial versions of copyrighted programs. If you like particular programs, register with their authors for a nominal fee and receive licenses, enhanced versions, and technical support. *Freeware programs* are copyrighted games, applications, and utilities that are free for personal use. Unlike shareware, these programs do not require a fee or provide technical support. *GNU software* is governed by its own license, which is included inside the folder of the GNU product. See the GNU license for more details.

Trial, demo, or evaluation versions are usually limited either by time or functionality (such as being unable to save projects). Some trial versions are very sensitive to system date changes. If you alter your computer's date, the programs will "time out" and will no longer be functional.

eBook version of UML Weekend Crash Course™

The CD-ROM also contains the complete text of this book so that you can keep it with you as a reference and to turn to when you need a refresher. You can read and search through the file with the Adobe Acrobat Reader (also included on the CD).

Self-Assessment Test

If you want to find out how you stand with your UML knowledge before or after the course, you can take the self-assessment test. The test consists of about 100 multiple-choice questions. Each answer is explained to make certain that you understand. The test is divided by topics, and is self-scoring for your convenience.

Troubleshooting

If you have difficulty installing or using any of the materials on the companion CD, try the following solutions:

- **Turn off any anti-virus software that you may have running.** Installers sometimes mimic virus activity and can make your computer incorrectly believe that it is being infected by a virus. (Be sure to turn the anti-virus software back on later.)
- **Close all running programs.** The more programs you're running, the less memory is available to other programs. Installers also typically update files and programs; if you keep other programs running, installation may not work properly.

- **Reference the ReadMe:** Please refer to the ReadMe file located at the root of the CD-ROM for the latest product information at the time of publication.

If you still have trouble with the CD, please call the Customer Care phone number: (800) 762-2974. Outside the United States, call 1 (317) 572-3994. You can also contact Customer Service by e-mail at techsupdum@wiley.com. Wiley Publishing, Inc. will provide technical support only for installation and other general quality control items; for technical support on the applications themselves, consult the program's vendor or author.

Glossary

abstract class
A class that cannot be instantiated because a *method* (an implementation) has not been specified for every operation of the class. See also *operation* and *method*.

abstract data type
A class created to encapsulate a type of information common to an application. It is often used for items such as addresses, which contain a number of individual fields combined in a specific way and edited according to rules unique to that combination. See also *encapsulation*.

abstraction
A unique representation of a real-world entity. The intent of the representation is not a comprehensive description, but rather a description that is useful for a specific application or purpose. For more information see Session 1.

abstract operation
An operation without an associated *method* (implementation). See also *operation* and *method*.

action
A response to an event in a Statechart diagram, typically part of the transition from one state to another and typically *atomic* (cannot be broken into subtasks). See also *event* and *Statechart*.

action state
A condition in an object where it is occupied with the execution of an atomic behavior. An activity in an Activity diagram represents an action state.

activation

The execution of an operation on an object, or another call to an object to initiate a behavior on that object. An activation is shown as a thick vertical object lifeline segment on the Sequence diagram. For more information see Session 16.

active object

An object in control of a thread or process that can initiate control activity. In a Sequence diagram, this is identified by adding an activation bar to the object lifeline, usually for the full length of the timeline. In an Object diagram, this is signified by making the object icon bold.

activity

Processing that an object performs while it is in a specific state. An activity is typically non-atomic (that is, it may be composed of any number of subtasks). Because an activity does not cause the object to change states, it may be interrupted. Contrast this with actions. For more information see Session 14. See also *action*.

actor

A person, system, or device that interacts with the system in a Use Case diagram. For more information see Session 6.

aggregation

A type of association in which one object represents a collection, assembly, or configuration of other objects such that the assembly is greater than the sum of its parts. Aggregation is characterized by focus of control in the one object representing the "whole," propagation from the "whole" object to its parts, and the fact that the entire assembly functions as a single, coordinated unit. For more information see Session 11. See also *composition*.

ancestor

Any class that resides higher than the reference class in a generalization hierarchy. See also *superclass, subclass,* and *generalization*.

association

A relationship between classes that specifies the type of links that may be created between objects of the associated classes. For more information see Session 10. See also *link*.

association class

Information about an association that has been abstracted into its own class. For more information see Session 10.

asynchronous event or action

A type of message that does not require a response and does not require the sending object to wait. For more information see Session 16.

attribute

A class member used to define a unit of information owned by the containing class, including such details as type and domain of values. For more information see Session 9.

automatic transition

A change in state triggered by the completion or termination of a state activity. See also *transition* and *activity*.

balking event

A message type in which the client can pass the message only if the supplier is immediately ready to accept the message. The client abandons the message if the supplier is not ready.

base class

A class that is further specified by subclasses. Also called a superclass or ancestor class. For more information see Session 11. See also *superclass* and *subclass*.

bound element

A class resulting from the specification of parameters in a template class. See also *template class*.

class

An abstraction of a set of related information, behaviors, and relationships that describes a type of entity. A definition used to create objects. For more information see Sessions 1 and 9. See also *object*.

classification

The process of finding common information, behaviors, and relationships among objects, in order to create a common definition for the objects. For more information see Session 9. See also *class* and *object*.

class operation

An operation that is specific to a class rather than to objects of the class. As such, it may be invoked without using an object of the class. For more information see Session 9.

class variable

An attribute that is specific to a class rather than to objects of the class. As such, it may be referenced within the class without using an object of the class. For more information see Session 9.

client

An object that initiates a request.

collaboration

An interaction between objects. The term is also used to describe a pattern, a standardized concept for configuring classes to fulfill a specific function. For more information see Session 12. See also *pattern*.

component
A physical unit of software that may reside in memory on a processor and *realizes* (implements) a set of interfaces. For more information see Session 25.

component view
A UML presentation dedicated to the description of software implementation *units* (components); may be used in combination with the deployment view. For more information see Sessions 25 and 26. See also *component* and *deployment view*.

composite state
See *superstate*.

composition
A type of aggregation relationship in which the part object cannot exist separate from the whole object. The whole object is responsible for the creation and destruction of the part object. For more information see Session 11.

concrete class
A class that may be instantiated because a *method* (an implementation) has been specified for every operation that is inherited or owned by the class. See also *abstract class*.

concurrency
The simultaneous execution of multiple activities by executing multiple threads or multiple processes. For more information see Session 14.

constraint
The UML extension of the definition of a model element that allows you to impose restrictions on the use of the element (for example, edit rules on an attribute value or limits on the participation in an association). For more information see Sessions 9 and 10.

context
The set of model elements that defines the frame of reference for the interpretation and implementation of a particular model element.

contract
An agreement between classes regarding the handling of responsibilities and implementations in the class definitions. For more information see Session 7.

coupling
A measure of the degree of dependency between model elements. A quantitative assessment of the communication volume, number of relationships, and the complexity of the communication that define the relationship. For more information see the Supplements on the CD. See also *dependency*.

data type
The format of information allowed for an attribute (for example, integer, address, or character data). For more information see Session 9.

decomposition
Separating an entity or process into smaller functional units.

delegation
Passing responsibility for a task to another entity, typically hiding the implementation of the task from the requestor.

dependency
A relationship between two model entities in which a change to one (the independent model element) will affect the other (the dependent model element). For more information see Sessions 5 and 24.

deployment view
A presentation dedicated to the description of processing architectures; may be used in combination with the component view. For more information see Sessions 3 and 26. See also *component view* and *node*.

derived association
An association shortcut created by relying on a series of other associations. For example, if Bill knows Mike, who knows Cathy, who knows Sue, then you could arrange for Mike to know Sue directly.

derived attribute
An attribute whose value can be determined by applying a rule or calculation using one or more other attribute values. For more information see Session 9.

domain
A subject area with an associated vocabulary and semantics.

element
See *model element*.

event
A system stimulus, often in the form of a message or signal from one object to another that can cause the receiving object to respond and/or change state. For more information see Session 16.

generalization
The process of organizing the information in a set of classes according to the similarities and differences between the classes. The objects of the classes must all share the same semantic purpose. The criteria for the organization process include operations, methods, attributes, attribute values, and associations. Also, a class that contains the shared properties of all the subclasses below it in the inheritance hierarchy. For more information see Session 11. See also *inheritance* and *specialization*.

guard condition
A statement, associated with a state transition, which must test true before the transition may take place. For more information see Sessions 14 and 16. See also *state transition*.

implementation inheritance
The sharing of both the *interface* (operation) and the *implementation* (method). See also *interface inheritance*.

import
A dependency stereotype between packages where one package obtains access to the other's contents by adding the "imported" package's contents to its own. For more information see Session 24.

inheritance
A relationship between a generalized class and a specialized class that allows the specialized class to incorporate the elements of the generalized class into its own specification. For more information see Session 11. See also *generalization*.

instance
The implementation of a class as an object.

instance method
An operation implementation that is only available through an object. Contrast this with a class method. See also *class method*.

instance variable
An attribute that is only available within an object. Contrast this with a class attribute. See also *class attribute*.

interaction
Communication between objects. For more information see Session 16.

interface
The visible part of a class. Typically used to describe the public signatures of operations in a class. May be used to refer to a single signature or the sum of all signatures for a class. For more information see Session 1.

interface inheritance
The sharing of only the signature or declaration of an operation, not the implementation.

iteration
To perform a function or set of functions more than once. The repetition may be based on a value, a count, time, completion of a task, or any other type of condition. For more information see Sessions 16 and 18.

link

A relationship between two objects. For more information see Session 13. See also *association*.

link attribute

A value that helps to describe a relationship between two objects. See also *association class* and *link*.

logical view

A presentation dedicated to the description of conceptual analysis and design work products for a software project. For more information see Session 3.

merge of control

To synchronize or coordinate the completion of multiple threads or processes and pass control to a single thread or process. Merge of control does not require the completion of all threads or processes. Merge may be conditional on the completion of one or more of a set of threads, time, or other conditions. For more information see Sessions 14 and 20.

message

Communication between objects, typically an event containing information and/or eliciting a response. For more information see Sessions 16 and 18.

metamodel

The specification of a language for describing the UML diagrams. Also, a model that describes the elements and the relationships between those elements that make up a specified domain (for example, the Class diagram). For more information see Session 1.

method

The implementation of an operation. For more information see Session 9. See also *operation*.

model

A representation of a view of a physical system, usually designed to simplify and facilitate understanding of the system. The representations may focus on the logical rules and relationships that define the system as well as the physical components used to implement the system. For more information see Session 3.

model element

The smallest unit of semantic definition in a model. The same model element may appear in multiple diagrams. For example, an event appears in Sequence diagrams, Collaboration diagrams, and Statechart diagrams. In all three contexts it provides the same semantic information. For more information see Session 3.

multiplicity

A constraint on the number of objects that may participate in one end of an association. For more information see Session 9.

navigability
A specification of the allowed direction of communication along an association.

node
A physical object that represents a processing unit, typically computing hardware or a person, capable of owning and performing a system function. For more information see Session 26. See also *deployment view*.

object
A uniquely identifiable entity composed of information, behaviors, and relationships with other entities. For more information see Session 1.

object activation
An object in control of a thread or process that can initiate control activity. In a Sequence diagram, this is identified by adding an activation bar to the object lifeline. In an Object diagram, this is signified by making the object icon bold. For more information see Session 16. See also *active object*.

object constraint language
A formal language used to express rules that need to be enforced on elements in a UML diagram (for example, to define which objects may participate in an association).

object lifeline
Used in a Sequence diagram, the timeline is represented as a vertical dashed line drawn from the owning object downward to the end of the scenario. For more information see Session 16.

object management group
The standards group currently overseeing the modeling standards related to object-oriented software development. For more information see Session 1.

object termination
The end of an object's lifecycle, usually denoting object destruction. Identified by an X at the bottom of a sequence diagram timeline for the specified object. For more information see Session 16.

Object-Oriented Analysis and Design Task Force
The group assigned by the OMG to generate and oversee the RFP for a metamodel for object design. For more information see Session 1.

operation
The declaration of a unit of behavior within a class. See also *method* and *interface*. For more information see Session 9.

overloading
Used to describe operations within a class where an operation name is shared but the arguments vary in number and/or type. Contrast this with polymorphism.

package
A general-purpose mechanism for grouping models and model elements, typically by similar functions or uses within the context of a system. For more information see Session 24.

pattern
A common solution to a common problem, describing a set of cooperating classes, the rules for their interactions, and consequences of using the pattern. For more information see Session 12.

polymorphism
Operations where the operation signature is the same but the *implementation* (method) is different. See also *overloading*.

post-condition
A statement that must test true at the completion of the responsible task or Use Case. For more information see Session 7. See also *pre-condition*.

pre-condition
A statement that must test true before execution of the responsible task or Use Case. For more information see Session 7. See also *post-condition*.

primitive data type
The smallest unit of data definition provided by the implementation environment (for example, integer, float, or char). For more information see Session 9. See also *abstract data type*.

private
A form of visibility constraint that prevents access to a model element from outside of the owning class. For more information see Session 9. See also *public*.

process
A "heavyweight" flow of control that can execute concurrently with other processes.

property
A named value describing a characteristic of an element.

protected
A type of model element visibility that allows only subclasses to have access to the protected model element (for example, an operation or attribute). In some languages, like Java, protected may also allow access from within the same package. For more information see Session 9.

public
A form of visibility constraint that allows access to a model element by any object outside the owning class. For more information see Session 9. See also *private*.

qualifier
A modeling element, used on associations, that identifies an attribute or attributes used to navigate an association. Synonymous in function with keys or indexes in a database or the data modeling domain. For more information see Session 10.

realization
When a class implements an interface specified by another class (or interface class as in Java).

reflexive association
An association that relates objects within the same class to one another. For more information see Session 10. See also *association*.

reverse engineering
The process of translating code into modeling elements. This typically results in a Class diagram. But new tools are providing Sequence and Statechart diagrams as well. For more information see Session 30.

role
Describes how an object participates in an association. For more information see Session 10.

scenario
A single logical path through a Use Case, often used as a test case. For more information see Session 8. See also *Use Case view*.

send event
A message or signal sent to another object from within a Statechart diagram. For more information see Session 22.

server
An object that acts only as a respondent in an interaction. Note that the same object may act as a client in another interaction.

signal
An asynchronous stimulus sent from one object to another.

signature
Synonym for *operation* and described as the name, the number, type, and order of arguments, and sometimes the return data type (implementation languages vary on their interpretation). For more information see Session 9. See also *polymorphism, overloading,* and *interface*.

specialization

The identification and encapsulation of properties that make a type of object unique within a larger set of objects that share the same purpose (for example, a description of the unique properties of Granny Smith apples within the larger group of apples). For more information see Session 11. See also *generalization*.

split of control

To initiate multiple and simultaneous threads or processes from a single thread or process. For more information see Sessions 14 and 22.

state

The condition of an object at a point in time, reflected in the values of certain attributes of the object. A change in the attribute values redefines the condition of the object. For more information see Session 20.

stereotype

A UML extension that provides a means of further describing or qualifying a model element without defining its implementation. For more information see Sessions 6, 9, 24, and 26.

subclass

A specialized class connected to a more general class (also known as *base class* or *ancestor class*) in a generalization class hierarchy. This relationship gives it inheritance access to all the properties of the ancestor class. For more information see Session 11. See *specialization, generalization,* and *inheritance*.

substate

A refinement of the condition of an object from within another state with a broader definition (composite or superstate). For more information see Session 22. See also *superstate* and *state*.

superclass

A generalized class connected to a more specialized class or *child class* in a generalization class hierarchy. The superclass contains properties that are common to all subclasses below it in the hierarchy. For more information see Session 11. See also *subclass* and *generalization*.

superstate

A state defined at a higher level of abstraction that can be broken down into smaller, more refined state definitions. For more information see Session 22. See also *substate* and *state*.

synchronous event

A form of communication that requires a response. For more information see Session 16.

tagged value

An extension of the properties of a UML element that allows you to add your own new information to an element's specification in the form of property name and value pairs, that is, property = last edited date and value = 04/12/02.

template or template class

A parameterized class that serves as a model for building other classes.

time event

An event that specifies an amount of time elapsed since the current state was entered. For more information see Session 16.

transition

A change from one object state to another object state. For more information see Session 21. See also *state*.

Use Case view

A presentation dedicated to the description of user requirements. For more information see Session 3.

view

A grouping of diagrams and other work products for a particular function in the overall process for developing software. For more information see Session 3.

visibility

A constraint on the access to attributes and operations within a class by other classes of objects. For more information see Session 9. See also *public, private, protected,* and *package.*

Index

Continued

Wiley Publishing, Inc.
End-User License Agreement

READ THIS. You should carefully read these terms and conditions before opening the software packet(s) included with this book ("Book"). This is a license agreement ("Agreement") between you and Wiley Publishing, Inc. ("Wiley"). By opening the accompanying software packet(s), you acknowledge that you have read and accept the following terms and conditions. If you do not agree and do not want to be bound by such terms and conditions, promptly return the Book and the unopened software packet(s) to the place you obtained them for a full refund.

1. **License Grant.** Wiley grants to you (either an individual or entity) a nonexclusive license to use one copy of the enclosed software program(s) (collectively, the "Software") solely for your own personal or business purposes on a single computer (whether a standard computer or a workstation component of a multi-user network). The Software is in use on a computer when it is loaded into temporary memory (RAM) or installed into permanent memory (hard disk, CD-ROM, or other storage device). Wiley reserves all rights not expressly granted herein.

2. **Ownership.** Wiley is the owner of all right, title, and interest, including copyright, in and to the compilation of the Software recorded on the disk(s) or CD-ROM ("Software Media"). Copyright to the individual programs recorded on the Software Media is owned by the author or other authorized copyright owner of each program. Ownership of the Software and all proprietary rights relating thereto remain with Wiley and its licensers.

3. **Restrictions On Use and Transfer.**

   (a) You may only (i) make one copy of the Software for backup or archival purposes, or (ii) transfer the Software to a single hard disk, provided that you keep the original for backup or archival purposes. You may not (i) rent or lease the Software, (ii) copy or reproduce the Software through a LAN or other network system or through any computer subscriber system or bulletin-board system, or (iii) modify, adapt, or create derivative works based on the Software.

   (b) You may not reverse engineer, decompile, or disassemble the Software. You may transfer the Software and user documentation on a permanent basis, provided that the transferee agrees to accept the terms and conditions of this Agreement and you retain no copies. If the Software is an update or has been updated, any transfer must include the most recent update and all prior versions.

4. **Restrictions on Use of Individual Programs.** You must follow the individual requirements and restrictions detailed for each individual program in Appendix B of this Book. These limitations are also contained in the individual license agreements recorded on the Software Media. These limitations may include a requirement that after using the program for a specified period of time, the user must pay a registration fee or discontinue use. By opening the Software packet(s), you will be agreeing to abide by the licenses and restrictions for these individual programs that are detailed in Appendix B and on the Software Media. None of the material on this Software Media or listed in this Book may ever be redistributed, in original or modified form, for commercial purposes.

5. **Limited Warranty.**

   (a) Wiley warrants that the Software and Software Media are free from defects in materials and workmanship under normal use for a period of sixty (60) days from the date of purchase of this Book. If Wiley receives notification within the warranty period of defects in materials or workmanship, Wiley will replace the defective Software Media.

(b) **WILEY AND THE AUTHOR OF THE BOOK DISCLAIM ALL OTHER WARRANTIES, EXPRESS OR IMPLIED, INCLUDING WITHOUT LIMITATION IMPLIED WARRANTIES OF MERCHANTABILITY AND FITNESS FOR A PARTICULAR PURPOSE, WITH RESPECT TO THE SOFTWARE, THE PROGRAMS, THE SOURCE CODE CONTAINED THEREIN, AND/OR THE TECHNIQUES DESCRIBED IN THIS BOOK. WILEY DOES NOT WARRANT THAT THE FUNCTIONS CONTAINED IN THE SOFTWARE WILL MEET YOUR REQUIREMENTS OR THAT THE OPERATION OF THE SOFTWARE WILL BE ERROR FREE.**

(c) This limited warranty gives you specific legal rights, and you may have other rights that vary from jurisdiction to jurisdiction.

6. **Remedies.**

(a) Wiley's entire liability and your exclusive remedy for defects in materials and workmanship shall be limited to replacement of the Software Media, which may be returned to Wiley with a copy of your receipt at the following address: Software Media Fulfillment Department, Attn.: *UML Weekend Crash Course*, Wiley Publishing, Inc., 10475 Crosspoint Blvd., Indianapolis, IN 46256, or call 1-800-762-2974. Please allow four to six weeks for delivery. This Limited Warranty is void if failure of the Software Media has resulted from accident, abuse, or misapplication. Any replacement Software Media will be warranted for the remainder of the original warranty period or thirty (30) days, whichever is longer.

(b) In no event shall WILEY or the author be liable for any damages whatsoever (including without limitation damages for loss of business profits, business interruption, loss of business information, or any other pecuniary loss) arising from the use of or inability to use the Book or the Software, even if WILEY has been advised of the possibility of such damages.

(c) Because some jurisdictions do not allow the exclusion or limitation of liability for consequential or incidental damages, the above limitation or exclusion may not apply to you.

7. **U.S. Government Restricted Rights.** Use, duplication, or disclosure of the Software for or on behalf of the United States of America, its agencies and/or instrumentalities (the "U.S. Government") is subject to restrictions as stated in paragraph (c)(1)(ii) of the Rights in Technical Data and Computer Software clause of DFARS 252.227-7013, or subparagraphs (c) (1) and (2) of the Commercial Computer Software - Restricted Rights clause at FAR 52.227-19, and in similar clauses in the NASA FAR supplement, as applicable.

8. **General.** This Agreement constitutes the entire understanding of the parties and revokes and supersedes all prior agreements, oral or written, between them and may not be modified or amended except in a writing signed by both parties hereto that specifically refers to this Agreement. This Agreement shall take precedence over any other documents that may be in conflict herewith. If any one or more provisions contained in this Agreement are held by any court or tribunal to be invalid, illegal, or otherwise unenforceable, each and every other provision shall remain in full force and effect.